Merleau-Ponty's Philosophy

Merleau-Ponty's
Philosophy

Samuel B. Mallin

New Haven and London   Yale University Press

Published with assistance from
the foundation established in memory of
Philip Hamilton McMillan of the Class of 1894, Yale College.

Designed by Thomas Whitridge and set in IBM
Baskerville type by A & B Typesetters, Inc., Concord, N.H.
Printed in the United States of America by The Murray
Printing Co., Inc., Westford, Mass.

Library of Congress Cataloging in Publication Data
Mallin, Samuel B.
  Merleau-Ponty's philosophy.
  Bibliography: p.
  Includes index.
  1. Merleau-Ponty, Maurice, 1908–1961.   I. Title.
B2430.M38M34   194   79–64078
ISBN 0–300–02275–1

11   10 9 8 7 6 5 4 3 2

To Sandra and Rebecca

Contents

Acknowledgments

I am especially grateful to Professor Henry Pietersma for the close and creative reading he gave the early drafts. I also wish to thank Jane Isay and Maureen Bushkovitch of the Yale University Press for their commitment to this book and their thorough and excellent editorial advice. Finally, I am indebted to Atkinson College of York University for making available the physical resources necessary for the preparation of the manuscript.

Abbreviations

References to the most frequently used works of Merleau-Ponty appear in parentheses using the code given below. References to the French text usually indicate that they are my own translation. However, if there are neighboring quotations within an argument from the same page of a text where I have made my own translation, I give the French reference, even when the translation agrees with the standard English translation. Page numbers alone within parentheses refer to the *Phenomenology of Perception* (Routledge and Kegan Paul, 1962). References to the *Phénoménologie de la perception* (Gallimard, 1945), have an *F* preceding the page number.

VI refers to *The Visible and the Invisible,* Northwestern University Press, 1968.

VI——F refers to *Le visible et l'invisible*, Gallimard, 1964.

EM refers to "The Eye and the Mind," in *The Primacy of Perception*, Northwestern University Press, 1964.

EM——F refers to *L'oeil et l'esprit*, Gallimard, 1964.

CO refers to "The Child's Relations with Others," in *The Primacy of Perception*, Northwestern University Press, 1964.

CO——F refers to *Les relations avec autrui chez l'enfant*, Centre de Documentation Universitaire, 1967.

Introduction

My purpose in this book is to provide a unified and comprehensive interpretation of Merleau-Ponty's philosophy, and my method of doing so is to analyze extensively the concepts that are central and original to his philosophy and the way in which they form an integrated whole. Thus I aim to present an articulation of his philosophy that will allow it to be comprehended as a unified and original philosophical point of view and methodology.

The present stage of Merleau-Ponty scholarship requires such an interpretation of his work. The great majority of the studies of Merleau-Ponty have been of an "introductory" character; that is, they have limited themselves either to explicating his particular phenomenological studies in a fragmentary and unconnected manner, to simplifying his major notions and purposes, or to comparing his philosophy to others and thus reducing it to a variation on the philosophies of the other prominent members of the phenomenological movement. There was good reason why the early analysis of Merleau-Ponty took this form, for his works contain such a wealth and diversity that one could only hope at the beginning to present helpful commentary on each major theme and study by itself. However, this type of treatment has made only the barest beginnings at an overall interpretation of Merleau-Ponty's thought.[1] For example, De Waelhens, Bannan, Barral, Heidsieck, and Kwant have all followed Merleau-Ponty's analyses in the order in which they were presented, without any major attempt to unify their themes or

---

1. Thomas Langan's *Merleau-Ponty's Critique of Reason* (and John F. Bannan's *The Philosophy of Merleau-Ponty* to a lesser extent) is noteworthy for its attempt to formulate such an interpretation. However, my interpretation essentially differs from his.

1

rediscover the purpose for that particular organization. Since they do not achieve a sufficient distance from Merleau-Ponty's own presentation, these studies do not permit us to rethink Merleau—Ponty's central insights or attain a coherent and total grasp of his work. Furthermore, because these commentators tried to cover all of Merleau-Ponty's studies they were rarely able to deeply analyze any of them, and were prevented thereby from explicating the main notions his studies were meant to reveal and support.[2]

A single and coherent view of Merleau-Ponty's work must be given. For he was presenting a new and complete philosophy, and it is this unique perspective, even more than the traditional philosophical problems to which he applied it, that needs to be made explicit. The other major form of studying Merleau-Ponty, in which the above participate to differing degrees, has been to attempt to thoroughly describe his philosophy by comparing it to those of other philosophers.[3] These projects have, unfortunately, tended to obscure Merleau-Ponty's original point of view, for they have stressed his similarity to his predecessors but have rarely attempted to come to grips with the unique use he has made of their thought and terminology. On the whole, these methods of exegesis have left Merleau-Ponty rather mysterious and have failed to reveal the positive aspects of his philosophy.[4] This, in turn, has frequently led to the general criticism that Merleau-Ponty's philosophy lacks completeness and is "ambiguous."[5]

2. For example, De Waelhens, who has given us the best general commentary (*Une philosophie de l'ambiguité*), merely indicates some of Merleau-Ponty's major notions and questions, although he relies upon them heavily to defend Merleau-Ponty (see, particularly chapter 18): for example, "primary faith," the "tacit *cogito*," the certainty of being-in-the-world, "facticity," and Merleau-Ponty's formula that "there is something." This occurred because he failed to see that Merleau-Ponty was constantly working out such problems as those arising from universality and generality, form and content, the one and the many, the relations between the reflective and prereflective selves (and the personal and empirical selves), and evidence and truth. Merleau-Ponty did not just point to these paradoxes and "ambiguities," but made their investigation central.

3. Richard M. Zaner's *The Problem of Embodiment* and Theodore F. Geraets's *Vers une nouvelle philosophie transcendantale* are the main examples of this type of treatment in book form. However, this is not to deny that these works are important as comparative studies. Geraets's is especially valuable as a study of the influences on Merleau-Ponty's early thought.

4. W. B. Carter criticizes Cowley for not revealing Merleau-Ponty's alternative to his criticisms of empiricism (see his "Review of F. Cowley's *A Critique of British Empiricism*," *Dialogue* 7 [1968] : 491-94).

5. This criticism, which turns Merleau-Ponty's notion of ambiguity on his own works,

I shall therefore argue for a way of viewing all of Merleau-Ponty's efforts that preserves the originality of his philosophy and unifies and remains faithful to its intent. Furthermore, I shall make claims about the interrelation of his diverse notions and phenomenological studies, and about the proper way to understand his key statements and texts. The interpretation will thus be tested by demonstrating how it sheds light upon generally misunderstood portions of Merleau-Ponty's thought, how it is able to unravel the complexity of his notions, and how it allows us to comprehend all of his studies as a coherent whole and as expressions of a distinctive and consistent philosophical point of view.

If we are to analyze Merleau-Ponty in this way, our treatment cannot pretend to be "introductory" in any sense; it must necessarily be complex, abstract, and difficult. The only way we can argue for a unifying interpretation of Merleau-Ponty is to presuppose a good acquaintance with his philosophy. A point-by-point explication is out of the question, for it would immensely expand the text and would frequently repeat studies that have already been done. However, one cannot merely present a dogmatic sketch of his philosophy, for the evidence on which such an overall interpretation would be based—his individual studies—often needs interpretative justification of its own. Thus the complexity of having to critically follow an argument which attempts to relate many separate studies is magnified by the fact that some of these studies will have to be themselves reexamined in detail.

Since Merleau-Ponty himself took his philosophy to be primarily metaphysical, we can gain a comprehension of its core by abstracting and closely examining his metaphysics. However, since he developed and supported his metaphysics through his phenomenological epistemology, it is impossible to understand the one without the other. We shall find that our initial study of the metaphysics in chapters 1 and 2 constantly relies on the main notions that have been discovered through the epistemological investigations. On the other

holds that his investigations end with the affirmation of the ambiguity of our knowledge of ourselves, others, the world, and Being. We shall show, on the contrary, that Merleau-Ponty took this affirmation as his starting point and that he develops a thorough analysis of the lived world and of prereflective subjectivity. See, for example, Langan's *Merleau-Ponty's Critique of Reason*, pp. 183-84, and Rudolph J. Gerber's "Merleau-Ponty: The Dialectic of Consciousness and the World," in *Man and World* 2 (February 1969): 104 (Gerber gives us a recent version of Alquié's original criticism).

hand, when we study his phenomenology of perception and cognition in chapters 3 and 4, we shall find that the conclusions from our study of the metaphysics will enable us to achieve a full and clear understanding of them. We shall justify the methodological separation, relationship, and order of these two parts at the beginning of chapter 3, when we have seen what can be gained from a concentrated examination of the metaphysics. The main reason for this organization is that it will permit us to examine both parts to an extent and in a depth that has never been attained. Although the metaphysics and the epistemology are separable by abstraction only, their integrated study is one of the main sources of confusion for readers of Merleau-Ponty (and one of the main reasons for their frequently unsatisfactory treatment by his commentators), because both are original and highly complex in their own right. We have a license for such an abstraction and rearrangement of Merleau-Ponty's philosophy, for our aim is not to reproduce it but to interpret it or talk about it. Finally, although we shall concentrate on his metaphysics and epistemology, since this is the simplest and shortest method for grasping his philosophy as a whole, we shall include in their analysis a less intensive study of his phenomenologies of action, aesthetics, and society in order to establish their essential place in his philosophy.[6]

In order to support our interpretation, we shall refer mainly to Merleau-Ponty's full-length works, the *Phenomenology of Perception* and *The Visible and the Invisible*, rather than to his numerous articles. This is necessary because Merleau-Ponty is notoriously difficult to read and easy to misunderstand. Since the books are systematic works wherein all the studies confirm or bear on one another, there is less room for erroneous readings, and by means of cross references one can reasonably defend one's understanding of a passage. For this reason, and because I intend to demonstrate the coherence of Merleau-Ponty's philosophy, I shall often support my claims with multiple references selected from diverse and different

---

6. Our principles of selection have also been dictated to a large extent by the current state of Merleau-Ponty research. We can presuppose more accurate knowledge of (and thus spend less time on) Merleau-Ponty's analyses of motility, language, psychology, and the socio-cultural world because of the extensive and adequate commentary that already exists. Furthermore, the issues and passages we shall stress in his epistemology and metaphysics are often those that have been generally ignored or misunderstood.

studies within these works. Furthermore, I shall constantly integrate references from both texts, for it is one of my main purposes to show that there was no substantive change in Merleau-Ponty's philosophy between the two.[7] This point must be stressed, for I shall not directly argue it but shall depend on my total explication and on continual cross references to prove that there is no "later" philosophy. If there is a break or change in Merleau-Ponty's work, it is between *The Structure of Behavior* and the *Phenomenology*.[8] Because of this change, and because Merleau-Ponty's philosophy is only outlined in the former work, which in any case is not generally known, it would not serve my aims to use it as a basic source. Finally, since I rely most heavily on the *Phenomenology* and since Colin Smith's translation is often misleading, I have had to retranslate at least half the quotations from this text. I have, nevertheless, used the English translations of Merleau-Ponty's writings whenever possible, correcting them when necessary, because I am writing for an audience whose first language is likely to be English and who thus primarily uses translated editions.[9]

7. These methods will allow us to overcome the pitfalls of Merleau-Ponty's dialectical mode of expression, which is perhaps the main source of current misinterpretations of his philosophy. His positions are frequently mistaken for those he wishes to reject, for he generally presents the latter in the first person and as convincingly as possible.

8. See Geraets, *Vers une nouvelle philosophie transcendantale*, who has adequately demonstrated (especially pp. 184–86) that there is a major change between these two texts.

9. However, since my translations are usually quite different from those they replace, it would be of no help to give the page numbers in the English version; in these cases I always refer to the original French text. Also, if there are neighboring quotations within the argument from the same page of a text that has been retranslated, I also use the French reference for consistency, even when my translation agrees with the English (cf. the List of Abbreviations for the way these retranslations will be indicated).

1　The Ontology of Situations

1. An Introduction to the Concept of Situation

Merleau-Ponty's philosophy may be characterized as a philosophy of situation. *Situation* (*situation*) is the most comprehensive term Merleau-Ponty uses to express the ultimate unity of man with his surroundings, and thus it is fundamental to the discussion of all aspects of his epistemology and metaphysics. The sense of *situation* in which we are interested is roughly synonymous with "involvement in circumstances" or "active concern with sets of natural, cultural, or human problems." We are using this sense when we say, for example, "The child is unable to deal with that type of situation," or "His situation is that of the worker, constantly disturbing and confusing." These situations occur whenever something is found to have a direct bearing at a certain moment on the total life of an individual. They generally arise from the way an individual must relate himself to his present milieu and understand it. We most often apply this sense of *situation* to the interchange between ourselves and others. What is most important is not to confuse this sense with two standard and frequent uses of the word *situation*: the location sense, which is synonymous with "place" and "position," is not of much danger to us, but we shall have to be wary of the "external circumstances" sense which makes *situation* refer merely to an unrelated group of entities, a "set of facts"[1] or a state of affairs.

If we understand situations to be sets of physical circumstances, we shall be misled into believing that Merleau-Ponty is referring to

---

1. This is the sense that P. F. Strawson attacks and attributes to Austin in his article "Truth," in George Pitcher, ed., *Truth*, pp. 39-40.

something entirely external to the subject, something in-itself, like an event or thing. On the contrary, when Merleau-Ponty says that a man is in a particular situation or is situated by something, he means that the subject or some state of the subject is thoroughly intertwined with the object, body, other person, or general milieu that is indicated. It is his aim to overcome the perpetual problems of Cartesian dualism and its resulting extremes of realism and idealism by showing that neither the subject nor the object is primary and that, when taken as distinct, both are theoretical abstractions from the unified situation that founds both. As will soon become apparent, Merleau-Ponty has created an ontology of situations. Situations are to be taken as the real constituents of the world in what Strawson calls the primary sense of *real*. Hence they are not just one type of entity alongside others, but instead they comprise the ontological possibility of every other type of entity.

This use of the concept of situation and some of the metaphysical processes that Merleau-Ponty includes in it are not alien to contemporary philosophy. Sartre uses the term extensively and entitles his many collections of essays *Situations*. But, as we shall see, although Sartre also wishes to make the term ontologically important, he takes it ultimately in the "external circumstances" sense, for he treats it as just another type of object that in the end has no more relevance to subjectivity than any other natural object. Fackenheim, in his *Metaphysics and Historicity*, relies heavily on the concept of situation and makes good use of it, although he too slips into a mistake similar to Sartre's by finally defining situations in terms of "events" and "actions."[2] Heidegger gives the concept immense importance by using "current situation" and "limit situation" to describe what is given in *Dasein*'s most authentic and metaphysically revealing disclosure. Later it will become obvious that Merleau-Ponty also relies on this privileged intuition of the existentialist for his understanding of every possible type of situation. In chapter 2.4, when we learn that the dynamics of situation reflect those of Being and temporality, we shall see that Merleau-Ponty owes much to Hegel's notion of the Concept (*Begriff*). Contemporary analytic philosophers have also used the term *situation* in important contexts. Philosophers of science who follow Popper rely heavily on

2. P. 26.

it.[3] Philosophers of history who are influenced by Collingwood and Dilthey (such as Dray and Berlin) make central the situation of the historical figure for understanding explanation in history, and the situation of the historian for dealing with the problems of interpretation and bias in historiography. One finds the concept of situation used frequently in normative philosophies, for example in Fletcher's *Situation Ethics* and Dewey's pragmatic theory of ethics, which Brandt aptly labels "contextualism."[4] Taking account of an agent's situation to determine his responsibility and culpability has become an important variable in modern ethics.[5] An interest in the logic of situation is also very close to the ordinary language philosopher's concern with rules and principles. Finally, Merleau-Ponty's work is relevant to all forms of contemporary structuralism, for in demonstrating that structure is essentially dependent on situation, it provides an existential-phenomenological clarification of the notion of structure and a critique of the formalism and intellectualism that dominates the structuralist school.[6] Because the concept of situation has an important position in such diverse philosophies, it must be explicitly analyzed if the ontology to which it commits us is to be made obvious. Merleau-Ponty has provided such an analysis, and it is part of our aim to follow its development throughout his metaphysics and epistemology.

It is the purpose of this chapter to familiarize the reader with Merleau-Ponty's ontology of situation. To do so, we shall describe the elements and logic of those common states and processes that most people would invariably and willingly label as situations. It will then be necessary to examine how Merleau-Ponty can apply this notion to every kind of entity: to see, for example, how thoughts, meanings, emotions, and actions, as well as sensations, properties,

3. For example, I. C. Jarvie, *The Revolution in Anthropology*, pp. 216 ff.

4. Richard B. Brandt gives an excellent but unsympathetic outline of this position in chapter 3 of his *Ethical Theory*.

5. For example, see Brandt, *Ethical Theory*, pp. 365 ff.

6. Because of the many shared concepts and interests (e.g., the arts and the social sciences), such a critique should be unambiguous and consequently productive of useful dialogue. There can be no doubt that structuralism has become a formalism, for the structures it favors are theoretical constructs that are hypothesized in order to explain the subject matter as scientifically (and, often, mathematically) as possible. (Chomsky's system of transformational grammar makes this clear, as does Raymond Boudon, *A quoi sert la notion de "Structure."*)

objects, and space, are ultimately situational. This will be accomplished by showing to what extent these objective and subjective phenomena are interdependent. At that point, we shall be able to give a sketch of Merleau-Ponty's ontology by analyzing how situations interrelate to form a unified world. The advantage of outlining all of Merleau-Ponty's ontology so early in the study is that it allows us to locate the central notions and problems of his philosophy and, therefore, to organize the discussion in the remainder of the book meaningfully.

Let us begin by establishing through illustrations what most would unhesitantly take to be situations in Merleau-Ponty's sense. By giving a detailed description of the dynamics of such situations, we shall be able to arrive at most of the essential characteristics of a situation and, thus, of Merleau-Ponty's philosophy. This study will leave us with a valuable paradigm for the terms and principles it introduces, but more important, it will give us what Heidegger calls a pre-ontological understanding of the notion.

At first glance, the main source of our situations seems to be our relationships with others—our family, our friends, our employers, and society at large. We readily speak of certain groups of people sharing a situation, such as academics, workers, Catholics, or women; of certain societies that are attempting to determine what their situation is, such as the French Canadian, the American Negro, the political Left. We also easily apply the category of situation to tasks in which we are actively and strenuously engaged. For example, the attempt to articulate Merleau-Ponty's philosophy presents me with a multiplicity of situations.

The term *situation* is most frequently modified by negative adjectives, such as *disturbing, confusing, troublesome,* and *difficult,* and a situation is described by enumerating facts, obligations, commitments, practical rules, and alternative courses of action and their consequences. The reason for this is that being in a situation implies being actively involved in trying to determine one's present circumstances. It is the engagement in a problem one feels he must deal with and work out. The agent is faced with sets of indeterminate and ambiguous elements that demand his attention but which he can never finally determine or control and a vague and uncertain awareness of his capacities to handle the situation. His purpose is to articulate and clarify it to the maximum. But this struggle to understand the situation is equally the attempt to work out a kind of principle of action that will both organize its diverse elements and establish his role in respect to them. It is a principle that comes into being only in the action itself, never verbally or self-consciously, and reappears whenever it is required in similar situations.[7]

We can broaden our understanding of situations by considering the personal development of the child, which consists of the encountering and mastery of a series of situations that arise from the cultural and natural world, and even from within himself. From his birth, he is perpetually confronted with the foreign, alien, contingent, and unpredictable. As Hegel has shown, his maturation is the overcoming of this otherness by appropriating it and making it non-other to himself. Hence, the child will expend much energy in acquiring patterns of behavior that will organize his cultural surroundings, giving him a measure of control over them. He will painfully learn how to act in standard social contexts, and his dealings with others will be arranged in terms of a perpetually evolving schema. He will also be occupied with situations of a personal nature which attempt to comprehend the bearing that inability, loneliness, anxiety, and independence have on his life.[8]

That nature is a source of situations can be seen very clearly in the case of the child. For him, nature is situational because it is there only to be used and manipulated, and it consists solely of obstacles and threats that he finds typical means to avoid. Nature has a similar meaning for the adult, but he attempts to obscure and deny it by interpreting nature as consisting of nonsituational entities or things-in-themselves. What is important to see here is that nature viewed from within a situation only exists insofar as it is relevant to the

7. R. M. Hare's understanding of principles occasionally comes close to Merleau-Ponty's notion of situation. Hare's chapter "Decisions of Principle" in *The Language of Morals* agrees with many of Merleau-Ponty's main points. Both broaden the scope of practical principles to include most types of subjective activity, and both describe these principles as habitual, a necessary ground of decisions, general but provisional, continually modified by specification, and not essentially verbal or cognitive. It is interesting to note this similarity since contemporary ordinary language philosophy shows great concern with the concept of principle. Of course, Merleau-Ponty combats rather than shares the intellectualist perspective of this school. Nonetheless, the comparison should help us gain a preliminary understanding of the concept of situation and, conversely, suggest the foundations for a situational theory of principles (which would describe verbal and thetic principles and rules on the ground of nonthetic, lived, and concrete practical structures).

8. Hare says: "To learn to do anything . . . is to learn a principle" (surprisingly, "even to learn or be taught a fact"), and "self-teaching, like all other teaching, is the teaching of principles" (*Language of Morals*, pp. 60 and 61).

concerns of the situated individual. The child is situationally involved in nature because he has prior interests which nature satisfies or with which it conflicts. Similarly, there is a common natural world because there is a common subjectivity or set of primordial concerns that all men share. Hence, we are pulled into situations and feel the need to become involved in the solution of the problems they present because we have concerns we always carry with us. The nature that counts for us inescapably puts these concerns into action.

We can see now that it is not third-person facts or neutral states of affairs that are encountered in situations. Rather, there are environments which have an undeniable relevance for me and already contain "lines of force," meanings, or patterns. We cannot describe these situations by isolating a set of pure circumstances and setting them over against a similarly abstracted set of actions, purposes, and thoughts belonging to a subject. Yet, we must not understand the situation as a subjective idealist would, for if there were nothing beyond our subjectivity there would be no need for that perpetual struggle which attempts to arrange and differentiate our resistant environment into ever more manageable situations. Nor must we take it as a naive realist would, for we have already begun to see that the environment can only appear as other than the subject if it becomes conspicuous in clashing with the subject's own purposes. There is, then, a dialectic between the two sides of a situation. In order to understand or experience one side, one must take the other into consideration: the subject's concerns only become available if they are triggered or secured by the setting and the setting can appear and be conspicuous only insofar as it resists these concerns.

Thus far we have discussed "creative" situations, where a subject struggles to overcome the situation's novelty and delineate its sense. This process leads to the acquisition of a sort of general principle. It is general because it will be reapplied habitually or with minimum energy in every subsequent situation that is similar. We can say, then, that the subject "sediments" these situations (or their "structure"), with the result that certain milieus will be immediately familiar to him and will automatically bring these situations into being. Sedimented principles, Hare agrees, allow one to *learn* how to act in certain kinds of circumstance; . . . learn to single out quickly the relevant aspects of a situation, including the effects of the various possible actions, and so choose quickly, and in many cases habitually."[9] We can now see that a creative situation is always problematic to the subject because his sedimented methods of dealing with the world are inadequate to it. In a creative situation our surroundings are already partially structured by our sedimented principles, but they also contain something beyond their grasp (its "otherness"). Since the mastering of a new situation comes about through noting exceptions to the subject's sedimented body of experience, this situation is seen in reference to these past sedimented structures and appears as a modification, recombination, or specification of them. Furthermore, by being used in this new context, the previous sediments are slightly altered to take account of their relationship to it. Therefore, we can conclude that every actual situation refers to sedimented situations and that these sediments are all closely interrelated in the form of a schema of sedimented structures.

We are now in a position to grasp one of the major principles of Merleau-Ponty's ontology. A separable "matter" or "content" or "otherness" is impossible to experience (and, for Merleau-Ponty, therefore cannot exist) unless the subject carries a structure of some sort that will permit it to appear. Thus, we have seen that the milieu of a sedimented situation is immediately given as organized by the subject. Although in the creative situation the subject does not possess capacities or structures that can satisfactorily deal with the milieu, the subject is not for all that presented with a pure and uninterpreted matter (like the hypothesized stimulus or sense-datum). On the contrary, that which one laboriously tries to comprehend is already structured *as* relevant or important to the subject's primary concerns. It is this original preparedness or openness for the novelty of a situation that makes it possible for the situation to disturb the subject, count for him, or motivate his articulation of it.

Another essential characteristic of any situation is the ambiguity that engulfs our awareness both of its objective features and of the actions and attitudes with which we attempt to organize it. Even when I have settled on a principle that will presumably unify the diverse and problematic elements of my situation, I am aware that I

9. Hare, *Language of Morals*, p. 61.

have by no means attained an exhaustive grasp of them. I know that I could return to meditate on this situation indefinitely and perhaps gain a more specific and deeper comprehension, but I would never arrive at an incorrigible determination of it. This ambiguity, which always leaves room for further specification, gives us another aspect of the situation's generality. It appears, then, that situations can exist at different levels of generality but that they will have a relation analogous to that between genus and species.

The same ambiguity and corrigibility adheres to our sedimented situations. We may think of these as structures or as capacities we possess; however, we are unable to give a clear and precise explication of the elements that will trigger them or of the principles that are used in dealing with these elements. The only way that I can "know" a situation and have it fully available to myself is by actually being in it when it occurs. It is possible to describe it with the aid of memory and imagination, but only by putting myself back into the situation as it concretely existed. Such a description must always remain vague and indefinite (even more so than its description at the time of its actual occurrence). One finds that the more cognitive or thematic one makes it, the more its "mood," "feel," or "atmosphere" disappears.

We have seen that the subjective and objective aspects of a situation cannot be isolated, that they interweave and are dialectically interconnected. Hence, when we examine a situation we find that it is equally an activity and a passivity. We talk, on the one hand, about the principles, patterns, structurings, and concerns that circumscribe and reveal; on the other hand, about the natural elements, settings, and circumstances that have motivated the former. Our language forces us to speak of them in one of these two ways. Yet we find that neither the subject- nor the object-terms alone provide us with an accurate vocabulary for describing situations. We only approach this goal if we constantly supplement our descriptions that refer to subjective phenomena with those that refer to the objective phenomena, and vice versa. In order to facilitate our talk about situations, let us adapt the Husserlian terms *subject-side* and *object-side*. The awkwardness of these terms plays a role, for it constantly reminds us that a situation is neither subject nor object, but both. These terms also keep before us the fact that *for* the subject within a situation the two types of phenomena do not appear as self-sufficient or ontologically distinct, but only have being within the context of the situation.

However, when I am in situation I know that the entities of the object-side have an import that goes beyond this particular situation and thus some degree of independence from it. This is what we have already called the *otherness* of the situation (the non-other part of the situation is made up of both the subject-side and object-side). It will eventually become clear that we can understand a kind of independence of the object-side while still maintaining the rule of the ubiquity of situations (i.e., Merleau-Ponty's rule that the subject can only be aware of the world by means of situations). First, we can do so by observing that the object-side's elements can be parts of other situations and thus correlative to other involvements. Secondly, the otherness that is characteristic of this object-side is manifest to us in the corrigibility and indeterminateness of any grasp we ever achieve of the situation. Similarly, my own subjectivity is given to me as going beyond my inherence in any one situation. I am aware that my existence stretches itself into many other situations in the present, the past, and the future. The subject and object are, then, independent to a degree from any *one* situation because both are the possibility of further situations. But this implies that neither is in the least free from the situational structure in general nor capable of being exhaustively defined except in situational terms.

There is one other property of these situations that must be noted early. Merleau-Ponty divides the ways we can relate ourselves to the world into the perceptual, the cognitive, the affective, and the practical, and we can note that any situation contains all of these to varying degrees. *Cognitively*, in every situation we may, for example, recite rules to ourselves, make inferences and judgments, or merely rely on linguistic categorizations. There is always a core of *perceptual* awareness of ourselves, others, and the natural world. *Affectively*, there may be emotional tensions, moods, attitudes, concerns, or desires. Of course, situations are essentially *practical*, but, besides their containing capacities and dispositions, there is an accompanying bodily or motor involvement (which is found in physical behavior or perhaps gestural or verbal action). We shall see that it is possible to make one of these types of involvement central (a temporary focus of one's life) but never to succeed in preventing the others from being at least generally present in its background. Since any situation occupies the whole subject in the above fashion, we can say that situations are modes of being-in-the-world or are expressions of our global existence.

Let us review the central characteristics of Merleau-Ponty's concept of situation with which we have become familiar through the above descriptions. Its main property is that it has two sides which are essentially interconnected. The best means we have for speaking about either side by itself is the use of a dialectical description that refers us to the other side and thus reestablishes the correlativity of the two. However, these sides point beyond themselves in the opposite direction as well to something more or other than what is made available in the particular situation. This otherness, which is beyond every sedimented structure, is ultimately explicable as the source of still further situations. None of the "external" entities of which the object-side may be said to consist can exist for a subject unless they are either (a) already structured by the sedimented experiences of the subject, or (b) given as relevant to and, hence, interpreted by, the essential concerns that open the subject to the world. On the other hand, the structures or principles of the subject-side cannot exist for the subject unless they are concretized to some degree within an actual situation. Even when the situation is present to the subject, his awareness of it is ambiguous, and what he can know of it cognitively (or thetically) is a mere abstract outline or sketch of the full experience. Situations are mastered (though never finally) through a process of articulation and patterning which at one and the same time is the formulation of actions and of dispositions. These creative situations are then retained as sedimented structures which are repeatedly actualized whenever they are appropriate to the present setting. Besides their repeatability, they are general because they can always be further specified and because their full sense refers to other situations together with which they form a schema of all the possible situations the subject can encounter.

2. The Objectivity of Situations

We now have in our possession a paradigm of Merleau-Ponty's concept of situation which has been established by describing the logic of certain kinds of relationships that are obviously situational. Our present task is to understand how Merleau-Ponty can take every conceivable type of entity to be similarly situational. The conceptual shift that is necessary to see that situation is not just one kind of thing among others, but is the ground or source of every form of existence, will take us to the heart of Merleau-Ponty's metaphysics. In carrying out the shift the discussion will at the same time act as a phenomenological reduction to the "lived-world" from the Cartesian and atomistic ontology that dominates the natural attitude. Our study must be very difficult and abstract, but we do have available to us the previous concrete illustrations of situation to which we can always refer to mitigate the formality.

This section will present an intensive analysis of each of the parts of a situation. We shall initially examine those entities that are normally taken to be objective or external to the subject. By noting their dependence in every case on subjectivity, they will be revealed to be abstractions of the object-side from the unified situation. We shall also explain their degree of independence from any one situation by explicating the otherness which the object-side always indicates. This will be followed in the next section by a similar study of the subject-side, where it will be necessary to gain a detailed understanding of Merleau-Ponty's use of the term *structure*. This notion profoundly challenges Merleau-Ponty's claim that there is no subjective phenomenon that is nonsituational or that does not inhere in the world.

Before proceeding, it is necessary to say a little more about the four elements into which we shall analyze the situation. Every situation has an object-side and a subject-side, but each of these sides points beyond itself, or, we might say, contains more than is revealed of it within the particular situation. We have already used the term *otherness* to refer to what is alien, strange, or transcending within a particular situation's object-side. We shall eventually see that this term describes an essential characteristic of Being, and that the more of the subject-side manifests this same aspect of Being, with the result that it too is otherness. But let us call the unknown, ungraspable, or other that adheres to the subject-side *subjectivity*. Hence the situation has four elements: a *subject-side*, which blends into the *subjectivity* to which it belongs; and an *object-side*, which merges into the *otherness* of which it is a concretion.[10] Hence, when

---

10. *Subject-side* and *object-side* are Husserlian terms that are not used by Merleau-Ponty (although he uses, occasionally, similar terms such as *subject pole*, etc.). He uses *subjectivity* frequently, but he uses *otherness* only rarely (e.g., *un Autre* [*F*372, *F*376, *F*486] and *altérité* [*Signes*, p. 156]).

we use the terms *subject-side* and *object-side*, we shall not only be referring to what is subjectively and objectively explicable within a particular situation, but also to the subjectivity and otherness in which the two sides inhere.

The immense power of the notion of situation is displayed by the fact that it constantly reminds us that in order to grasp any one of these four elements it is necessary to take the other three into consideration. If we analyze or attempt to experience subjectivity by itself, we find that it is differentiated into and articulated by the subject-sides of all its possible situations. We have seen that every subject-side projects itself or shows itself in the world; that is to say, it has an object-side. Finally, when we try to pin down the object-side we discover that it is permeated by ambiguity and inexhaustibility, which is the phenomenological expression of its materiality or concreteness. This brings us to otherness, which is the last of the four elements. If we now attempt to grasp otherness by itself, our path is reversed. We immediately find that it is given to us only as a multiplicity of past and future object-sides. These, in turn, demand that we consider their correlative subject-sides if we are to understand how such organizations or structures are possible in the world. On analyzing the latter, we discover that they must be comprehended as states or modes of subjectivity; but these modes must always remain obscure to us since their ontological source is hidden in that ungraspable otherness of the subject-side which we are here calling *subjectivity* (a notion that ultimately points to the facticity and historicity of a subject). These four notions, therefore, are vague or indistinct concepts which blend into one another and which are only ideally separable. It is in this sense that the situational relation is dialectical. Merleau-Ponty, in his later words, would call this a "good" dialectic, because, unlike the "bad," which he extensively criticizes, it does not postulate an all-encompassing synthesis into a rigid category, but preserves the diversity of its elements (*VI*94-95).

The reader need only be warned now about the one other situational term that will be important to us, *structure*. It will be used as a way of referring formally and abstractly to situations without explicitly considering their concrete inherence in otherness or their actual possession by a particular subject. In the following chapters, we shall also use the terms *noematic* and *noetic* to refer, respectively, to descriptions that favor the object-side or the subject-side of a structure. These terms are appropriate; for at this formal level structure approximates to our traditional understanding of intentionality.[11] Although the concept of structure will not be analyzed until the next section, it is necessary to begin to use it immediately.

Let us begin our outline of Merleau-Ponty's ontology by considering some objective entities that are commonly and naively taken to have an external existence independent of the subject. If Merleau-Ponty is correct that the situation is the metaphysical foundation of every type of entity, he must show that the being of these objective entities can only be adequately understood when they are taken either as they appear within situations or as the abstractions of the object-sides of different types of situations. Indeed, a great deal of Merleau-Ponty's philosophy is an attempt to understand in this way such entities as things, events, sensations, properties, other people, history, society, truths, space, and time. In order to see how the logic of situation can be used to come to an understanding of Merleau-Ponty's ontology and to guide us to the essential features of his theories about these entities, it will be sufficient to take sensations and objects as examples. What will appear at this stage as rather dogmatic explications will be deepened and extensively supported in the following chapters, particularly in chapter 3.

One can demonstrate that all these entities are object-sides of situations by establishing either that they are dependent on the presence of subjectivity in general or that their ontological status is equally determined by their correlative subject-sides. Hence, we shall constantly be refuting the claim that external objects are pure particulars, discrete material atoms, or things-in-themselves, by revealing that they are always general and meaningful, that they are permeated by structure and form, and that the subject's actual presence and particular activities supply the transcendental possibility of their being.

If we hold that the sensations or qualities given to us through our senses are *situational*, what are we implying about their being? We cannot maintain a causal theory according to which sensations are

11. We are adapting these and other Husserlian terms to Merleau-Ponty's thought (as he himself does), for they are basic to phenomenology. However, Merleau-Ponty's radical development of the theories of intentionality, horizon, synthesis, etc., implies that these concepts are similarly modified. Therefore, one must not assume that our (or Merleau-Ponty's) use of Husserlian terms suggests that he accepts Husserlian analyses.

stimuli, for we have seen that in a situation there can be no passive reception of pure contents or matter. What is given must be, instead, already interpreted and organized by the structures the subject possesses. For the same reason, we cannot understand these qualities in a realist manner, for as structured they must originally be given as meaningful, thus implying subjectivity. Finally, they cannot be the phenomenalist's sense-data, understood as mental entities, for they display all the following characteristics of inhering in otherness: we can never specify them exhaustively and we are captivated by their unconquerable plenitude; they constantly direct us beyond what we can articulate within any one situation; their source is obscure and they are not willed or projected, but are contingently out of our control.

The originality of Merleau-Ponty's theory of sensations becomes clearer when we make explicit the implications of the fact that sensations have a subject-side, or are necessarily *structured*. First, no sensation is possible unless it is of a certain type, for it can be sensed only by means of a structure the subject has already sedimented or one he will create in distinction from other typical structures. The sensing of any color, for example, presupposes that the subject possesses a structure that is correlated to the series of colors. In other words, every particular sensation must be given with an aspect of generality, such that it is always qualitatively repeatable and similar to other sensations. Furthermore, this generality indicates that one's grasp of a sensation can always be made more specific and that there is the possibility of apprehending the numerically same sensation through different degrees of generality. Sensations, then, are presented through *constant* (299ff.) structures, and thus in principle they are always related to other occurrences or tokens of them.

Secondly, Merleau-Ponty shows that sensations are not related only to those of the same type. Rather every type is closely bound up with every other type of sensation (at least those belonging to the same sense) to form a unified schema of sensory structures. The reason for this gestalt is that sensation situations always have more than one quality present as their object-side. Merleau-Ponty calls such situations *levels*. Contrary to our expectations, there is not, for example, a different structure for each different color quality (nor for each different tactile constant, etc.). The entire series of colors is contained as the object-side of one structure (although there are many of these structures corresponding to different lightings). Hence, a color (that is, either its structure or correlative property) can appear only if it is differentiated from, or distinguishes itself from, at least one other color in the same visual field. Given the activation of this all-inclusive color structure, even those colors which are not contained in the field will have a presence to the subject within his spatial and temporal horizons. Therefore, a constant of any sense will be defined as "for-another," or by its differentiation from every other constant of that same sense.

The third implication of sensations being structural is that they are meaningful. Since they are given as constants or general types, they subsume many tokens in a way similar to that of linguistic meanings. Because they are defined by their position in a gestalt of sensory structures, they also resemble the members of a conceptual schema, which is the traditional model of a subject's meaning-giving activities (Merleau-Ponty will insist, of course, that it is a bodily rather than a cognitive schema).

Lastly, with the above in mind we can begin to see why Merleau-Ponty insists that sensations, like every other subjective act, are intentional (F247); they are a reference beyond the subject to an individual by means of a constant or typical structure. But according to Merleau-Ponty the intentional object or object-side is, for lived perception, a fully intersensory thing. This is the case because a structure of any one sense is normally created or acquired through the interrelation of the body-subject (using all its sensory capacities to some degree) and the thing (which is the unified correlate of all the senses). One is certainly able to ignore the thing with its own constant properties and make the sensation instead the focal point of one's attention; but even then the quality on which one concentrates is taken to be objective or to have an existence within the world. Because sensations have an object-side, even when taken in the restricted subjective sense, and because objective qualities can only exist insofar as they appear, Merleau-Ponty does not make a sharp distinction between sensing and perceiving, or between sensations and qualities (281).[12]

There are a number of further characteristics we would expect to belong to sensations when we take cognizance of their subject-side.

12. *The Primacy of Perception,* p. 42.

We have learned that a subject-side displays certain activities that are essential correlates of the object-side. Thus Merleau-Ponty discovers that a bodily motility and a temporal synthesis are the conditions of the structures that make sensing possible. These accompanying activities are most obvious in touch, where, for example, the hand's superficial movements (which test surface texture), its deep muscular movements (which test density), and the duration of these movements synthesize the tactile entity with which the hand is in contact. However, we must not let this example mislead us into taking these movements merely as physical responses of the objective body. Instead they might be thought of as bodily dispositions. Or, more precisely, they are touch's version of a distinctive type of intentionality that Merleau-Ponty calls "operative" or "motor intentionality" and which defines the nonthetic subjectivity of the body-subject. Hence, one must be prepared to find that even in color vision there are certain motor attitudes, the adduction and abduction of the whole body, which must accompany color sensations if they are to appear. The temporal synthesis that is also presupposed in all sensing directs us to the subjectivity that goes beyond the subject-side, for Merleau-Ponty will ultimately find the meaning of subjectivity in temporality. Subjectivity is, then, undeniably present in every sensation at least as an ongoing synthesis that holds the starting point or initiating contact of sensation and its final structured accomplishment in one unified grasp. We shall return shortly to this investigation of subjectivity in its relation to objective phenomena in the immediately following study of objects. What is described there is easily applicable, *mutatis mutandis*, to sensations.

If sensations are to parallel our initial paradigm of situations, they must be modes of existence that involve the whole subject. Sensations are structures that are concentrated in a certain perceptual region, but they still owe much of their constitution or meaning to all the other regions of the body. Let us consider some examples. The cognitive structures that are given to us by our language have a direct influence on the formation of sensory structures. Hence we may find that one language-group delineates its sensory structures in a way that differs from another group, with the result that certain sensations are *more readily* identifiable by one of the groups. The degree to which structures are specified and sedimented will be partially determined as well by the practical importance they have for a subject and by their relationship to his most basic bodily concerns. Similarly, emotions, attitudes, or moods always accompany sensations, since they are what determine whether and to what degree the subject will make available the structure that will allow the sensation to appear. The overall motility of the body (for example, its posture or state of health) will have a direct bearing on sensations, since, as we saw, the senses must make use of this same motor body.

Because sensing is a mode of being-in-the-world, a sensation belonging to any one sense also implies structures proper to all the other senses. A sensory structure is acquired normally only when the body with *all* its sensory capacities relates itself proximally (most thoroughly and completely) to an object. This means that the way in which a particular constant structure has been creatively determined is arbitrated and limited in consideration of the constant structures of the other senses that are formed in one and the same originating experience.[13] Subsequently, whenever this constant structure is concretized, it will signify these other related sensory structures. Hence, Merleau-Ponty will repeatedly state that a certain color would not be qualitatively the same unless it were the color of a similar object (*F*361).

Finally, as is the case with all situations, it is always possible to analytically reflect on a sensation by limiting one's knowledge of it strictly to those types of characteristics that can be transparently revealed through one's cognitive structures. The result is that one is left with a fully determinate and thetic entity, for example, a sense-datum or a *quale*. This thematization has "reduced" (*F*370) or left behind all the obscure involvements of the subject, as well as the indeterminate and implicit references of the sensation. However, as we have just discovered, these constitute the interdependence or "union of the subject and of the world" (*F*370), and are essential to the original givenness of a sensation.

---

13. The situations that are epistemically (we shall always use *episteme* in the broadest possible sense) the most ideal are not the same for the determination of different kinds of qualities. For example, consider the difference in the positions most advantageous for grasping, alternately, the shape, texture, color, or weight of an object. The compromise that each sense must make when all attempt, through a single and common situation, to attain the best possible grasp of an intersensory object (thereby forming the object structure) becomes part of the meaning of each resulting constant sensory structure.

By examining the dependence of natural *things* on subjectivity, we shall both complete our study of external entities and deepen our understanding of subjectivity itself and the way in which it permeates every situation. Like all objective phenomena, a thing can be encountered only through a structure. Hence a thing is necessarily a constant and is given as the object-side of a typical and general structure. However, an object structure is different from a sensation structure as it is essentially intersensory, that is to say, a coherence and intertwining of the relevant structures from each sense. We have already touched on the fact that a particular sense structure is formed simultaneously with structures of the other senses when the subject, using all his perceptual capacities, attempts to achieve the fullest possible grasp of the entire intersensory thing. This originating experience leaves the "accent" (*F*368) or mark of the object on every sensation structure, so that whenever these structures are concretized they immediately refer to the thing itself. It is for this reason that Merleau-Ponty holds, contrary to traditional philosophical doctrine, that things are logically prior to sensations. Hence the object cannot be understood as a mere bundle of qualities or as constituted from a conjunction of sensations.

This primacy of objects is due to the fact that they are the full correlates of subjectivity. Not only does the object unify the subject's perceptual capacities, but it also provides the objective nucleus for every other type of activity. Thus practical, affective, and even interpersonal predicates will always be rooted in the natural object. Merleau-Ponty will finally explicate subjectivity or Existence as the perpetual action of interrelating, and the temporal drive to unify, all subjectivity's primordially given capacities—those of the senses, cognition, motility, and affectivity.[14] Since each object structure is an articulation of subjectivity as a whole, it has a central role in the schema of structures that constitute the subject. Hence, just as we discover natural subjectivity itself in the "intertwining" (*VI*130) of the structures of the different senses, we find the object itself strictly in the intertwining of its qualities. Further, just as the subject continually strives to determine itself but only manages to

---

14. We shall capitalize *Existence* whenever we use it in Merleau-Ponty's technical sense, in which it is almost synonymous with *subjectivity*, in order to distinguish it from the much broader and more common use of *existence*.

achieve a presumptive unity of its functions in each and every present, so the perceived object always remains corrigible, tentative, and to some degree indeterminate.

Our naive faith in the object as the primary constituent of the world is metaphysically justified in two ways. First, Merleau-Ponty insists that our senses are in direct contact or actually merge with otherness, to the extent that Being "runs through" them (*VI*185*F*, *F*250 and *EM*178). Hence, the natural world can be divided into a number of material regions that are correlative to subjectivity's natural or sensuous capacities. The perceptual object has the importance of being that entity which "gathers together" (*recueillir*) or manifests all these regions simultaneously. Secondly, we saw that the structures of each sense are levels, that is, their object-side consists in a series of qualities. This means that, whenever one quality is actualized in a field, there has to be at least one other of the same series also present (the remainder existing either in the field or on its horizon). Since an object situation must bring into play the structures of every sense, the perception of an object implies a perception of its whole field. An object must always be given in contrast to and on a background of other objects. Moreover, through this "chiasm" (*VI*130) of levels, every present perceptual field contains every other field on its horizon. The result is that the perception of any one object provides a global perspective on or a focus for the entire world. Since the world can then be understood as an immense schema of interwoven object structures (and this is what, in fact, constitutes spatiality and temporality), we can understand Merleau-Ponty's central claim that "the world is wholly inside and I am wholly outside" (407-08).

We can now explain, in the case of object situations, the equivocalness that characterizes their structures and the obscurity or "opaqueness" (*F*384) that is essential to their concrete occurrence. We can never fully explicate our immediate situational hold on an object, because it entails, noematically, a perspectival presentation of the world as a whole, and, noetically, a reference to the entire schema of our sensory structures. Like all sedimented situations, these have a necessary connection to the past where they were created through an only partially successful struggle to determine otherness. Hence, whatever determinations they might have are founded on a provisional synthesis or on an interpretation that is forever open to question. Finally, every perceptual situation refers back to the senses, which, as we have just noted, merge with or are primordially open to otherness. Merleau-Ponty describes the natural facticity of the subject in terms of this contact, which thus must in principle be beyond the comprehension and control of the subject. This obscurity that is at the source of all our structures can be attributed indifferently to the thrownness of subjectivity or to the denseness (*épaisseur*) of otherness.

We have shown how Merleau-Ponty grounds objective phenomena in situations by disclosing the essential dependence of these phenomena on subjectivity and structure. In this examination of sensations and things, we also had to take cognizance of their degree of independence, which was attributable to their otherness. Since we shall continue to rely heavily on the difficult notion of otherness, it has become mandatory to clarify it. However, at this stage our study will be provisional, for otherness is a theme that runs throughout our metaphysical analyses, and it is in fact possible to consider the whole of the three metaphysical chapters as a working out of this notion. Its full comprehension will coincide with our final study of Being.[15]

We have seen that a consideration of any phenomenon or experience (terms which Merleau-Ponty usually uses as synonymous with *situation*) gives us something with which we are familiar and at ease, something we in some sense know and possess. Blended into this aspect of the experience which is "non-other" or "human," we find something more that is undeniably "other" and "non-human"; Merleau-Ponty says that it is "hostile and alien . . . a resolutely silent Other . . . which escapes us" (*F*372). This combination of the non-other and otherness in every phenomenon is a basic fact with which a metaphysics can begin, and the label *otherness* is as neutral as a metaphysical term can be. Merleau-Ponty states, "Our first truth—which prejudges nothing and cannot be contested—will be that there is presence, that 'something' is there" (*VI*160). He defends the

---

15. Langan's final criticism of Merleau-Ponty is that he did not analyze the concept of otherness, but we shall show that this is not the case. In general, we shall argue that Merleau-Ponty has in fact done what Langan says he must do to complete his philosophy, that is, explained the independence of things, how subjectivity transcends to things, and how otherness can be comprehended at the level of Being and its primordial *écart* (*Merleau-Ponty's Critique of Reason*, pp. 177-87).

neutrality of this fact by showing that it can lead to a realist, idealist, or situational metaphysics (*VI*158-60). He establishes the notion at this rather unsophisticated level because it is necessary for him, as it is for us, to use it in most descriptions, while its final comprehension must await the understanding of Being. Hence, we can feel justified in using the term *otherness*, but we shall reinforce this naive but valuable hold on it with the following outline of its phenomenological characteristics and its role in Being. This study will also attempt, of course, to contribute to our understanding of situation and of Merleau-Ponty's metaphysics.

It is thus essential to the thing and to the world to present themselves as "open," to send us beyond their determinate manifestations, to always promise us "something else to be seen". (*F*384)

One of the key properties that characterizes otherness is inexhaustibility. This notion can be unpacked in two ways. First, we have seen in some detail that we cannot exhaust the sense of any situation, because every concrete situation holds every other possible situation on its horizon and is ultimately a focus for the entire articulated world. Secondly, as the above quotation shows, otherness signifies something more than this determinate world or sedimented system of structures. It points to the infinite structurability and openness of any phenomenon. Our understanding can never fully coincide with any object because it is essentially indeterminate or incompletable; that is, we can structure and articulate an object infinitely but never reach a point when we can claim to have exhausted all its detail or even be sure of the grasp we have already achieved.

It may appear prima facie that this second and more interesting aspect of otherness suggests an unknowable material substance or Kantian thing-in-itself. But such an in-itself, and the dualism it entails, are out of the question for Merleau-Ponty, and he will constantly show that otherness is eminently experienceable. We have already been able to characterize otherness as infinite structurability, which means that our powers of existential understanding are not stopped and negated by a self-subsistent something that shows them to be lacking and ineffectual. It means that otherness is totally amenable to structure, since we can always succeed in articulating it further and make some progress toward the truth.

We experience otherness within every situation as the tension between our structures and what they aim to encompass, or by the resistance of the latter to the former. We shall make clear in chapter 3 that when a constant structure is actualized it is never given purely for itself, like an idea, because it must always appear. Merleau-Ponty explains appearances *qua* appearances as the "blurring" (329) or imprecision with which the object-sides of our structures are presented, and this is just the otherness in which they inhere. We can begin to understand this theory by recalling that the structures through which entities are revealed are general and that they roughly approximate a series of categories. When an entity is placed within this series, it falls within the vicinity of one of these structures; but, since no one structure is ever perfectly adequate to it, it tends to call up neighboring structures as well. Hence it blurs or strains the differentiations by which these structures are defined in such a way that they "pass into each other" (324) and yield an inexact presentation. There are a number of reasons why a phenomenon never perfectly "fits" one of our sedimented structures. First, the structure was initially formed in response to a present which can never again be duplicated. Secondly, because the structure had to be created through the use of a vocabulary of previously sedimented structures which were themselves types, there had to be some discordance, from the beginning, between the structuring and the phenomenon that motivated it. Therefore, appearances present us with otherness, but they are not the appearances *of* things-in-themselves but *of* those constant properties or objects that *are* strictly the correlates of our structures.

Merleau-Ponty will describe otherness in many further ways. He will show that we experience it in the way that it demands, solicits, or motivates our structures (I shall discuss this dynamic interchange thoroughly in the section on contact). He will show how it guides the formation of new structures and calls forth, or triggers, those already sedimented. We shall see that the corrigibility of all our experiences has its source directly in their manner of inhering in otherness (as does their *évidence*) and in the finitude of Being itself.

The great extent to which otherness is intimately tied to structure, and hence dependent on subjectivity, establishes that it too is in some sense situational. In other words, its being is impossible without it essentially implicating that of subjectivity. Such a statement can be made comprehensible only by showing that all situational relationships are rooted in a similar relationship within Being. Furthermore, since Being is univocal, we should be prepared to find that at this ultimate level it is in the relating per se that Being is disclosed rather than in either of its poles, subjectivity or otherness. Hence in his later works, Merleau-Ponty will say that Being is reversibility and intertwining and that these poles are the obverse and inverse of one another. We have seen that otherness is discovered in its tension with the subject-side; that it is the stretching away, or splitting off, from any structure; and that this being-outside-of-itself is its essence. In order to comprehend otherness, it is paramount that we deny our first impulse to take it as a static thing. Rather, it is the pole of a dynamic movement, thrust, or transcendence; while the other pole, subjectivity, is like it in being merely an ideal and limiting notion attached to this primordial movement.

The relationship between otherness and Being is made clearer through the following quotation:

Subjectivity is not an immovable identity with self: like time, it is essential to it in order to be subjectivity to open itself to an Other and to go out from itself. (426)

Merleau-Ponty agrees with Heidegger that we find the meaning of subjectivity in time and that temporality in turn reveals the structure of Being. Hence what Merleau-Ponty says here about subjectivity and time applies as well to Being, with the result that Being must be understood as a going-beyond-itself and, consequently, as intrinsically possessing otherness within itself.

We shall later understand how Being is the "outside of itself" with the aid of temporality's *ekstase*, lapse, or flux. For now we can only give a rough report of our conclusions. Merleau-Ponty tells us that we must discover time's *ekstase* in the present, for there we can see time revolving on itself. A present is time's positing of itself; but even while the posit is being performed, the inadequacy of this grasp becomes plain, and thus this present has already become a part of its own past history of such attempts. This inadequacy within time itself *is* the indeterminate future which is the tension within, or pressure on, this present both to abandon itself to the past and to leap out or burst forth (*éclater*) into a new and more tempting present. Being is a similar becoming that constantly attempts its own articulation, gains some hold, and then in the same movement experiences its insufficiency and finitude and plunges on into ever-renewed attempts. Merleau-Ponty's most important characterization of Being is his labeling this movement *écart*, that is to say, a splitting off from itself, a spreading and dividing of itself (or it can be thought of as the more mundane process of differentiation or articulation).

In order to comprehend this dynamic Being, we must resist understanding Being as absolute plenitude and, instead, understand it as radically finite. This means that it is indeterminate and ambiguous, that it has an emptiness and "fissures and gaps" (333) that are inherently incompletable, and that it is essentially foreign and other to itself. Temporality is a result of this finitude; for Being is a spreading which hesitates, and which loses itself as it unsuccessfully moves on. Hence, otherness is not a representation or rationalizing of the finitude of man's understanding; for otherness is just the finitude that permeates Being. It is in this finitude that we discover the necessary inexhaustibility, indeterminacy, and corrigibility of all our situations, and it is in Being's spread and thrusting outside of itself that we find the primordial bond that defines every situation.

Being is not common to every situation in a nominalist sense but actually displays its whole character in each, for ultimately the logic of situation is grounded in the *logos* of Being.

To designate it, we need the old term "element" in the sense it was used to speak of water, air, earth and fire, that is, in the sense of a *general thing*, midway between the spatio-temporal individual and the idea, a sort of incarnate principle that brings a style of being whereever there is a fragment of being. (*VI* 139)

It is undeniable that this description of Being is equally a description of situation, for the latter is also an incarnate structure and a particular permeated by generality. The Greek "element" was an accent present in every concrete existent but not contained by any one individual. Yet this general thing is as much form or idea as it is materiality. Hence we locate the being of a phenomenon by establishing its situational form rather than by looking for its existence or being as a property or mark (or, as Kant would say, as a predicate).

We have said that every situation is, by definition, existent insofar as it inheres in otherness. This locating of Being beyond the object-side of the situation seems to conflict with the above, where Being was seen to be manifest through or parallel to the full constitution of situation. But it is not misleading to speak of a situation's existence as being due to its present blend with otherness, and this schema will be simpler and more useful for most of our discussion. Therefore, otherness must ultimately be understood as a noematic expression of how Being escapes the interpretative grasp of every situation, while still merging with the situation to the extent that this finitude of the situation is itself an expression of Being's primordial finitude.

3. The Subjectivity of Situations

Up to this point our study of the object-side of situations has concentrated on sensations, objects, and otherness. We have not considered cognitive, sexual, cultural, and practical objects, but when we come to examine them later we shall find that they can be shown to be situational in the same manner as perceptual entities. The reason for this uniformity in what Merleau-Ponty calls "existential analysis" (136) is to be found in Merleau-Ponty's thesis of the primacy of perception. It holds, first, that perception gives us the clearest case of our relationship to Being; secondly, that all other types of objects have a natural nucleus in or must be based on this perceptual relationship; and, thirdly, that all the regions of a unified Existence necessarily interact in such a way that they "borrow" or "imitate" the logic of the most primordial region, perception. Because the core of Merleau-Ponty's philosophy is found in his analysis of perception, our discussion up to this point will be useful throughout the first two chapters where we shall most frequently look at his philosophy in terms of the metaphysics of the natural world. For the same reason, the whole of chapter 3, will be devoted to a detailed analysis of the phenomenology of perception, which we must now presuppose.

In order to complete our study of situation, we have still to discuss its subject-side and subjectivity. Since we have already learned much about these topics we can spend less time on them and treat them more generally. We can achieve the most with this discussion if it is organized around an explication of the concept of structure. Chapter 4 will analyze entities that are normally believed to be entirely subjective, such as all types of *cogitationes*, images, and linguistic meanings. We can assume for now that this analysis will establish that such entities are most fully grasped as the subject-side of situations or as *structures*. Nevertheless, one then encounters a serious question about the ontological status of these types of structures, especially when they are not concretized in the present field. The idea of structure then appears to be a great threat to

Merleau-Ponty's monistic ontology; for one is tempted to take structures as self-subsistent transcendental categories, essences, potentialities, or meanings. But if a structure were any of these, we would have an example of a kind of subjective entity that existed purely for-itself, was completely private, and hence lacked the requisite factor of otherness. In that case, Merleau-Ponty's claim that all entities are situational would be overthrown.

Although *structure* has these dangerous connotations, we shall use it in the remainder of this book as frequently as *situation*, as Merleau-Ponty himself does. It permits us to speak of situations in a general and formal manner, without constantly having to be concerned about a particular subject's involvement in a particular field. By beginning our study of Merleau-Ponty with a discussion of situation and by showing presently how the concept of structure is parasitic on the concept of situation, we shall be able to keep these notions within the bounds Merleau-Ponty has set for them. Otherwise, we might make the serious error of interpreting Merleau-Ponty as a transcendental idealist, a gestaltist, or a structuralist. This type of misinterpretation of existential phenomenology is inevitable if one gives primacy to structures rather than to situations. Merleau-Ponty himself occasionally fell into such intellectualism, most notably in parts of his early work, *The Structure of Behavior*, where he relied too heavily on the idea of symbolic function.

If situations are taken to be actual only when they are occurring within our present field, then we can approach the limiting notion of pure structure through those sedimented situations, capacities, or potentialities that are on the far horizon of this field. We shall attempt to demonstrate that for Merleau-Ponty, no matter how distant a potential situation may be from our present concerns, it must somehow still inhere in otherness, have presence or actually exist. Therefore, although there can be no pure structures, it is helpful to be able to use *structure* to distinguish between situations that are present, or fulfilled, and those that are on the far horizon, or empty. A structure, then, is not merely the subject-side of a situation; but, as the abstract form of a situation, it must also be outside the self and in the world. Its noema is an object-side abstractly isolated from its existing roots in otherness. We shall finally see in chapter 4 that this object-side in isolation is what some have mistaken for an objectively existent gestalt, and that it best explains the epistemology of imaginative activities such as painting and abstract behavior (i.e., that of which Schneider was incapable).

In order to show that every structure exists or is as much a part of Being as any presently actualized situation, we shall have to return to our explication of Being, temporality, and subjectivity. Only then shall we be in a position to understand Merleau-Ponty's original theory of *horizonal being*. Once this is accomplished, we shall be able to look at some of the unique features of Merleau-Ponty's theory of intentionality.

We have noted that Being is ecstatic, that it spreads away from itself (*écart*), and that both subjectivity and otherness are founded in this singular movement of Being. If we can show that any structure is an actual mode or "part" of subjectivity itself, we can conclude that, like subjectivity, these structures must always exist situationally or in a bond with otherness.

We traced otherness to temporality's future, which we also found to merge with the inexhaustibility of every present. The source of this *ekstase* is Being's essential becoming, which can be conceived as its drive to articulate itself or as the finitude which prevents it from ever fully accomplishing itself. We find that we can trace subjectivity's transcendence, projection, or freedom to this same *ekstase* and thus can meaningfully grasp the way in which otherness and subjectivity merge. We can equally understand their independence by locating subjectivity within the past as well. This past consists of those previously acquired structures which are used in every present and already determine the outline of any future. Or it can be located to that side of Being which contains the dimensions that have already been determined. The distinction is between that which articulates and that which is articulated, but both are aspects of one and the same movement. Hence subjectivity is a drive that is perpetually ahead of itself into a future, a future that it attempts to make present and non-other to itself, and does so by means of capacities that it has already acquired or which were originally given to it.

This total merging of subjectivity and otherness can be found in every subject in that primordial set of structures that constitutes the subject's facticity or throwness (*Geworfenheit*). In the following sections we shall discuss at length Merleau-Ponty's account of *thrown structures*. We shall show that these primordial structures are generally the regions into which subjectivity can be divided (the linguistic-cognitive, the motor, the affective and intersubjective [sociality], and the perceptual). For the present we shall continue to limit our discussion to the perceptual. This region is basically structured by the different senses which, in turn, are further differentiated into such thrown structures as the light-dark, large-small, soft-hard, and rough-smooth levels. Merleau-Ponty holds that these thrown structures, which are not created by the subject but are given to him and constitute his Existence, have Being "running through them" or are necessarily open to otherness. They in fact coincide with the basic dimensions or characteristics of Being itself. For this reason, there can be no distinction between structure and structured at the level of the senses. They are necessarily in contact with otherness to the extent that any new structure that is created in the future is "simultaneously" (189) and correlatively, both an articulation of these thrown capacities and an articulation of the world and of otherness. "Sensibles are cut out (*découpés*)" of the "Being of Nature" (*VI*267-68*F*). Therefore, the subject's capabilities to experience otherness reveal Being as it is itself and do the work of Being, and are not the distorting lenses that most philosophers have taken them to be. There is not "another being beyond apparent being" (397). Because the subject serves Being's drive to articulate itself and because it gathers together Being's many dimensions within a field, as Heidegger states, the subject has the privilege of being *Dasein*. Inversely, because the "matter" of the senses and the world is continuous or one and the same, Merleau-Ponty can label Being flesh, visibility, and sensibility.

If Merleau-Ponty's argument is to work, it must explain how a specific structure manifests its general region; for only then can it be claimed that such structures share in the region's facticity or contact with otherness. Merleau-Ponty establishes this connection through his theories of horizon and generality, which in addition give us the logic of the interrelations of structures. As this logic will be extensively analyzed in chapter 2, I shall only give a sketch of it here.

We have seen that a structure is defined as "for-another," and thus gets its sense through its differentiation from every other structure of the same category. These structures may be taken as species of a more general structure (the single structure that encompasses the category itself). This more general structure is also defined through its distinction from other structures at the same level of generality. The final genus of these structures (genera, their species, the subordinate species of the latter, and so on) will be the region or regions of which they are the determinations. Therefore, the system of structures approaches a classificatory and hierarchical schema.[16] However, this is merely a thematic and cognitively abstract representation of the system, for Merleau-Ponty will hold that these genera and species are not related merely through a shared meaning but more essentially through a shared being. Hence, when a highly general structure is concretized, this situation may be taken to contain, but in a vague and equivocal manner, all the more specific structures into which it can be articulated. Even before the subject has created these new specific structures, the more general situation can also be said to delimit the same Being or otherness which will be further delineated by these future specifications. Hence the relationship between the region, its thrown general structures, and its acquired more specific structures is that of a hierarchy of genera and species that is real or rooted in Being.

This hierarchy is not merely a theoretical construct to explain away our problem, for we actually experience it every time we perceive a specific object. In our study of contact (chapter 2.3) we shall describe in detail the way in which the otherness of a particular field is able to as Merleau-Ponty says demand, solicit, contact, or motivate exactly the structures most appropriate to it and which give the subject the maximum possible grasp of this field. There we shall see that the field itself sorts out the most general structures and then works through their hierarchies until the most specific structuration to which the subject is open at that moment is selected and concretized. Hence, as Merleau-Ponty frequently stresses, we most often perceive general objects, groups of objects, or even fields. He explains the process of intentional achievement in just this way. As a consequence, a fulfilled intention of a highly general object, or a region, may at the same time appear as the unfulfilled mode of a more specific object which may or may not be achieved in the future.

This complex argument, which tries to establish that structures cannot be purely subjective nor totally independent of otherness, is completed by Merleau-Ponty's theory of *horizons*. We can demonstrate this conclusion, first, by showing that every potential structure

16. Merleau-Ponty variously speaks of it as "a whole architecture . . . of phenomena 'in tiers,'" (*VI*153F), a "polymorphic matrix" (*VI*221), "symbolic matrices" (*VI*192), and a "hierarchized system" (*VI*239).

exists horizonally and, secondly, by showing that every horizonal entity is concretized to some general degree by the present field. The first follows from the fact that each of our thrown regions is manifest in every present field by at least one of its structures; and, as we have repeatedly seen, this structure refers to or horizonally maintains every other possible structure within that region. Hence Merleau-Ponty can say: "The perception of the world [the full system of structures] [17] is only an expansion of my field of presence, it does not transcend the latter's essential structures" (F351).

The first point also serves to support the second concerning the actuality of every horizonal entity. However, the latter needs to be reinforced by clearly refuting the counterclaim that horizonal entities may be pure possibilities that do not inhere in otherness. It is refuted by showing that, although every possible structure cannot be completely present in any one field, the genus under which each is organized and subsumed must be intentionally fulfilled or fully concretized in that field. In other words, these potential structures are actually present to us but in an unfulfilled manner and are never absolutely empty. They can only be conceived of as potentials or capacities (and hence exist within our past, future, and present horizons) insofar as the generic structures in which they are grounded are actualized in every particular field.

Through my perceptual field . . . I am present to my surroundings, I coexist with all the other landscapes that stretch beyond . . . I am present . . . to the whole past that has preceded it and to a future. And, at the same time, this ubiquity is not actual [effective] , it is manifestly only intentional. (F381-82)

We are present to the world as a whole, but only through varying degrees of generality, and the present field actually contains those fields that are horizonal. It must be stressed that our field is not constituted exclusively by structures that are highly specified. If we make the figural or focal mode of a situation paradigmatic for existence, we quickly slip into an atomistic ontology. As the quotation repeats, we are "present" to our horizonal entities, and thus they are parts of our field of presence (Merleau-Ponty insists on this broad understanding of a "field of presence" [415]). To say that something in particular is on the horizon is not to deny its presence

17. Square brackets within quotation marks will henceforth indicate that the comments are my own.

and reality, but only to affirm its distinction at this moment from those situations that have achieved a high degree of determinacy. It is gradually becoming apparent that the world consists of a fabric of interwoven structures; it is, as the title of chapter 4 of *The Visible and the Invisible* calls it, "the intertwining—the chiasm," yet it is also a flux where these structures merge with and separate from one another, their existence being variably manifest at one of their many levels of generality.

It will be helpful to look briefly at what Merleau-Ponty says about these general and horizonal beings.

> The horizon is not . . . a collection of things held together, or a class name, or a logical possibility of conception, or a system of "potentiality of consciousness": it is a new type of being, a being by porosity, pregnancy, or generality. (*VI*195F)

Merleau-Ponty has just warned against limiting reality to fulfilled, focal entities, for most of reality consists of beings that are general, ambiguous, and indeterminate. The horizonal entity can be as evident as the one on which I am presently focusing: The kind and extent of the claim I make about what is beyond my perceptual range is just general enough to be fulfilled by my present field. The horizonal entity is potential in two senses. First, it is potentially a goal of my attention, for it exists in the background of my present figure. When I turn my attention to it, I do not attain a highly determinate entity but rather a general being. Secondly, the horizonal entity is one that can potentially be articulated to the most specific degree desired through certain means and within certain circumstances of which I am aware. I know that this specification must follow the outline I am given through my present general grasp. Even the reproductive imagination will stabilize itself within and follow these indications of our present concrete situations. Horizonal situations are empirical, and not simply "logical" (*VI*195F), possibilities, for they have all been derived from a previous experience of otherness and are subsequently confirmed and indirectly presented in *every* field. Similarly, the horizon cannot be understood as a "potentiality of consciousness" (*VI*195F), as if it consisted of possible *cogitationes* or thematic ideas that could be posited at will. These general entities are incomprehensible in terms of a collection of things because they have a different and more genuine type of being and are interrelated through their hierarchies of specification. It is "a being by porosity" (*VI*195F) because it is incapable of final determination but is nevertheless pregnant with the structures into which it can be resolved inexhaustibly. One of Merleau-Ponty's most important characterizations of the horizonal entity's generality is that it exists only "within a certain degree of indeterminacy" (*F*382). He means by *indeterminacy* that these entities merely circumscribe, or delimit within the world, a possible set of vague alternatives which are themselves ultimately indeterminate. When they become focal, these more specific entities may be found to be contrary to one another and to share no identifiable characteristic. Hence, we must avoid thinking that the general entity is indeterminate in the sense that it lacks a number of the exact details that its specifications might possess. In fact, we shall see that the most determinate phenomenon never gives us even one detail that is in-itself and incorrigibly present.

Although it may be tempting, it would be very misleading to identify a structure with a thetic intention. Merleau-Ponty does hold that the situation is operationally intentional, but he explicates this intentionality through the characteristics of situation that we have already discussed. For him, thetic intentionality, that which makes a definite claim or judgment about its object, is uniquely characteristic of the cognitive realm. As we have seen, structures cannot be identified with cognitive meanings, essences, or acts. Merleau-Ponty maintains that thetic intentionality is the cognitive version, or reflective representation, of operational intentionality (*F*478). Thus he states:

Idealism (like objective thought) passes by the side of true [*véritable*] intentionality which *belongs to* [*est à*] its object rather than posits it. (*F*509)

Since belonging to (*être à*) is the subject-side of being-in-the-world (*être au monde*), operative intentionality's essential characteristic is to be outside of itself through its inherence in otherness. This is why Merleau-Ponty says that "it [operative intentionality] renders the first [thetic intentionality] possible and is what Heidegger calls transcendence" (*F*478).

We are now in a position to put into perspective one of the more frequently voiced criticisms of Merleau-Ponty, which concerns the relationship of intentionality to the real world. Many commentators, for example, Zaner, have claimed that Merleau-Ponty has made a serious error in his use of intentionality, in that he has given the intentional relation and the intentional object real status.[18] Since intentions are essentially situational, and as we have just noted are also concrete, intentionality must indeed be "real" in some sense. But it is most important to remember that the situation is not real in the objective physical sense of this term (for example, what Strawson has in mind when he says that "persons and material bodies are what primarily exist").[19] Merleau-Ponty has devoted a great deal of time to showing that objects, acts, and relations are real in themselves only for the analytic attitude or the "prejudice of the world in-itself" (F527). Such entities are parasitic. They exist only on the ground of and as a cognitive sublimation of the preobjective relation of the subject to the world. We can hardly say that the situational relation or its object-side exists in this naive physical, causal, or objective fashion. Rather, it is real in the same sense that we might say being-in-the-world is real or that our thrown inherence in otherness is real. We have seen that the situation has the primordial ontological status of having the reality of Being and not that of beings. (It is *the Being of this* [objective] *being* [*VI*151].) It is inexcusable for Zaner to equivocate on these senses of "reality," for he takes the Being of an entity to be itself an entity and thus forgets the "ontological difference."[20] Merleau-Ponty of course agrees with traditional phenomenology's caveat against taking the intentional object to be one and the same as the physical—real—object. But he goes further and grounds all types of intentionality in the *ekstase* of temporality and thus in the movement of Being itself. For example, he unmistakably describes the temporal meaning of intentionality when he says: "This *ek-stase*, this projection of an indivisible power into a term that is present to it, is subjectivity." (F487) Like any phenomenological reduction, Merleau-Ponty's discloses an intentional realm; but for Merleau-Ponty this realm is also metaphysically primary, for it is here that one finds the situational unity of subject and object. It shows us "the intentional tissue" (F65) and "the intentional threads that bind the phenomenal body to its

18. Richard M. Zaner, *The Problem of Embodiment.*

19. Strawson, *Individuals,* p. 247.

20. Heidsieck makes a similar mistake when he equates Merleau-Ponty's use of the word *being* to refer to the beings of the objective analytic attitude with his use of the word *being* to refer to the being of phenomena or situations (see François Heidsieck, *L'ontologie de Merleau-Ponty,* p. 109 and also p. 108).

surrounding and finally will reveal to us the perceiving subject as the perceived world" (*F*86).

4. A Comprehensive View of Merleau-Ponty's Ontology

In the first two chapters and the final chapter our purpose is to disclose Merleau-Ponty's metaphysics in its entirety. Thus far we have been able to achieve a broad preliminary view of his ontology by examining the concept of situation.[21] Through our analysis of the major elements of a situation, we have established a basis for our exposition that will keep us from slipping into a Greek ontology or Cartesian metaphysics. It will show us what still remains to be done to make Merleau-Ponty's metaphysical system comprehensible, coherent, and clear. It can already be seen that the major notions still to be discussed will include the ideas of primordial contact or original faith, facticity, specification, Existence, the world, temporality, spatiality, Being, finitude, otherness, and *écart*.

However, before we conclude this chapter we must give a comprehensive sketch of the unitary constitution of Reality and the world. The bulk of this task can be accomplished by unifying and summarizing what has already been discussed. Yet, in order to gain the overall grasp of Merleau-Ponty's philosophy that the analysis of situation has promised us, it will be necessary to introduce and explain a number of other major notions, such as meta-structure, spatial level, and the prepersonal, and the regions of sociality (*Mitsein*), motility, and cognition. The key to comprehending Merleau-Ponty's ontology is to study the four major regions of Existence and their "primordial contact with Being" (*F*255). This section will outline these regions and their interrelation, and chapter 2 will analyze the notion of primordial contact in depth.

In order to obtain a preliminary and concrete grasp of this notion and to initiate our discussion of the perceptual world, we shall begin by describing Merleau-Ponty's theory of the primordial contact of the senses. We shall see that the facticity of the senses and the

21. We find the distinction between ontology and metaphysics useful. We understand ontology as the study of the character and status of entities that may be said to exist in some sense, while metaphysics includes this study but ties it closely to the further investigation of Being itself.

givenness of perceptual entities are one and the same, and that the senses, as thrown transcendental structures, are actual and material parts of Being. A review of the logic of the perceptual region and world (the relationships between sensations, objects, and fields) and the introduction of the idea of spatial level will show us how the ontological world and the entire subject can be discovered in each and every focal situation. We shall then take note of the other existential regions (motility, sociality, and cognition), with the aim of demonstrating both how they merge with one another and how their worlds (the cultural, social, and linguistic) blend with the presentational nucleus of the focal situation. In our examination of intersubjectivity, we shall be introduced to the prepersonal status of the senses, which will show us that a sense is not possessed by an individual, but is instead a singular dimension of Being itself, in which individual subjects participate and share. At this point, we shall have achieved a unified view of Merleau-Ponty's monism and the way in which the single reality of the lived-world can irreducibly accommodate every type of entity.

In the following quotations it is clear that Merleau-Ponty does not use *given* in the phenomenalist sense of contents presented to an ego by something outside of it. "My perception . . . expresses a given situation: I can see blue because I have a *sensitivity* [*sensible*] to colors" (*F*249). "Through sensation, I grasp . . . a life of given consciousness . . . , the life of my eyes, my hands, my ears, which are so many natural Selves" (*F*250). Here, *given* is synonymous with *thrown* and indicates Merleau-Ponty's rigorous interpretation of the existentialist notion of facticity. The phrase "given consciousness" could mislead us into understanding it in an idealist fashion, for instance, as the prepossession of transcendental categories; but "given situation" obviates this mistake. Like all situations, this primordial one involves simultaneously a structuring of, and a contact with, otherness. It is this primordial contact of the senses that is the source of any subsequent more specific inherence in otherness (328). The otherness of even the most highly specified, or most culturally influenced structure can be traced to the general region that it articulates. Hence all of Merleau-Ponty's applications of *given* to the most mundane phenomena will carry a connotation of this facticity. For example, he refers to the givenness of an object equivalently as "its carnal presence and facticity" (109). It is not an accident that he often does this; nor is he being careless with terminology (as he sometimes is) in using *facticity* instead of *factuality*.[22] The facticity of the natural thing and the senses are one and the same (*VI*140).

It is misleading in the case of these thrown regions to speak of a contact between two sides, for at this basic level there is absolutely no distinction. In his later works, he describes this bond better as "flesh" and "visibility," but even in this early text he speaks of it as "sensibility" (*F*250). Through sensation I experience

another self which has already sided with the world, which is already open to certain of its aspects and synchronized with them. . . . I experience the sensation as a modality of a general existence, one already destined for a physical world and which runs through me without my being the author of it. (*F*250)

The frequent use of *already* suggests the close connection of these passages to Heidegger's explication of facticity as already-being-in. The senses are open and synchronized with the world to the absolute extent that Being "runs through" them. The corporeal subject is not face to face with Being; for corporeity is Being itself. "General existence running through the senses" is perhaps the best description Merleau-Ponty can give of his intuition of Being as uncompromisingly univocal or unitary. What must be understood is that Being is wholly a dynamic thrust which does not start from or arrive at a place and that the senses and otherness are poles of this unitary movement. Hence, it is true that I at the same time discover "Being . . . surrounding me and in a sense traversing me"(*VI*114 and *EM*60F). Existence is general in the sense that we can grasp it either noetically, as the undifferentiated thrown structures of the senses, or noematically, as the sensory fields whose contentless "atmospheres" (*F*249) account for the Being of all entities.

The core of the idea of thrownness is that there is meaning in the world before I initiate it, but at the same time this meaning discloses my "connaturality" (*F*251), that is to say, that the nature of myself is the same as the nature of the world. Thus Merleau-Ponty occasionally says Nature is as much *naturans* as *naturata* (naturing as natured) (240). Our double facticity of being open to Being in definite ways as well as having this Being constituting our prepersonal selves is excellently illustrated by the senses. Our senses are "gifts of nature" (*F* 251) and we are thrown not because we have

22. Heidegger uses this distinction but never clearly shows the interdependence of the two terms. See *Being and Time*, p. 82.

limited perspectives on reality, but because Being is undeniably in touch with us. Our bond with it is inescapable and our every act must be grounded in it. Merleau-Ponty understands philosophy as the attempt to explicate this Being which we discover in our senses. He says that our means of doing so, dialectic, is "a situational thought, a thought in contact with being" (*VI*92) and "a way of deciphering the being with which we are in contact" (*VI*94).[23]

All of the senses whose distinctive structures provide the thrown articulations of the perceptual region are involved in every present field and, as a consequence, every actual entity must be intersensory. We saw when we examined the structure of a sensation (its constant) that it was necessarily bound to the structures of our other senses, with the result that a sensation normally intends a full intersensory object. Thus, objects were found to have a primary importance in our field, for they are the accent that holds all our perceptual regions together. But we also saw that our sensory structures were levels, which meant that they always revealed simultaneously more than one entity. Hence the field does not consist of totally discrete and disparate things-in-themselves, for every object is imbedded in an irremovable background and, thus, is tightly interwoven with every other entity that occurs in the field. Since our sensory structures are our initial opening to the natural world and since they always constitute a number of entities, we can see that the perception of an entire field is logically prior to the perception of its constituent objects. The noetic correlate of this gestalt of all the constituents of a field is the synergy of the senses. It is here that we first discover the essential "reversibility" (*VI*142) or translatability of the regions within Existence. The unity of Existence is made apparent in its perpetual interrelating of its different senses, which will even borrow one another's structures or translate them into the logic of their own (225 ff.).

The field itself can be grasped, similarly, only on the background

---

23. The metaphysical importance of this theory of primordial contact can be seen by putting it in the context of the dilemma that arises if we try to reconcile the idea of human nature with the idea of self-making, the dilemma which Fackenheim delineates so clearly in *Metaphysics and Historicity*. Man is neither bound to essential and determinate ways of experiencing the world nor is he totally free to create his own world. Rather, in compromising between these two extremes, primordial contact shows that although man is given very general capacities for being-in-the-world, their articulation or specification is due to his creativity.

of the subject's other past and potential fields. This interweaving of fields has already been shown to be necessary because of the horizonal relationship of our potential structures to our present ones. Yet any present field is essentially a part of the spatiality that constitutes the actual world, and thus it horizonally maintains directions and distances to every other field.[24] In order to understand how this is possible, we must become familiar with the most important concept of Merleau-Ponty's theory of space, the spatial level (248 ff.). The spatial level is the global structure that is correlative to the entire field. It is constituted by every type of structure that is involved in the field, with every region being at least minimally present. It represents the unique equilibrium and balance among all these capacities which yields the maximum grasp the body-subject as a whole is able to achieve on this particular field. These levels are the source of ontological space because they give us a cross section of Existence in its attempt to posit a unity of all its thrown regions, or similarly, to overcome otherness in all its dimensions. This is the movement of temporality, for the way in which a new spatial level is created (and equally a new field made present) is by taking account of the way in which otherness demands a reorientation of the immediately preceding existential level and a differentiation from every previous level. Therefore, through the spatial level that structures a field, all other fields are placed within a spatial and temporal horizon; moreover, because the spatial level consists of every region, it also holds every potential structure of which the subject is capable. Although this latter system of potential structures is ultimately engrained in the spatio-temporal system, it initially directs us to the possible inner horizons of any focal entity and to the individuality and historicity of a particular subject. We can now make sense of one of Merleau-Ponty's key metaphysical formulae, which states that the constancy of a sensation is derivative from the constancy of the thing, which in turn depends on the constancy of the world (313). The last-mentioned constancy is that of our entire system of structures, whose permanency is a result of their being modifications or expressions of the thrown regions of the body-subject (and noematically, of the world).

24. Compare Heidegger's notions of directionality and de-severance in *Being and Time*, pp. 138 ff.

We discover the entire natural world and natural self in each and every focal situation. The totality of space, time, the subject, the world, and Being itself are always found at the focal point of a field of presence (100-02). Hence Merleau-Ponty speaks of the subject as a "peak" or "wave" of Being, or he could, like Heidegger, speak of the "clearing" (or the *Da*) of Being as a whole. (The pure subject or ego of traditional and analytic thought can be taken as the ideal extension of this point, abstracted from its inherent background [*VI*222]; while the objective world of things-in-themselves, or isomorphic and homogeneous space, is the ideal extension and leveling of the horizon, abstracted from its foundation in this same point [*VI*84].) The subject and the world, then, are equally concretized through the present field. Merleau-Ponty will define the body-subject as the present realization of Existence's system of structures, which exactly describes a field of presence. I am "identical with my presence in the world and to others, as I am now realizing it" (452), because my "body is nothing but that very situation insofar as it is realized and actualized" (340). Therefore, when Merleau-Ponty asserts that there can be no purely subjective phenomena because all can be shown to be embodied or incarnate in the body-subject, he is making a noetic statement which is identical to the noematic statement that all structures are materialized in one's present field. If it were not the case that the embodiment of our structures was equivalent to their concretization in otherness,[25] then his repeated arguments to show that all subjective phenomena are embodied would have failed to reach the desired conclusion, that is, that all these phenomena are situational or are "in the world." Just as we have seen that the whole natural world is rooted in a focal situation, we shall also see that the motor-practical, the social and cultural, and even the world of ideas form about this same focus.

The perceptual world is not distinct from the motor-practical. But we shall only be able to see the close interconnection of our perceptual and motor capabilities in chapter 3, after they have been investigated in great detail. Our perceptual structures will be shown there *to be* motor intentions and, hence, to have an intrinsic connection to the body's capacities for gross or wide-ranging motor behavior. Therefore, we can add two further qualifications to our

25. Merleau-Ponty even makes *incarnates* synonymous with *concretizes* (319-20).

above outline of Merleau-Ponty's ontology: first, the object structure is not constituted merely through its unique interweaving of all of our sensory capacities, for these sensory structures are further limited and compromised in their attempt to attain their own clearest and most distinct grasp. The object's constitution must equally take account of the constant movement and postures of the body-subject, as well as the practical uses and significances that the object may have for it. Secondly, the entire organization of our field and thus all of natural space will rely heavily on the subject's motor capacities to cover distances and potentially to orientate the field from any point within it.

A third region of Existence is sociality.[26] Like the other primordial and thrown regions, it merges with otherness in a unique manner and is ultimately a dimension of Being. It is because of this region that we have a thrown openness to other persons, social behavior, and distinctively human gestures, all of which are given as clearly different from natural objects.[27] Merleau-Ponty, following Freud, traces intersubjectivity's main condition to the body-subject's sexual capacities. Neither, of course, means that the structures of this realm are merely those of sexual desire as ordinarily understood; instead they consist of all the ways in which we deal with others. Thus sexuality, when maturely articulated, will be the material ground of our affections, of our sentiments, and correlatively of our socio-cultural world. Given the presence of this world, natural objects will gain a cultural and practical significance which will bind them to the uses and roles they have for societies of persons. This intertwining of cultural, motor, and sensory structures in the object

26. We have decided to use the term *sociality* (*F*495 and *F*511 are examples of its rare use by Merleau-Ponty) in preference to the more frequently used *interpersonal, intersubjective, social, cultural,* or *historical world,* because it includes all of these notions without their more distinctive connotations. It is meant to function in the same way as Heidegger's *Mitsein* and it appears to be the closest English equivalent for that term. Schutz uses it in our sense in some of his English essays (in *Collected Papers,* vol. 2, p. 199, and vol. 3, p. 71), and he may well have taken it from Husserl's use of *Socialität* (e.g., *Die Krisis der europäischen Wissenschaften und die transzendentale Phänomenologie,* p. 175).

27. "We must consider the relation with others not only as one of the contents of our experience but as an actual structure in its own right" (*CO*140). "We must rediscover ... the social world ... as a permanent field or dimension of existence" (362). "If other people who empirically exist are to be, for me, other people, it is necessary that I have that with which to recognize them; it is necessary, therefore, that the structures of the for-another already be dimensions of the for-oneself" (*F*511).

is so thorough that the experience of a purely natural or sensory object is empirically impossible.

However, sociality and the world that arises through the interchange of subjects also find their source in the other regions. All the thrown structures of a subject are shared in the strongest sense by every other subject, such that there is immediately a recognition between body-subjects of all their basic modes of behavior, and all share a common world. Thus almost every movement or action of the body will have a gestural significance for others; and the most articulate form of gestural behavior, the linguistic, is essential to the formation of a socio-cultural world (and, as we shall see, to the cognitive as well).

This sharing of thrown structures is most spectacularly demonstrated by the prepersonal status of the senses. Let us return to the consideration of the senses in order to see why Merleau-Ponty insists that it is not an "I" which senses but a "one." This will lead us to the important tenet that the senses are universal to all subjects; it will reveal a subjectivity in general, which gives us a glimpse of Being itself, and will thus show us concretely how consciousness is "implanted in Being" (*F*485). The following discussion will be thorough, for it will demonstrate most of the arguments made in this section and give us an invaluable base for the next section's study of primordial contact.

The subject is not in complete touch with himself, for all his most personal acts are grounded in his given and prepersonal existence. Every perception allows him to experience this existence but "it takes place in an atmosphere of generality and gives itself to us as anonymous. . . . I ought to say that *one* [*on*] perceives in me" (*F*249). When these structures are in use they are anonymous, because I do not coincide with the Being that "runs through them." Since I am not their author or originator, I am aware of them strictly in their generality as the mere exercise of pregiven capabilities. I know them as potentialities that possess me and whose actualization is not due to my creativity but to their preexisting bond with otherness. I am conscious of these primordial situations through my awareness of being perpetually open to the unforeseen dictates of otherness which nonetheless are articulated by means of the structures that found my selfhood.

The most astonishing property of primordial structures is that their generality not only implies their anonymity and ability to be infinitely actualized but also that they are intersubjective or universal to all subjects. "Universality and the world find themselves at the heart of the individual and the subject" (F465).[28] We can now comprehend the full implication of *anonymity* and the *on*, for the facticity of these primordial situations implies not merely that their origins are unknown (this is the aspect of facticity that Heidegger stresses), but that these situations exist apart from any particular individual who partakes of them. Just as we saw that any concrete sensation is ontologically a manifestation and specification of one of our senses that is general and given, we now see that the individual's own possession of this sense situation is a manifestation and specification of something that is broader than the individual himself. In other words, the universality of these primordial givens is traceable to the structure of Being itself. All our structures, being articulations of our initial primordial contact with Being, have a "cohesion which cannot be denied them since they are all differences, extreme divergencies of one same something" (VI84). A subject does not possess a sense like vision; the sense, rather, as a dimension of Being, possesses him. Hence Merleau-Ponty will use *visibility* to name the metaphysical ground of both the visual sense and the visual field, and use *sensibility* to name that aspect of Being of which my own perceptual capacities are only a contingent appearance.

It will only be possible to clarify the metaphysics involved in this claim in our discussion of Being in the last chapter, but we can at least note some of its relevant implications. All subjects will have a common natural world and their being co-present in it will greatly deepen and strengthen its total horizonal presence. Two subjects within the same field will be in contact with otherness through the same basic and thrown structures, only specifying them to different degrees. Hence each subject's field will be a further structuring of the other's. In fact, the other subject's field will fill in and be continuous with my own because, given my awareness of his body-subject, the

28. For Merleau-Ponty, this statement is both a paraphrase and the ultimate analysis he gives of that phrase of Husserl's with which he is constantly preoccupied (e.g., 371): the transcendental subject is intersubjectivity (xiii). It occurs as well in *Signs*, pp. 97 and 107, in *Sense and Non-Sense*, p. 134, and in *The Primacy of Perception*, p. 51. This is a good example of Merleau-Ponty's style of constantly returning to and meditating on key phrases and terms of Husserl's.

field will in a sense be actualized for me from his point of view (this is comparable to Husserl's notion of intentional transgression).

> My body . . . discovers in that other body a miraculous prolongation of my own intentions, a familiar way of dealing with the world. Henceforth, as the parts of my body together comprise a system, so my body and the other person's are one whole, two sides of one and the same phenomenon, and the anonymous existence of which my body is the ever-renewed trace henceforth inhabits both bodies simultaneously. (354)

The other's body is a "prolongation" because it further articulates the same entities at which I am directed. Merleau-Ponty's comparison of the unity of the parts of the body to the relation of many bodies must be taken literally (see also *VI*141), for it again directs us to a one of which each is a manifestation. Together all form an intersubjective system which articulates Being, in the same way as the intersensory system articulates a perceptual world. Just as my different perspectives on a thing are interwoven by being all specifications of this general object situation, the global perspective that I am (that definitively characterizes my reality and individuality) is interwoven with that of every other, all being specifications of general Being-in-the-world. Like two sentences that express the same meaning, these perspectives are not discrete but cohere. "In reality, the other is not enclosed in my perspective on the world . . . because it slips spontaneously into that of others" (*F*406). The result is that our fields merge, overlap, and are doubly articulated. The co-presence of many subjects within my world justifies, confirms, supports, and actualizes to some degree the infinite horizonal connections that form the background of my present field. In other words, a body-subject is actually presented and given to me essentially as another perspective or organization of the world itself.

The last existential region is cognition, which is also founded in the materiality of the body-subject, most particularly in that distinctive type of motility that is used in our verbal gestures and behavior. Cognition is grounded in our linguistic body. In alliance with sexuality, the extremely precise structures that the cognitive-linguistic realm possesses help give rise to a society and culture which even further deepens the complexity of our world. Language and cognition make possible the precise and sophisticated communication between subjects which results in the formation of societies and the binding of every subject's perspective of the world tightly together. It also, however, develops a mental world or realm of ideas, which achieves a pseudo-independence from the natural and cultural world (*VI*144). Its extensive analysis will be given in chapter 4, where we shall investigate *cogitationes* of all types, language, imagination, *évidence*, and truth.

We shall stipulate that the structures of cognition, as well as of sociality and motility, be called *metastructures*; for, like meta-languages, they are second-order structures that necessarily refer to first-order structures (perceptual situations). The object-side of a metastructure is the full perceptual situation. We shall see that for the most part metastructures work to modify, direct, and regulate our inescapable perceptual openness to otherness. Therefore, once again it is maintained that nonperceptual structures are found as layers about the presentational nucleus. Furthermore, they are frequently acquired through the adaptation, or translation, of perceptual structures to the logic of their own general and thrown capacities. Hence moods, attitudes, interests, affections, gestures, movements, and all types of *cogitationes* will show themselves in the way they affect the organization of our perceptual field. The concept of metastructure will be further discussed in chapters 2 to 5, for its mode of inherence in otherness is less direct than that of perception. It is mandatory for us to understand these indirect situations, for they are of central importance to a number of aspects of Merleau-Ponty's thought: other minds (the perception of persons and gestures), the interrelations of the four dimensions of Being or regions of Existence, analytic and reflective perceiving, the depen-dence of *cogitationes* on otherness, and freedom.

We have now demonstrated how one can approach the totality of Merleau-Ponty's ontology both through studying the primordial contact of our existential regions and analyzing the constitution of any focal situation. The natural world is thus found to be an abstraction when taken as separate from the social, cultural, and cognitive worlds; for every object's essence is modified by its practical use, its socio-cultural significance, and its corresponding cognitive-linguistic structures (for example, the activities of naming and thematic classification). These worlds intertwine as tightly as do the senses and, being correlatives of our thrown regions, they have the unity of Existence. We shall see that even the plurality of individual subjects is part of the multiplicity into which Being must divide itself in order to position itself. And, given this plurality, the socio-cultural and cognitive worlds can be viewed as necessary parts (in Hegel's retrospective sense) of Being's self-articulation. We were already on our way to grasping this notion when we saw that, since Being needs a subject in order to articulate a world, a plurality of subjects would infinitely enrich the gestalt of this world and make it, throughout, more concrete and explicit. Let us, then, turn to the detailed study of primordial contact in order to fully comprehend how Merleau-Ponty supports these positions and grounds his ontology.

2 The Logic of Situations

1. Primordial Contact

In this chapter we shall continue to study the themes we have already introduced which are relevant to the logic of situations. We shall examine in detail the major concepts it compromises: primordial contact, creative specification (or acquisition), productive specification (or contact), articulation, and metastructure. The method of this chapter will differ to some extent from that of the previous, for we must now not only continue to develop Merleau-Ponty's theories in detail, but also prove that he holds them in the way that we have thus far attributed to him.

Since I have already shown the importance these notions have for Merleau-Ponty's situational analysis (which he also calls "radical reflection" or "existential analysis"), there is no need to justify studying them. However, it should be noted why such an analysis is necessary at this point. First, situational analysis will be crucial to the phenomenological studies of perception and cognition (chapters 3 and 4), and we shall be able to give our complete attention to these studies only if we have Merleau-Ponty's main methodological notions already to hand (complete descriptions have rarely been achieved because of the need to explain these notions every step of the way). Secondly, this study will help us to comprehend Merleau-Ponty's understanding of Being and temporality, for we shall be able to see how he has transferred these basically phenomenological notions to his metaphysics. It is Merleau-Ponty's practice to use for his most basic metaphysics concepts that are packed with meanings and uses they gained initially in his most concrete phenomenological studies.

This chapter, although schematic and abstract, will help convey this practice and show how Merleau-Ponty, as an existentialist, remains faithful to a philosophy of the concrete.

I have already introduced the notion of primordial contact and demonstrated its central role in Merleau-Ponty's ontology. Now we must examine the notion in depth. This is necessary, not only to prove that we have not misinterpreted Merleau-Ponty, but also to understand the relationship of the notion of primordial contact to his other essential concepts, to establish it as a cohesive theme that runs throughout his epistemology, and, most important, to get a concrete phenomenological comprehension of it. Merleau-Ponty often says that his entire phenomenology is meant to be a reduction to the lived and preobjective realm where primordial contact is disclosed (256, VI101-03, VI160). We shall proceed by first discussing it as a theory of innateness, noting its similarities to some contemporary structuralist theories of this type. We shall then show briefly how primordial contact can be discovered through Merleau-Ponty's analysis of space. This preliminary sketch of space will provide us with an irreplaceable expression of the original and material bond between the subject and the world. The examination of the world's individuality will bring us to a consideration of the "tacit *cogito*." The latter is important, for it yields the purest possible experience of thrownness and introduces us to Merleau-Ponty's central notions of primordial faith, openness, and the unique certainty that "there is something." By studying these in depth, we shall arrive at an epistemological and phenomenological description of primordial contact, finally replacing our abstract and formal comprehension of it. Since it will also relate some of Merleau-Ponty's own extensive phenomenological descriptions to primordial contact, this section will turn our explications more directly toward what Merleau-Ponty believes is the only proper method of doing metaphysics, that is, phenomenological description.

Merleau-Ponty's theory of thrown structures relies heavily on the fact that understanding and interpretation are equally primordial and essentially interdependent. It concretizes and clarifies this shared primordiality by showing that even the most highly articulated situations "comprehend Being," because of their ontological and genetic roots in our originally given perceptual structures. These basic structures are equally an openness to Being (understanding) and an initial articulation with which every subsequent interpretation of otherness must cohere. In this section we shall attempt to isolate the "understanding" (53 and 327) character of primordial situations, while in the next we shall study its unity with articulation. This second section will also begin the explication of the logic of situations by examining the way in which our acquired structures are creative specifications of our thrown regions. The third section will analyze productive specification in order to reveal how these highly determinate and sedimented structures are triggered or actualized by their contact with the otherness of a present field. We shall complete this chapter by a discussion of temporality, which, as the structure of all structures, unifies the features of situation that we have discussed in this chapter.

Merleau-Ponty occasionally refers to our given situations as "innate"; but he does not stress this term, and they must not be confused with the innate ideas of traditional theory.[1] Yet they do satisfy many of the following aims of such a theory. We have seen that these structures are given to us from birth and set limits to our future comprehension of the world. Since they are our basic openings to the world, they are a given power of understanding in the deepest sense. We shall see that they are transcendental, for they are the condition for and possibility of any experience or existent. For consciousness even to appear, it must "play upon significances given either in the absolute past of nature or in its own personal past" (137). "My history must be the continuation of a prehistory and must utilize the latter's acquired results" (254). These "natural absolutes" will become the basis of all our lived and objective certainties. They present us with the indubitability of "primordial opinion," which is just the certainty of our inherence in the world, and thus they overcome epistemological skepticism or solipsism. Finally, they are universal and necessary to all men.

However, Merleau-Ponty is not susceptible to the traditional pitfalls of innatism. Everything we have so far learned about the logic of situations militates against such a charge. We have seen how different situations are from Platonic essences, Cartesian ideas, or Kantian categories. Structures are ambiguous, indeterminate, and general, and they can be known only insofar as they are concretely actualized within the world. They do not give us knowledge

---

1. He uses "innate" explicitly on *F*99, *F*527, and *VI*139, and in *Sense and Non-Sense*, p. 21; also it is implicit every time he uses the important phrase "original faith," for we would not betray his meaning if we translated *originaire* as *innate*.

independent of an experience with the world, and they are not clearly and thematically detailed nor distinctly and thetically defined. "The psycho-physical equipment leaves a great quantity of possibilities open, and there is no more here than in the realm of instinct a human nature given once and for all" (F220). Rather, all human conduct "eludes the simplicity of animal life, and diverts [détourne] the sense of vital behavior through a sort of *leakage* and by a talent for the equivocal which can serve as a definition of man" (F221). The body-subject provides us not only with a given material but also with the power of Existence, or transcendence, which, from the first, makes us creatively and historically modify this corporeity. Our thrown structures yield the most general and indeterminate regions of Being, and with our first experience they are already specified and hence transcended. Furthermore, they are so distant from our focal concerns that Merleau-Ponty calls them the "horizon of horizons."

Chomsky and other structural linguists feel a similar need for innate structures, even beyond the realm of language.[2] Chomsky's argument, although ultimately spoiled by its rationalism and scientism, is instructive. It turns on the insight that "we must postulate an innate structure that is rich enough to account for the disparity between experience and knowledge."[3] He means by this that it is impossible to account for the structures of behavior, even though occasioned by singular, deficient, and short-lived data, by means of any theory of induction or intellectual subsumption. Rather, we must already have general guidelines or directions which, in conjunction with these givens, can yield a structure that will continue to hold for us. In our terms, an encounter with otherness can yield a new and more specific structure because our approach to this particular experience has already been delineated by sedimented and more general structures. Hence man's experiences, even his first, depend on there being some degree of organization which forms the

2. Cf. for example, E. H. Lenneberg, "The Capacity for Language Acquisition," in Jerry A. Fodor and Jerrold J. Katz, eds., *The Structure of Language*.

3. Noam Chomsky, *Language and Mind*, p. 78. The reader should be warned that, although these comparisons are useful because of current knowledge of Chomsky, they are not meant to encourage a synthesis of Merleau-Ponty and Chomsky of the kind that James Edie promotes, for example ("Can Grammar Be Thought?" in Edie et al, eds., *Patterns of the Life World*). Chomsky's rules and capacities are so formal and constructivist, and thereby nonexperiential and nonphenomenological, that they can be of only minor interest to a phenomenology of language.

past and on which all future articulations can be grounded. Chomsky agrees with such a theory of specification; all evidence, he says, acts on our present structures (he mistakenly thinks of them as "hypotheses") as "corrective action, confirming or disconfirming."[4] When this evidence (which again is not strong enough to yield a new structure through induction) disconfirms, then, through a sort of ad hoc process, the structure is slightly altered. It is restructured rather than banished or totally rejected because it has its roots in immovable but modifiable innate structures. Chomsky also argues that these structures and their modifications must have a high level of "complexity," but only the needed degree of "richness" or determinability.[5] The vast generality of Merleau-Ponty's natural absolutes, the great but graspable complexity of his hierarchy of specifications and the diversity of particulars it can contain, meet these requirements.

If we look briefly at three of Merleau-Ponty's central concepts—primordial space, world, and the tacit *cogito*—we shall begin to grasp what is meant by this contact or "understanding" apart from the articulations given to it in the course of our normal existence.[6] In discussing spatial levels, Merleau-Ponty shows that the present level which is anchored in the milieu is the global adjustment of all the body-subject's diverse capabilities to its present field. The only way one can notice and be aware of this present orientation is if it results from a readjustment of a previous level (which describes the body's past hold on the world). Therefore, every new anchorage of the body-subject presupposes a previous level. In other words, every new field can only appear in its particularity and conspicuousness by its differentiation or disorientation from the previous field to which the body-subject adjusted itself. Hence, Merleau-Ponty proves through a finite regress from each level or field to the previous one on which it depends that there is a primordial level which describes the original bond between body and world and which is, thus, a level of levels.

---

4. *Language and Mind*, p. 78.

5. *Language and Mind*, pp. 32 and 69.

6. It is important to comprehend understanding and interpretation separately as well as in their unity because Merleau-Ponty's treatment of them gives his solution to the corresponding troublesome epistemological dichotomy between the given and the interpretation (or, equivalently, between reference and sense, content and form, and passivity and activity).

Since a first perception, that is to say, the taking notice of a particular and distinctive phenomenon, is only possible through a rebalancing of the body-subject's general grasp, before the first perception we must be "already at work in a world" and spatiality "already acquired" (F293). "It is necessary that my first perception and my first hold on the world appear to me as the execution of a most ancient pact between 'x' [a "natural or captive self"] and the world in general" (F293). The "anchorage points" of this original world cannot consist of particular contents, for these can only appear as such through their resistance to a previous level. Nor must one believe that anchorage points are things-in-themselves which exist prior to and independently of their spatialization through levels. The least appearance of particularity demands the immediate readjustment of our levels, and thus the primordial world must be "nothing" (in the sense of containing no things). Merleau-Ponty says that such contents "cannot be found anywhere" (F293). This level of levels is our most general structure and hence is a description of Existence or being-in-the-world as a whole. When Merleau-Ponty says that it is "executed" by our first experience, he means that through this first actualization it begins to specify itself and fulfill itself. It can be thought of as the only perfectly empty intention, for the whole of life will be dedicated to articulating this initial grasp. Yet from another point of view it can be taken as the only totally fulfilled intention, for it is pure presence and contact with Being.

This x or natural self is "the system of anonymous 'functions' which envelop every particular fixation in a general project" (F294). This is not the intellectualist sense of "project," as it is the bringing of our past inherence in otherness to bear on the present. This quotation conclusively shows that for Merleau-Ponty original spatiality, or the world, is correlative to our given bodily potentialities. Merleau-Ponty says that the aim of his study of space is to "describe the phenomenon of the world, that is to say, its birth for us in that field where each perception puts us back" (F296). This pure world cannot be found in isolation from the "world" that consists simply of a conjunction of entities (the sense that Heidegger in *Being and Time* encloses in quotation marks) because, from the first, our original and thrown level is captivated by and constantly adjusting to its particular surroundings. Similarly, understanding and interpretation are only artificially distinguished.

Our "primordial comprehension of the world" reveals it to be a "unity" in the sense of a "style" and an "open individual" (327). We are now in a position to understand why these descriptions hold. The comparison of this constancy with the style of an individual person is more than an analogy or anthropomorphism; for the world's unity is the object-side of the unified thrust of Existence or of subjectivity as expressed by our innate structures. For example, Merleau-Ponty characterizes the self as "a single 'cohesion of life' [a reference to Heidegger], a single temporality that progressively explicates itself from its birth and confirms it in each present" (F466). Because Existence must necessarily structure itself within certain innate regions, its style remains constant and its facticity is inescapable. "I am from my origin in communication with a single being, an immense individual from which my experiences are taken" (F378). The world's individuality as well as the self's is due to the characteristics of our primordial contact. Being expresses itself or "runs through" man by means of innate situations which have a definite sense. Again, we must stress that these givens are not categories but structures of Being itself or, we might say, of "Existence-Otherness." The world is not merely a projection or noema but consists of the most material of regions. It is what Merleau-Ponty calls a "concrete a priori" and which we may call an "experienceable transcendental." It is transcendental because all future experiences will be specifications of it and it will constantly give us "the fact of our birth, the perpetual contribution of the subject's corporeity" (F294). It is experienceable because it is our inherence or primordial contact and it "recommences at every moment" (F294).[7] Finally, the world is "open" or incomplete because these innate situations are extremely general and indeterminate. Just as our perceptual functions will be repeatedly specified but never exhaustively, so our primordial world will be articulated but never made totally determinate.

The tacit *cogito*, which is the most intimate experience of ourselves, is just the experience of our primordial being-in-the-world.

7. Langan's book, which presents the best overall interpretation of Merleau-Ponty to date, in missing the notion of primordial contact, misses Merleau-Ponty's realism. Thus Langan goes wrong in his last critical chapter, where he understands Merleau-Ponty as presenting only a variation on "idealist" transcendental philosophies and criticizes him for his lack of realism (*Merleau-Ponty's Critique of Reason*, pp. 169 ff. and 186-88).

"To be conscious" is here [in perception] nothing but "being-in . . . " (*être à*),
. . . my consciousness of existing merges into the actual gesture of "ex-istence"
[a reference to Heidegger's *Existenz*]. It is in communicating with the world
that we indubitably communicate with ourselves. (*F*485)

My ultimate consciousness of self is thus not a second-order
reflection that could reveal a separate realm, but it is given to me by
means of and indistinguishably from my contact with the world. I
find myself in my throw into otherness (which is similar to Sartre's
neg-intuition) or through the separation (*écart*) that occurs with my
first attempt at specification. "What I discover through the
cogito . . . is the deep-seated momentum of transcendence which is
my being itself, the simultaneous contact with my being and with the
being of the world" (377). Transcendence, then, is necessarily
structured and is a going beyond the self in the sense that it is
already in a world whose contingency is unconquerable.

"We have no other way of knowing what the world is than by
retaking this affirmation that is made by us at each instant . . . we
only know it by the sole fact that we are" (*F*379). Hence, in
experiencing our existence, we experience the world. More generally,
our "indubitable communication" and "affirmation" *is* our awareness of Being. The primordial "there is something," the *cogito*, and
the *sum* all express this primordial contact. We shall now look closely
at these concepts and at the notion of primordial faith on which
Merleau-Ponty relies heavily.

What cannot be doubted in the experience of the tacit *cogito* is
that our existence makes direct contact with Being and truth.[8]

---

8. It has been argued on the basis of two early notes in *The Visible and the Invisible*
(especially *VI*170-71) that Merleau-Ponty repudiated his notion of the tacit *cogito* and
thereby much of the *Phenomenology* (most notably by Remi C. Kwant, in *From
Phenomenology to Metaphysics*). Merleau-Ponty is much too hard on himself in these notes,
for his criticism applies, if at all, to some nonessential arguments on two or three pages of
the *Phenomenology* where he may have begun to slip into a Cartesian mode of description.
As our following references and explication should make clear, Merleau-Ponty's normal and
intended use of the expression "tacit *cogito*" in both texts is just the opposite of a
rationalist one. In any case, the conclusive consideration here is the fact that Merleau-Ponty
ignores these notes and continues to use repeatedly the concept of tacit *cogito*, in the main
sense of the *Phenomenology*, in the notes that follow the two in question (and in the text
proper of *The Visible and the Invisible*, which was composed after these notes). Therefore,
these particular notes are of little merit and very misleading. They can hardly be used as a
main argument for establishing the existence of a major change in Merleau-Ponty's
philosophy, and without this argument the thesis that there is such a change is greatly
weakened.

Merleau-Ponty variously calls this affirmation, which is the condition of any particular perception, "primordial" (*F*279), "original" (*F*278), and "perceptual" (*VI*103) "faith or opinion" (*F*372). The type of certainty that it gives us is different from logical certainty or the certainty of belief; for it is impossible to doubt, and thus its *évidence* coincides with its truth.[9] "*Certainty is doubt*" (396) because we can always stand outside the most binding of our particular certainties and reveal their dependence on an infinitude of horizonal structures which can never be made explicit. However, we cannot distance ourselves from nor find motives or more primitive sources for our inherence in Being, and thus we can neither justify nor doubt our facticity. This "naive certainty" (49) is the ontological ground of Husserl's *Urdoxa* (343) and is "the primordial certainty of being in contact with being itself" (*F*408).

It is important to recognize that this singular type of certainty is a phenomenological or experienceable presentation of primordial contact. It is the epistemological equivalent of our metaphysical unity with Being. Like Heidegger, Merleau-Ponty holds that this certainty is to be found in that mode of man's being that most directly and genuinely discloses Being and that as a modification of anxiety it accompanies the revelation of our thrown existence.[10] This coincidence of a subject's being and his awareness of his own being is possible because, at the stage of the tacit *cogito*, the subject's actual mode of existence and his "consciousness of existing" (*F*485) are one and the same. This most basic experience of Existence founds all our most mundane experiences of truth and reality. Every other certainty we may possess will be a modification of this primordial faith that is presented to us with our facticity. Although we shall not discuss Merleau-Ponty's theories of *évidence* and truth fully until chapter 4, we can now begin to see how *évidence* is itself a metaphysical relationship and can be explained as a specification of primordial contact. If this is the case, an experience of *évidence* must be in some way the experience of a truth, for our being-in-the-world

9. Merleau-Ponty insists that even analytic truths can be questioned, for their certainty presupposes that of their axioms or regional principles. These are "assumed without question" but still always "hold a coefficient of facticity" (*F*451). Ordinary language philosophers of science hold a similar view about the corrigibility of the regional principles that found a science and the status of the "facts" that result from these principles; for example, Stephen Toulmin, *The Philosophy of Science*, chapter 3.

10. *Being and Time*, book 2, chapter 3.

is equally a "being-in-truth" (452). Therefore, we can experience pure worldhood, understanding, or primordial contact through the certainty of the tacit *cogito* and more commonly in the *évidence* of any entity within the world (object, event, or state of affairs). We shall also see in our discussion of cognition in chapter 4 that this being-in-truth or primordial contact that every experience must possess supplies the principle for Merleau-Ponty's refutation of skepticism.

The notion of openness, which is central to existential phenomenology, is often misunderstood. When Merleau-Ponty says that we have an "*openness to being* which is perceptual faith" (*VI*122F), he means not only that our thrown regions enable us to experience Being as it is, but that Being itself *compels* us to experience it. The subject's essential power to disclose Being is frequently taken in the idealist sense that our transcendental capabilities can be activated at will or are entirely due to a projection by the subject. But we have seen that this view is mistaken, for in being open the subject is also "not closable." "With the first vision, . . . there is initiation, . . . the opening of a dimension that can never again be closed" (*VI*151). The subject cannot escape or stop the "demands," "interrogation," "saturation," and "penetration" of Being. He must always be in a situation and every situation has otherness. "There is always something before him, a being to be deciphered, an *omnitudo realitatis*" (*F*379 and *VI*106). The subject cannot retreat to a private realm, for even during sleep (465) or the most intellectual activity he is still in contact with the perceptual world. Yet the subject is not passive, for the element of truth in intellectualism is that the subject does have the power to regulate or select what is given to him. His interests, attitudes, moods, emotions, and so forth, are metastructures, in the sense that they pattern what the subject will attend to by means of his unclosed senses. Hence the subject is able to choose among types of fields and entities and their degrees of generality but never able to close them off entirely. When he is not actively engaged in regulating these openings, their correlative fields do not disappear; on the contrary, they impinge on him all the more. For example, in the case of illness, when he is merely "in the world without actively assuming it" (266), it is found that colors become dense and voluminous. Still more extreme: in the case of schizophrenia, visual objects so overwhelm the subject that he takes them to be literally on his eyes.

The formula Merleau-Ponty uses to express the basic truth that primordial faith yields is: "There is something and not nothing" (330, 354, and 397).[11] By examining this phrase, we can better understand the original intuition of our thrown existence. "Our first truth ... will be that there is presence, that 'something' is there" (*VI*160). Merleau-Ponty stresses the importance of this formula since he understands his philosophy as just the attempt to make primordial contact or presence as explicit as possible. In his last notes, he says that the central concepts of his phenomenology "represent a getting in contact with being as pure *there is*. One witnesses the event by which there is something" (*VI*206).

Since this "There is something" is an articulation of our primordial situation and displays the correlative certainty of the subject and object, we can best analyze it by looking at both of its sides. Noematically, the "something" indicates that the subject always inheres undeniably in otherness and that his existence is inescapably fascinated by a certain presence. In every present an "object in general" is also necessarily given, for this "something" is not undifferentiated but an entity which unifies and manifests all our thrown regions. It is "not nothing," for it is already a separation (*écart*) in Being and an organization of otherness, which are thus structured or interpreted from the beginning. Thus Merleau-Ponty can equivalently say: "There is meaning (*sens*)" (*F*454), and "There is some determination, at least within a certain degree of relativity" (*F*381).

However, this "something in general" which is the foundation of objective truth is not the correlate of the "I think," but of a "thinking" which comprehends "all of Being" (*VI*145) and merges with the "general existence of my body" (331). Our primordial thrownness is given to us merely as *"there is"* (*VI*145), "something appears to me" (400), or "the power of something in general which is the phantom of the world" (407). Thus, noetically, we are certain of our existence in general as a being which is already outside of itself, which finds itself in its articulations of otherness, and which is an active transcendence that establishes and illuminates the Being of which it is part. In his last notes, Merleau-Ponty states that the "there is" is merely the separation (*écart*) from the "something"

---

11. This is, of course, comparable to Heidegger's famous question in *An Introduction to Metaphysics*, chapter 1.

(i.e., the original *écart* of Being) and can ultimately be understood as the general separation of figure from ground (*VI*191, *VI*192, and *VI*197). All these characterizations of Existence show that the subject *is* the "there" or "there is" of Being (in Heidegger's sense of *Da*, not *es gibt*). It is distinguishable from Being itself only insofar as it creates a field within Being by making it appear, or by organizing it into a unified and meaningful "something." Once again, it should be recalled that in making use of the notions of primary faith and the "there is something" Merleau-Ponty is presenting not a metaphysical construction of the tacit *cogito* but a phenomenological description of the foundational experience of ourselves and the world.

Merleau-Ponty holds that an important aspect of the primary faith found in every perception is the affirmation that all our experiences coalesce in a unified world and are "compatible and compossible" (*F*378). There cannot, logically, be more than one world, just as there cannot be more than one space. We can now see that the necessity of the world's unity and individuality results from the fact that the otherness into which we are originally thrown is "something." As the object in general, the world is the single, interwoven noema of all our thrown regions.[12] Since every subsequent experience is an articulation of these regions, every phenomenon must immediately be given as a part of the one Being. The belief in this original unity which is exercised in every perceptual act can be called faith or opinion, first because like all aspects of our facticity it cannot be justified or explained but must merely be accepted, and, second, because it is "presumptive" (330), since this highly general bond with otherness can never be fully explicated or determined.

The coherence of all our experiences has some interesting implications for Merleau-Ponty's theory of truth (which will be analyzed extensively in chapter 4). All errors, falsehoods, mistaken certitudes, illusions, and even hallucinations must in some way have truth. This follows from the fact that all are attempts to manifest the inescapable presence into which we are thrown, and hence they are articulations of primordially given truth. Merleau-Ponty thus holds that there are degrees of truth and that any experience must give us at least a partial truth. "There is an indefinite chain of concordant experiences . . . and a 'teleology' of consciousness" (*F*454), because a

12. Its concreteness would therefore make it very different from Husserl's formal object in general and the pure cognitive categories that constitute its empty outline.

phenomenon can only be shown to be dubious or untrue "in the name of a truer one" (360). We shall see that whatever is taken mistakenly as true and *évident* can be "crossed-out" (*VI*88) by another experience which is more *évident*, such that these previously held truths will gain the status of irreplaceable stages on the way to the present truth. Finally, we should note that this coherence and compossibility are not the criteria of the world's truth and unity, but are, rather, the results of this unity. One can indeed begin to understand the world's individuality through its cohering elements, but it cannot be defined as such. Coherence is only a reflective or cognitive sign of the world's reality and truth, which are primordially given to us in an immediate and direct fashion. In a similar way, the rationality of our world is a result of the *logos* of Being or the thrown structures of primordial contact. It too is unjustifiable through a deeper metaphysics, for it too is a basic contingency that must merely be accepted (408).

2. Articulation and Creative Specification

In the next two sections, I shall analyze the specification of situations through the processes of articulation and acquisition. We saw in chapter 1 that these processes were major elements of the logic of situation and thus essential to Merleau-Ponty's whole endeavor. We shall therefore have to clarify them and describe the way Merleau-Ponty understands them before proceeding further. This section will focus on the primordiality of articulation (the abstract capacity for determining, organizing, or structuring the world) and the concept of creative specification (the specific process of creating new structures). However, since the logic of productive specification (i.e., the centripetal or involuntary specification of our hierarchy of sedimented structures by otherness) is implied by that of creative specification (it must always follow the steps that have been constituted in the creative originating act), we shall learn about it as well. The following section will complete and concretize the study of productive specification by applying it to touch and color vision.

Once we have analyzed the originality of articulation and a detailed model of creative specification, we shall turn to a brief discussion of the principle of the identity of indiscernibles, for we shall have to show how it is possible for specification, which only seems to apply to qualitative differentiation, to account for numerical difference. We shall close this section with a discussion of interpretation as it is understood in ordinary language philosophy, and this will summarize the chapter by showing how Merleau-Ponty's analysis solves one of the crucial problems implied by the concept of interpretation.

We shall begin by establishing that "articulation" (what Heidegger calls "interpretation")[13] is for Merleau-Ponty a primordial dimension of subjectivity and a necessary manifestation of an essential characteristic of Being itself. We shall discover that for him the Being of every being is to be found in its articulations rather than in its substance or matter. It will be seen that, like Heidegger and Cassirer, he believes that all higher modes of expression (intellectual and linguistic signification) are founded on this thrown capacity for articulation (*F271-72*). After establishing the primordiality of articulation, we shall demonstrate that articulation and primordial contact are essentially interdependent. Their shared primordiality follows from the fact that our understanding of or blending with Being presupposes that we also partake of Being's own movement of explication (*écart*) which results from its own finite attempts to grasp and unify itself.

We have already noticed that *écart* is an original movement of Being which refers to its splitting apart in order to determine itself. Hence when Merleau-Ponty says that "this *separation* [*écart*] . . . is a *natural* negativity, a first institution, always already there" (*VI216*), he confirms that it must be an innate or primordial function of Existence. This negativity is the most general description of articulation, for it is the process of creating distinctions within our field and within entities through specification and differentiation. "Philosophy precisely as 'Being speaking within us', expression of the mute experience by itself, is creation. . . . Being is *what requires creation of us* for us to experience it" (*VI197*). Although Merleau-Ponty is here characterizing philosophy, the conclusions can be generalized. He is saying that Being speaks or delimits itself through and within us by means of the articulating of structures. We genuinely experience Being when we are creatively specifying our present hold on the world by finding new articulations of it. "It is being that speaks within us and not we who speak of being" (*VI194*).

13. Compare with *Being and Time*, pp. 188 ff.

In other words, the creative ability of Existence, which is experienced whenever we authentically grasp new specifications of our present, is thrown and irremovable. Further, these moments of creative specification define temporality's movement from one present to another, and they are the closest we come to the analytic conception of the present as an extensionless point or to Sartre's notion of the instant. Like our natural capacities, articulation is anonymous, universal, and general. Merleau-Ponty further characterizes philosophy as that which "continues an effort of articulation which is the Being of every being" (*VI*127 and *VI*151). He is very close to Heidegger's view that philosophy awaits the *logos* of Being and lets Being be.[14] Given that the majority of our structures are differentiations that cover the entire field, that beings or entities (*Seiendes*) can be taken as the meeting points of these numerous levels (there "knots" or "nodes"), that the levels that constitute our field are specifications of our innate openness to otherness, we are able to reach the important conclusion that articulations or structures are in fact the Being of any entity within the world.[15]

There is an important source and need for creative specification that will help explain how primordial contact and articulation are interdependent and have a shared primordiality. Creative specification results from the "intertranslatability," "reversibility," or "intertwining" of all our thrown regions of openness. For example, Merleau-Ponty says:

14. Merleau-Ponty was aware of *On the Way to Language* (*VI*250). On pp. 126-27 of *The Visible and the Invisible* he shows that he interprets the prelinguistic speaking of Being as the articulations and structures of our prereflective life and, correlatively, of the world. When we come to analyze cognition in chapter 4, we shall see that its main function is to express, within the limits of its distinctive linguistic categories, the nonverbal situations of the other regions.

15. This similarity to Heidegger is also obvious in Merleau-Ponty's earlier works. Although Merleau-Ponty formally uses Cassirer's distinctions between *Ausdruck, Darstellung,* and *Bedeutung* (235 and 291), he puts as much emphasis on the cognates of *expression* and *explication* as does Heidegger and he uses them in the same way (cf. *Being and Time*, p. 190). He says that all our given capacities "in a word, 'have it out' [*s'expliquer*] with the world" (*F*464). In defining the important process of *Fundierung*, he says that the founded is "a determination or making explicit [*explicitation*] of the founding" (*F*451). The Cassirer quotations refer to our lived structures as "expressive experiences [*expressives*]" (*F*337), which found the more subtle forms of articulation, "verbal expression [*Darstellung*] and intellectual significance [*Bedeutung*]" (*F*271-72).

the visual and auditory experiences are pregnant with each other and their expressive [*expressive*] value founds the pre-predicative unity of the perceived
world. (*F*271-72)

Each region not only expresses its own contact with otherness but
also attempts to express the distinctive forms of contact (thrown
situations) that define the other regions of Existence; each region
transposes and adapts the given situations or structures of the other
regions in order to specify its *own* grasp. These regions and senses are
open to one another because all are directed at, or are articulations
of, whatever is other to them, and they are all interconnected
because they are the primordial differentiations of a unified
Existence. We shall see that these regions manifest Being's own *écart*
or original split into a number of dimensions. Therefore, because
each is given to the other, their disparity or lack of total coincidence
with each other is lived or prereflectively obvious to them; that is,
the distinctive modes of contact of the other regions are part of the
otherness to which each individual region is open. Hence, all work
together in an ever-renewed attempt to realize a single and unified
world.

Because we have a number of diverse and partial primordial
contacts with a single world, Existence has a thrown drive to
articulate itself in such a way that it gains a unified grasp of itself.[16]
Only because we have more than one original opening (for example,
of the senses) is there a need for articulation, which is the attempt,
through explication, to unify the givenness of all functions and
regions. Furthermore, because the self is not imprisoned in the
inherence of any one sense, it can attain a distance that allows it to
explicate any sense from the point of view of another; this provides
the ultimate possibility of self-consciousness and reflection. The
finitude or intrinsic incompleteness of Being, which requires it to
"separate" and "coil over" in order to grasp itself, is expressed by,
and manifested in, the nature of subjectivity itself.

I am never quite at one with myself. Such is the lot of a being who is born,
that is, who once and for all has been given to himself as something to be understood. (347)

16. We shall have to await our analysis of temporality in order to grasp fully how
subjectivity is a one that is identical with itself through the many.

Although we have a primordial contact with otherness, it remains alien and contingent because each of our openings gives a disparate cross section of Being: our single world is necessarily vague and perpetually indeterminate. Thus, paradoxically, we have a primordial understanding of the world, but what it gives us is still "something to be understood." If we can resolve this paradox, then we can also comprehend the equal primordiality of understanding and articulation. We have seen that to understand Being means to merge with it in each of our regions; but in another sense we never fully merge with or understand Being, because our diverse methods of making contact with it conflict and never perfectly cohere. However, this lack of coincidence with itself is also an essential feature of Being, which we have learnt is radically finite and necessarily indeterminate and inexhaustible. Furthermore, the fact that we merge with Being means that it "runs through us" and thus that we take up Being's own processes or manners of being present to itself. Yet Being is as much a drive toward its own unity through articulation and acquisition as it is a comprehension of itself by means of its various dimensions or regions (one implies the other).[17] Therefore, when we fully comprehend our thrown understanding as a manifestation of Being itself, we find that it must involve a "teleology" of articulation which invokes the same disparity or finitude that makes Being a never-finished process of self-comprehension. We can conclude that given *subjectivity's* primordial contact, there must be in the subject a drive to articulate this contact. (In chapter 5 we shall analyze the characteristics of Being we have used to explain this necessity.)

Thus we can understand Merleau-Ponty's central assertion that "our body . . . is a grouping of lived-through meanings which moves towards its equilibrium" (153), or that articulation is the drive to achieve the greatest possible balance correlatively of ourselves and the world.

---

17. Therefore Merleau-Ponty's deduction of the multiplication of Being's attributes (its articulation of a multiplicity of structures) is the reverse of Spinoza's. Spinoza deduces, from the unity of a Being that is absolutely self-identical, an infinite (but theoretically determinable) number of modes and a set of permanent and essential attributes. Merleau-Ponty, on the contrary, begins with a Being that is outside of itself and already fragmented by its regions or dimensions. He then shows that it expands into multiplicity because it seeks its unity, and thus because it is primarily diversity or finitude.

We ourselves are one continued question, a perpetual enterprise of taking our bearings on the constellations of the world, and of taking the bearings of the things on our dimensions. (*VI*102)

We interrogate the world with the structures we have been given, while at the same time the "something" to which these structures open us interrogates the appropriateness of the present balance of these structures. There is a perpetual and necessary testing of the world's givenness against its own articulations. This argument is similar to Hegel's difficult claim that "knowledge tests itself" or that "consciousness furnishes its own criterion."[18] For example, we have seen that the spatial level is the present maximum balance of the body's global set of capabilities. When this field demands a new level, its otherness becomes conspicuous, revealing the disparity of our thrown openings. "The instability [*labilité*] of levels gives . . . the vital experience of vertigo and of nausea which is the consciousness and the horror of our contingency" (*F*294). We adjust to this disjointed field by articulating a new level that correlatively allows a unified grasp on the self. Therefore, "the positing of a level is the forgetting of this contingency and space is based on our facticity" (*F*294). We shall see that this is also the essential movement of temporality (its "lapse" or "autoposition"), which is a never-ending striving for unity that makes partial gains (each present) but then must try again on the basis of these new articulations. Our thrown primordial contact spontaneously gives rise to articulation, and these two aspects of Existence (understanding and interpretation) are inconceivable apart from one another.

In the remainder of this section, I shall examine how situations come into being and are retained by discussing the main process of articulation and acquisition, and its correlative aspects of creation and sedimentation. The section will end with discussions of numerical identity and ordinary language philosophy's use of the concept of interpretation.

The systematic ambiguity of the term *acquisition* is what makes it useful to Merleau-Ponty, for it encompasses the active sense of "acquiring" and the passive substantive sense of "the acquired." When he says that "the world structure" has "two stages of

18. *The Phenomenology of Mind*, p. 140.

sedimentation and spontaneity" (130), he means that situations are either the result of creative structurings or the actualization of already sedimented structures. These alternatives are closely related, for sedimented situations must have been acquired or primordially given and all newly created situations are grounded in previous acquisitions. The process of acquisition, the creation of new transcendental structures on the ground of the old, characterizes a movement which will later show itself to be the essence of temporality and subjectivity.[19] Merleau-Ponty here takes up Hegel's notion of overreaching (*Aufheben*) and gives the dialectic whose movement it expresses a more convincing ontological basis. We shall begin by explicating Merleau-Ponty's description of attention, whose primary sense refers to the process of acquisition. This will provide us with a detailed model of all types of specification.

The adult's world of color is:

a secondary formation founded on a series of "physiognomic" distinctions: those of the "warm" and "cold" shades, of the "colored" and "non-colored" . . .
The first perception of colors, as they are normally understood, is thus a change in the structure of consciousness, the establishment of a new dimension of experience. (*F*38)

These bare articulations of the primordially given visual region are physiognomic because their high level of generality has not yet allowed the subject to separate them *as* colors from its perceptual world as an integrated whole. Correlatively, the entities of the child's world do not consist of distinguishable types of properties, for the indeterminate structure, warm or cold shades, discloses the touch, sound, and shape of the entity as much as its brightness. With the coming to be of the color dimension, not only is the simple division of colored and non-colored specified into a large series of colors, but the perceiver is capable of isolating and focusing on this type of attribute in isolation from an entity's other sensory properties (something that the Maoris, for example, never learned to do). Merleau-Ponty goes on to point out that:

19. "Time and subjectivity are nothing else than a spontaneity 'acquired' once and for all, and that 'perpetuates itself in being in virtue of being acquired' [a critical reference to Sartre's rejection of this notion]" (*F*488-89). Merleau-Ponty concludes that "acquisition must be admitted as an irreducible phenomenon" (450).

It is on the model of these originating acts that attention must be conceived, since a secondary attention, which limits itself to recalling a knowledge already acquired, just takes us back to acquisition. (F38)

Secondary attention can be described as a mere reproduction of already sedimented situations because this form of attending to or aiming at an entity grasps the entity strictly by means of structures already in its possession. In this frequently used analysis, Merleau-Ponty is stating that sedimented situations always carry a reference to the original experience in which they were acquired and that they are thus parasitic on originating attention. In the present example, our ability to attend to colors is always a reproduction of our first accomplishment of such an act.

Normally, when we make something the focus of our attention, we specify (make richer and more precise) our present horizonal and highly general manner of understanding it. (Of course, in a phenomenological attitude we can attend to its present general mode without specifying it.)

To activate attention is not merely to further clarify some pre-existent givens, it is to realize a new articulation of them by taking them as *figures*. They are preformed only as *horizons*. (F38)

Specification can be accomplished in two ways: if we already possess structures capable of revealing the entity to the extent desired, we let the entity solicit, or select, the appropriate structures and "reconstitute itself." If our sedimented structures are insufficient for the task (that is, they cannot articulate and give us the degree of detail our interests demand), we must create new structures to make up for the deficiencies in the old. In the first case, we reveal details with which we are already familiar. In the second case, however, we acquire a new kind of transcendental knowledge of the world and actually "create" the details themselves, which exist only insofar as they are the noema of the new structures. We cannot speak of these details, entities, or attributes as existing in themselves before their discovery, since they are a function of my creativity and transcendence and are thus essentially bound up with the totality of the personal, cultural, and natural structures that constitute my subjectivity. These newly discovered givens are not, however, created *ex nihilo*, for they were present in a more general fashion in the relevant horizonal situations to which I turned my attention. Furthermore, when I no longer attend to these specific details, they do not disappear but are held on my horizon through basically the same general structure that existed before. When I create a new species, I do not banish its founding genus but only alter it to the extent that this genus will henceforth be my way into a new system of specifications. The latter are indissolubly bound to the former, for the originating experience was as much a creative manipulation of and variation on these more general situations as a creation of a new structure.

It is precisely in disrupting [*bouleversant*] the given that the act of attention reunites itself with the previous acts, and the unity of consciousness is progressively constructed through a "synthesis of transition". . . . This passage from the indeterminate to the determinate, this retaking [*reprise*] at each instant of its own history in the unity of a new sense, is thought itself. (*F*39)[20]

Merleau-Ponty has just given us a major formula of his philosophy, for what he means by "thought" here includes all types of subjective activity. Since all structures are grounded in the pregiven primordial structures of the body-subject, and since every level of specificity (or degree of generality) of our structures is intrinsically connected to the next level or degree, the fantastic number of specifications we acquire throughout life does not leave us with an absurd conjunction of disconnected entities. (Merleau-Ponty is not open to the charge of multiplying entities.) Ultimately, we hold the entire articulated world within the unity of our thrown regions. Therefore, although consciousness has the power to create infinitely new situations, it remains rooted in its thrown past, and its development, which is correlative to the world's, has a consistency, coherence, and historicity that can never be broken.

We can deepen our understanding of the process of specification by producing a paradigm or model that applies equally to creative or productive specification. (It will apply to both since the latter must follow the steps the former has created.) This model will show how

20. We shall translate *reprendre* and its cognates as *to retake*. Because this is an important technical term for Merleau-Ponty, it is best to indicate its use by a single English term, and, although *retake* is extremely awkward, there appears to be no better equivalent. Furthermore, any longer or more accurate and explicit phrase would frequently interfere with the context in which Merleau-Ponty uses the term. This translation also has the advantage of making more obvious this term's relation to other important terms such as *reconstituer, reassumer, engager, recueillir,* and *avoir* (*F*203, n.).

new structures must be grounded in the old, will give us a sketch of the schema the body uses whenever it either creatively or productively specifies an entity or its field, and will demonstrate how the generality and indeterminacy of situations are essential to Merleau-Ponty's theory of specification. Although our model is applicable to all types of specification, it is oversimplified and favors some, for it speaks in terms of two structures on the same general plane that give rise to a third, more specific structure. For example, object structures will fit this model better than the structures of the senses, which, as differentiation structures (levels), simultaneously maintain a large number of contrary qualities in the same field.

Whenever an entity does not perfectly "fit" or fulfill an available structure, it can, by means of originating attention, give rise to a new and more specific structure. Since this lack of adequation of our structures to the given is the rule (cf. chapters 3 and 4), we can always articulate our phenomena to a greater degree. However, because it requires a creative or authentic act, it is comparatively rare that we do so. We are usually content to experience an entity only as far as our sedimented structures will take us, and we are unconcerned about, or do not even notice the "tension," "blurring," "fuzziness," or "indeterminacy" that points to the possibility of further specification. (These terms that describe our experience of the otherness of a situation are used by Merleau-Ponty to characterize the way objects must appear [cf. chapter 3] rather than being wholly consonant with their structures.) Before the subject creatively specifies this indeterminacy, it is "nothing but a vague solicitation . . . a badly formulated question" (F248), a "vague uneasiness" (F25), and an "imprecise expectation" (F24). The term *vague* is instructive if it is understood in the sense it has when applied to linguistic entities, for it tells us that the entity we shall attain by specification presently falls between two structures and is thus a blurring or confusing of both. Hypothetically, if the "question" that otherness puts to the subject were well formulated, it would actualize a single structure which would be perfectly adequate to it. Thus the ambiguity or indeterminacy of any phenomenon is due to the fact that the structure we are using to articulate it is not sufficiently differentiated from another similar structure (on the same level of generality) and that the entity also motivates or concretizes this second structure to some extent.

If we decide to specify such a given, our new structure (let us label it and its correlative entities D) will be defined in terms of the two structures it previously actualized (B and C). In other words, the newly articulated phenomenon D previously fell somewhere within the extension of B and C, for it was then given merely as a tension between these structures or a blurring of one by the other (let us say of B by C, which implies that B was the more fitting of the two). Therefore, there are genetic relationships between the three structures, and their objects will disclose these relationships by means of their resemblance to one another. However, D's (the entities correlative to structure D) will resemble either B's or C's or both more than B's or C's will resemble one another (for D's fall between them). Since structures with the same degree of generality are defined by the extent of their differentiation from one another, we can say that D is a specification of B and C (or, less precisely, of B) and is not on the same level of generality as B and C. Let us now notice that there *may* be a still more general sedimented structure A which subsumes both B and C, such that B's and C's could be taken more generally as qualitatively identical A's (in other words, B and C are "species" of "genus" A). The subject can creatively articulate this more general structure (A), if he has not already done so, even after the acquisition of what are to become its species (B and C), that is, if it is relevant to his concerns to ignore the difference between B's and C's. In any case, given structure A, entities of type D would be exactly as appropriate to structure A as entities of types B and C, and all these types of entities would equally resemble one another at this more general level. Similarly, D's can be taken as B's at the next level of specificity, and so on. The phenomenon of resemblance is made possible by the structures we use to articulate the world, and thus it has as much stability, permanence, and truth as does our present system of structures (*EM*171 and *VI*220).[21]

It should be clear from the above that creative specification, besides being a subjective act of origination, presupposes a contact or blending with otherness. Unless the two structures B and C could be actualized or simultaneously demanded by otherness, there would be

21. These structures are, of course, not universals or essences, for they are noncognitive and nonthematic. However, as will become clear by the end of chapter 4, universals are grounded in or are the cognitive version of these lived and prereflective situations (but so is the cognitive notion of a particular or an object).

no need or motive (31 and 262) for any further specification. This has the important consequence that all situations must be both general and particular, or, more properly, at this level of lived structures there can be no such distinction. Because two such structures can be actualized by the same entity, situations must be general. However, for the same reason we experience particularity within these overlapping stuctures, for it is otherness that actualizes them and shapes the hierarchy that describes their interrelation. Furthermore, since the only way we can encounter a particular entity is by means of a structure, however much we have specified an entity there always remains the possibility that we can mistake it for another. In other words, we can grasp an individual object only generally: numerical identity, for lived experience, is indistinguishable from qualitative identity. Merleau-Ponty thus accepts the principle of the identity of indiscernibles.

Merleau-Ponty would not deny that we can experience the numerical difference of two or more qualitatively identical objects in the same field. However, he would hold that such an experience is exceedingly common and that one does not have to create artificial cases like perfectly symmetrical entities to prove it. This is understandable if we recall that he maintains that most objects are perceived at a very general level. We see trees, cars, parking meters, and poles, but it is comparatively rare that we see their different types and even rarer that we see the differences within a type. This kind of experience of numerical difference merely points to the possibility of further specification that will ultimately reveal a qualitative difference. Similarly, the particularity of the entities is to be found in their otherness, which is finally understood as "infinite and inexhaustible structurability." If we recall Merleau-Ponty's study of monocular images (*F*267-69 and *VI*7-8), we can see how he would handle the extreme case of two perfect spheres suspended in an undifferentiated space.[22] Monocular images are, after all, easily

---

22. See Max Black, in Michael J. Loux, ed., *Universals and Particulars*, pp. 204 ff. However, such invented cases are not particularly appropriate to Merleau-Ponty's understanding of the principle, for they are directed against those who must resort to the claim that a difference of position within a homogeneous space is sufficient to save the principle. Merleau-Ponty's lived space is qualitative in the strong sense since it is constituted strictly by means of our structures, which all spatialize. Thus for him it is begging the question to state that spatial relations are the final and irreducible qualities that will qualitatively distinguish two such individuals. Spatial position *indicates* qualitative difference but does not constitute it.

accessible and identical qualitatively. He shows that in such cases we experience entities as "phantoms" (*F*269) and refuse to give them the status of, or place them in the same "order" (*F*268) as, real things "within the world" (*F*269). The principle of the identity of indiscernibles abstractly describes part of our primordial faith; for we are absolutely certain (and we live this certainty) that we can specify, if it is of interest to us, any two entities to a degree that will reveal their qualitative difference. As for the hypothetical spheres or monocular images, where this possibility no longer seems open to us, we treat them (prereflectively) as illusions or mere images (or as lacking the otherness that all real entities must possess (cf. 3.2). At best we would take these spheres *to be* monocular images and set about adjusting our gaze and our whole body to perceive them as one. As Stratton's experiments indicate (244 ff.), we might well succeed! Even if we could not succeed in seeing them as a single entity (perhaps if there were more than two present), we would still not admit that they were cases of mere numerical difference. We would experience them instead, like the schizophrenic, as disturbing hallucinations or as visual manifestations of our complete disorientation and disequilibrium (339-40).

Before concluding, I want to stress Merleau-Ponty's central notion that we never experience otherness except as already structured and its converse that there is no pure datum that can be said to be empirically or logically prior to our activity of structuring or interpretation. Merleau-Ponty states that prior to the actual discovery of a novel detail within the field, it "had been only foreshadowed in our perceptual or practical field and . . . had only announced itself in our experience as a certain lack" (*F*179). We can understand how what is specified exists before it is articulated by comprehending how it is grasped, noematically, as merely "foreshadowed" in the field and, noetically, as a "lack" in our experience. The new detail or entity is foreshadowed because it gives itself as that which strains and stretches beyond the grasp that our sedimented structures have on our present field. The otherness of which we take notice is never experienced as an objective datum in itself or even as an undifferentiated manifold (matter or content), nor is the originating act of attention experienced merely as the turning of an "empty" (26) light on a preexistent given. Otherness merely "motivates" creative specification, because only if the individual has interests and purposes that specification will help fulfill will he create new structures richer than those he already possesses. Only from the need to seek more detail can the previously given indeterminate entity be judged as lacking. Therefore he experiences or "feels" this lack as belonging to and within his presently actualized structures. Only retrospectively, from the point of view of the newly created structure, can he judge that this lack indicated particular missing details or a certain kind of entity. Since our sedimented structures are in contact with otherness even when they are horizonal, *what* has been determined or specified is, noetically, our previous structured grasp of otherness and, noematically, the indeterminate entity which is present to us by means of these structures. Merleau-Ponty does not need to posit an awareness of contents, *hyle*, or things-in-themselves because he can show that attention is solicited by the otherness already apprehended in our present horizonal situations. The argument that otherness is always given to us as already structured does not lead to an infinite regress because of Merleau-Ponty's theory of pregiven primordial structures. In other words, from the beginning we are in contact with otherness through our primordial structures, and the future creative specifications of these thrown structures are equally specifications of the otherness to which they are necessarily open.

I shall conclude this section with a discussion of how Merleau-Ponty's concept of interpretation solves one of the more puzzling and important problems in contemporary Anglo-American philosophy (a modification of the traditional problem of form and content or activity and passivity). Ordinary language philosophers, especially in the field of philosophy of science, made a significant contribution to Anglo-American philosophy's understanding of the nature of facts (or observation statements) when they argued that all facts are theory-laden.[23] However, this conclusion gave rise to the problem of what it is these theories are applied to initially, if any fact is already the result of theory. Or to put the question in more strictly epistemological terms: if all knowledge involves interpretation, what is being interpreted and how do we reach it? The answer given usually resembles what Firth has called a "sensory-core theory."[24]

---

23. Cf. Norwood Russell Hanson, who states the position exceedingly well in chapters 1 and 2 of *The Patterns of Discovery*.

24. This is Firth's phrase. His characterization of the position is accurate and enlightening; see Robert J. Swartz, ed., *Perceiving, Sensing and Knowing*, pp. 216-19. We shall discuss Firth's answer to this theory in some detail in chapter 3.

But this is unsatisfactory, for it merely reasserts that all givens are already interpreted while at the same time trying to maintain that there is some sort of distinction between the interpretation and the subject matter (the "sensory core"). Philosophers of science have given a more satisfactory answer by claiming that the facts to which we apply theories are already interpreted in another way in that scientific theories are meta-interpretations of lower-level, first-order interpretations.[25] However, this leads either to an infinite regress or to the question of what privilege first-order interpretations have (both reproduce the problem in a new guise).

Merleau-Ponty has given a satisfactory solution to these problems with his concept of thrown regions that are simultaneously open to otherness and a structuring of otherness, or to put it another way, his idea that understanding always involves interpretation.[26] The basic facts that are interpreted by our scientific theories or thetic judgments (reflective and cognitive interpretations) are those given in and belonging to lived experience, the noemata of prereflective life and perception. They are indeed already interpreted, for perception is always structured. There is a basic layer of interpretation that is given to us as part of our thrownness, and one cannot go any deeper than this primordial contact with and articulation of Being. Thus two subjects who hold radically conflicting physical theories or belong to different cultures will indeed encounter different facts (406), yet in some sense they will perceive the same thing.[27] They perceive the same thing not because they encounter the same data, which they subsequently or simultaneously interpret, but because, like all men, they share the same thrown and primordial structures that open them to these phenomena in the first place. One man can always understand the lived world of another, at least at a high level of generality, for the cultural and cognitive interpretations about which

25. Cf. J. O. Wisdom, "Observations as the Building Blocks of Science in 20th Century Scientific Thought," in *Boston Studies in the Philosophy of Science*, vol. 8.

26. As we have seen, he uses "interpretation" in the same way as Heidegger, but also in the same way as the philosophers of science we have mentioned (*F*318 and *F*303). We shall see that he successfully unifies the two uses.

27. Hanson uses the example of Kepler and Tycho watching a sunrise; the former sees the earth falling away from the sun, while the latter sees the sun rising above the earth. However, Hanson does not succeed in showing that what is the "same" in their experiences is not identical sensations or a pure datum of sense (cf. chapter 1 of *The Patterns of Discovery*).

they differ are found only in the more specific sedimented specifications of these shared general structures. Therefore, there are in some sense natural as opposed to conventional facts, a universal "common sense," and it is to these basic givens that all our subsequent interpretations will apply. Merleau-Ponty's theory of primordial contact and primordial interpretation prevents the infinite regress that must result from a pure relativism in our knowledge of the natural world, just as we shall see that it avoids a pure historicism in our knowledge of the cultural and historical world.

3. Contact and Metastructures

Up to this point our studies of specification, acquisition, and articulation have tended to stress the subject-side of our bond with the world. In this section, the "realist" aspect of Merleau-Ponty's philosophy will be closely examined. We have seen that every situation inheres in otherness, but we have not shown concretely how otherness is able to intertwine with our structures. Merleau-Ponty uses many metaphors to describe this movement of productive specification: he calls it centripetal, triggering, and soliciting; he says that the world understands and teaches us; that otherness questions, interrogates, commands, and demands; that it specifies itself and articulates itself. We have decided to use *contact* as our major term for referring to this phenomenon (Merleau-Ponty uses the term in this sense at *F*366, *VI*65, *VI*73, and *VI*74). Although *demand, triggering* (28), and *centripetal* (111) are useful, as they highlight the activity of otherness, *contact* is more neutral and has the important advantage that it reminds us that this process stems from our primordial contact with otherness.

Even though we have discussed the logic of productive specification or contact, we have not seen how it applies to a particular sense. It is only on the basis of such a concrete description that this central theory of Merleau-Ponty's can be presupposed and relied upon in the following discussion. Therefore, we shall briefly examine the process in the cases of touch and color vision. We shall begin with touch (*VI*133), because the theory is most easily applicable to this sense; because of the apparent lack of distance between touch and its objects, the way otherness can directly manipulate and select its structures is not as mysterious prima facie as in vision. We shall then turn to a consideration of vision in order to show that its relationship to otherness, when it is either active or passive, is comparable to what holds for touch. Although we shall examine color in great detail in chapter 3, it is necessary to give a sketch of its logic at this point, because vision, which is ontologically the most significant sense, seems least amenable to a theory of contact. In addition, this sketch will prepare us for the detailed study of color vision by giving us an overview and summary.

We shall complete this section by discussing how Merleau-Ponty's notion of metastructure compliments his theory of contact. Once again we shall examine a concrete example of this process. We have selected free action for this purpose, since it gives us a particularly clear case of this type of structuring and we have already noted how the other regions are matastructural (chapter 1.4). Furthermore, freedom is philosophically interesting in itself and there will be few other opportunities to discuss it directly.

Every perceptual situation is an attempt to apprehend otherness. However, this specification of our primordial hold on Being is not due only to the subject but is guided, "put to us," and "suggested" (375) by the present contact with otherness. Merleau-Ponty says that the object "triggers," "calls forth" (28), "awakens" (26), and "sets attention in motion" (30). Since we are always perceptually open, the present field necessarily activates our sedimented structures (or our secondary attention), with the result that we are perpetually situated in the natural world, all our structures being brought into play at some level of generality. Similarly, our structures "differ-entiate themselves by coiling over . . . a certain visible wherein it [the system of structures] is redoubled and inscribed" (VI153F). We may previously have understood differentiation solely as the process whereby a subject sorts out and articulates his field. But the reverse holds equally; the subject is also differentiated by the present field. Just as the world must have a figure around which all its potential structures can be horizonally held and located, so must the body-subject. The dialectical interplay of the two sides of the situation becomes plain when we notice that the visible concretizes and organizes our set of sedimented situations, at the same time that it is given its Being by them. It is because the arrangement of our entire hierarchy of structures is triggered by contact that the perceiver "feels that he is the sensible itself coming to itself and that in return the sensible is . . . as it were his double or an extension of his own flesh" (*VI153F*). Merleau-Ponty provides an image for the way in which otherness selects amongst our sedimented structures until it finds the species most appropriate to it. He calls otherness "a current that will traverse . . . all these channels, all these prepared but unemployed circuits, . . . making of an embryo a newborn infant, . . . of a body a mind or at least a flesh" (*VI147*). Without contact, our body as our presently actualized system of structures would be "blind" and not even exist. However, even actualized, these structures cannot be said to constitute a Kantian phenomenal world; for not only does otherness trigger and synthesize them, but it actually *guides* and *demands* the newly acquired structures that we "create." The naive realist intuition that the entity exists with its own constitution outside our personal and intellectual control is accurate to this extent.

Let us now turn to a concrete study of the sense of touch, which can be introduced with a key quotation from the *Phenomenology of Perception*.

Movement and time are not only objective conditions of the knowing touch, but a phenomenal component of the tactile givens. They effectuate the patterning of the tactile phenomena just as light sketches the configuration of a visible surface. (*F364*)

Weight and secondary tactile qualitites like smoothness are correlative to the structures, respectively, of our gross muscular movements and of our extraceptive or superficial bodily movements. The tactile sense uses its own types of motor capacities to articulate the world of touch, and, as we have just seen, these structures are redoubled and are themselves inscribed on these tactile givens. Once this innate tactile motility has acquired specific structures and differentiations through its creative dealings with the tactile world, whenever the body makes contact with a touchable entity, the appropriate sedimented structure will be actualized or chosen. "A surface utilizes the time of our tactile exploration and modulates the movement of our hand" (*F364*). The "surface" denotes a tactile aspect of otherness that "modulates" and "utilizes" our capacities to touch (movement, pressure, and time). When a subject touches an entity, it guides his general and undifferentiated tactile motility through its acquired alternative structures to a greater and greater degree of specification until the entity is recognized. "The style of these modulations determines so many modes of appearance of tactile phenomena"(*F364*). Otherness will *resist* our movement in different ways by using up a defined amount of exploratory time and by alternating the amount of pressure used by this movement. For example, "there are 'surface tactile phenomena' . . . in which a two-dimensional tactile object offers itself to touch and opposes itself more or less firmly to penetration, three-dimensional tactile milieu, . . . and tactile transparency" (*F*364). Each of these "modes of appearing" is an acquired specific structure of the general ability to touch and noematically gives a certain type of objectivity. On touching an object (for example, a smooth surface) our tactility (that is to say, the most general "structure of exploratory movement" [*F*365] we possess) is triggered and actualized by otherness. If the subject is interested (holds himself open), the surface, which until now has presented itself merely as general tactile objectivity, will specify itself, by selecting, for example, the structure, tactile surface phenomena, or, equally, by negating the other alternative modes or types of objectivity. These structures have still more specific differentiations, such that the surface can further specify itself. somewhere on the smooth-to-rough scale. (The three-dimensional structure would be specified according to the hard-to-soft range.) Hence, when the subject perceives a smooth surface, this means that he has let his tactile structures be specified by otherness to that degree. If the subject were an "expert," who had even acquired species of each "degree" on the smooth-to-rough scale, then the surface would also sort out these alternatives and present the subject with a more specific type of objectivity.

Through this schema we can see how otherness and the subject-side of a situation are inextricably bound together. Furthermore, it should now be clearer how otherness is present to the subject in a situation, for it has called up and delineated his structures. The entity transcends subjectivity and is out in the world, because its articulations were not projected and created at will by the subject but rather were specified by otherness at every step of the way. Otherness is still present to the subject even when his most specific sedimented structure has been actualized, for its inexhaustibility calls for further creative specification. Since contact is essential to the occurrence of such structures, we can understand why Merleau-Ponty has so frequently stated that lived significances are available to the subject only when they are concretely actualized. Let us only note now that this theory of specification through contact explains the process of intentional fulfillment and achievement[28] (it will be discussed in detail in chapter 3). For example, when a subject wishes to identify a touchable entity to a particular degree of specification (for practical, affective, or cognitive reasons), his intention will be fulfilled if his epistemic position is such as to allow otherness to select the structure with the intended degree of specificity. It will be unfulfilled if otherness is able to specify his tactile capabilities only at a more general level. Finally, by means of this schema Merleau-Ponty will show that the perceptual act and the perceived object have the same degree of certainty (cf. chapter 4.3).

It may appear doubtful whether our study of contact in the case of touch can be broadened to cover all perceptual experience. Vision might seem to put this theory into question, for entities are not in contact with the eye as they are with the touching body. But to hold the view that *contact* has two different senses is to confuse our belonging to otherness with a mere physical contiguity. We can clarify this problem by noting the essential phenomenological similarities between vision and touch. We shall show that the visible is as much or as little "on" the eye as the tactile object is "on" the body. In doing so, we shall be able to understand the truth of the schizophrenic's experience of his body as "the power of joining up with all objects through sight and hearing" and of visual objects as "entering his head" and being "concentrated in the gaze" (290-91).

Direct contact with otherness seems to be epitomized in passive touch where we supposedly have a tactile quality presented to us without effort. But "pressure without movement produces a scarcely identifiable phenomenon. . . . And like the exploratory gaze of true vision the 'knowing touch' throws us outside our body through

---

28. This process needs explanation, for in Husserl its description is dominated by the primitive model of a filling in, and that by means of a purely passive reception of fully determinate contents or details. Merleau-Ponty's theory of generality and indeterminacy goes well beyond Husserl, for it allows one to seriously countenance degrees of fulfillment and indeterminate objects. This is possible in Husserl only if one takes the object to be a composite of details (each fully determinate in itself) that can be assembled piecemeal, a prejudice to which Husserl too often succumbs, even in the later works (see, for example, *Formal and Transcendental Logic*, p. 62). Husserl cannot see that there are grades of evidential generality (and thus degrees of truth), for even while he speaks of the "familiar or determinate indeterminate," he equates the indeterminate with the "empty" (e.g., *Experience and Judgement*, pp. 125 ff.) and says that determination is equivalent to a "correction" of the indeterminate (*Crisis*, p. 163).

movement" (F364). Hence, if we are not willing or able to hold ourselves open by putting forward our potential specifications, otherness can only trigger our most general regional capacity and be given to us as a simple "touchable" or as a "painful" something. If the subject-side is able to respond with the structures of movement, the tactile becomes a transcendent entity within the world and space, and no longer something "on the surface of the skin." It is true that our visual capacities, by their very nature, distance their objects and give them in greater detail, but this differs from the action of touch only in degree of articulation. Yet, most important, we must realize that "there is also passive vision without gaze [regard], as in the case of dazzling light, which does not deploy an objective space before us, and in which light ceases to be light and becomes something painful which invades the eye" (F364). Vision does not deal with the surface of an entity directly (for this is what defines our sense of touch), but entities do modulate vision through its direct merging with light. Lighting is the middle term to which the body adjusts and which the object resists. In the case where the eye may be incapable of accommodating this light, it will be apprehended as the simple regional property "visible" or, even more generally, as "painful." Touch's experience of an undifferentiated given which it does not immediately and prereflectively identify as a particular type of entity (for example, if it is struck by a great force) is as rare as undifferentiated painful vision.[29]

We shall now outline how otherness, through its direct contact with vision, can specify vision's structures of color and light. First, let us note that color is not a sense-datum we passively receive but is the result of a high degree of specification. For example, the phenomenalist's paradigm of a flat and perfectly determined red "requires a focusing, however brief; it emerges from a less precise, more general redness, in which my gaze was caught, into which it sank before ... fixing it" (VI131). This less specific red which we ordinarily encounter in lived perception is itself a specification of a genus of lighting.

Merleau-Ponty's concentration on lighting is an important first

29. Merleau-Ponty provides an instructive discussion of the parallel between vision and touch in terms of the motor attitudes that are presupposed by both in part of the Sorbonne series of lectures recorded in the Bulletin de psychologie no. 236, volume 18 3-6, 1964 (p. 175).

step in his argument, for it is easier for us to accept that the eye merges with light than that it merges with the colors of external objects. "The lighting is not on the side of the object, it is what we assume, what we take as the norm" (F359). The lighting of a field is the level that the eye adopts before it reveals any specific colors in the milieu. Just as a spatial level must be assumed by the body before objects can become conspicuous in their individual orientations (that is, by the way they differentiate themselves from these levels), colors can only reveal themselves by differentiating themselves from the dominant shade of the lighting. Hence, lighting is the first "impact of the world" (EM165), with the result that it triggers and actualizes one of the eye's general openings to light.

It is necessary to say [for example,] that the yellow light [*lumière*], in assuming the function of lighting [*éclairage*], tends to situate itself beyond all color, tends towards the zero of color, and that correlatively the objects distribute among themselves the colors of the spectrum according to the degree and the mode of their resistance to this new atmosphere. (F359)

This important quotation contains Merleau-Ponty's entire theory of color and visual contact. He is saying here that light is no longer a kind of colored entity (just as a particular spatial field no longer has a particular orientation) when it is taken as the body's present level that is, as lighting. On the contrary, colors can only be perceived when otherness modulates the present lighting, which is already assumed. When we notice the color of a particular light, such as the yellow light streaming through a window, it is because it clashes with another and predominant lighting which we hold as our level. (The same occurs when we say that a whole area of our spatial field is disorientated.) Each type of lighting contains as subordinate structures the entire range of colors, such that the degree of an object's "resistance" (F359) (and this, of course, is a key contact term) to this lighting will place it somewhere on the color scale. Further, each lighting contains different "modes" of appearing (parallel to those of touch), such as the structures of surface, transparent, reflective, and luminous color. Thus, whenever we perceive a color, its structure must include one of the above modes as taken under a particular lighting; for example, a red might be given as surface red in blue light but never as mere red. Each type of lighting is a distinctive differentiation structure, in the sense that colors are differentiated one from the other to the particular degree of precision that is definitive of that particular lighting. This is why the lighting only "tends" (F359) to invisibility; for we do have an awareness of it by means of the way in which the colors of our constant series blend with and distinguish themselves one from the other. In other words, the colors of the constant spectrum differ in every lighting in the way their "edges" merge with their neighboring colors. We shall see that if the lighting were to become entirely neutral we would not have appearances of colors but would possess their ideal constant form.

The notion of resistance is vital to Merleau-Ponty's realist theory of contact. The color level does not project the given color but only sets the tone for the specifications demanded by otherness. An entity of the same color as the light which has become the present lighting will offer the least degree of resistance. This lowest level of resistance will manifest itself as this color, for the gaze has made this color its standard or dominant. The degree to which every other present colored object resists the lighting (or equally its correlative field color) will place it on a scale of values (abhorrence to the dominant) that directly corresponds to the series of colors that we find in a spectrum. In this way, any object that has a different opacity to light than an object of the dominant color will appear as another color, which, depending on the extent of this difference, will be situated somewhere within the spectrum's range. Hence there are bound to be many indeterminate and vague colors in our field that fall between two neighboring constants within this spectrum. In summary: a field will contact the gaze, yielding one species of lighting. Entities within this lit field will then actualize the types of colors and modes of appearing (superficial, transparent, etc.) which correspond to their resistance to this lighting.

We have shown that we are inescapably open to otherness in such a way that it always triggers the innate and acquired structures we possess. Yet at the same time we were forced to qualify this "unclosedness" by saying that the degree of specification which otherness actualizes depends on our interests and concerns. If this were not the case, our perceived world would always consist of entities specified to the highest degree and would be inconceivably complex. But experience shows that at different times these entities are presented at different levels of generality. What is inescapable is that our perceptual world must be given at all times but with varying degrees of generality, if only as the most general and indeterminate something. We are able to stem the demands of otherness because we attend to otherness "according to our interests."[30] We have stipulated that the concerns which limit the degree of contact be called *metastructures*, a term which indicates that they too are structures with a situational logic but are of a second order which modifies our first-order perceptual situations.

Merleau-Ponty says that perception gives us a "genuine in-itself-for-us" (F372); that is, situations which inhere in otherness.

Ordinarily we do not notice this because our perception, in the context of our concerns [*occupations*], alights on things just enough to find again their familiar presence and not enough to rediscover the nonhuman which is hidden there. (F372)

The "nonhuman" is always present in perception, for it is what has triggered the perceptual structures upon which our higher-order interests are based. This otherness is not obvious to lived perception, for our grasp is rarely specified to the most detailed degree. It is when the most specific of our acquired structures is actualized and we still have a need to specify it further that the nonhuman obtrudes. Since our everyday concerns are rarely centered on perception, we normally deal with our perceptual field at the highest level of generality that meets our requirements and do not in fact care that these situations can be specified inexhaustively. In other words, the degree of specification that is acceptable to our present tasks stops the triggering process at that level and is taken as the fulfillment of our present perceptual intentions. We can experience the non-human "if we put in suspense our concerns and give to it a metaphysical and disinterested attention" (F372). In order to experience an entity in its maximum degree of givenness, we have to drop all other concerns and concentrate our attention strictly within our perceptual region. We may do so in order to take up a philosophical attitude or as a first step in a psychological experiment, but in everyday perception this attitude usually results from a crisis where our sedimented structures are inadequate to the degree of specification our present interests require. But, again, in most cases this "hostile and alien ... resolutely silent Other" (F372) is not

30. Husserl, *The Crisis of European Sciences and Transcendental Phenomenology*, p. 108.

noted, for we deal with the world well above the lowest level of specificity. When our aim is to get somewhere, the sidewalk on which we walk is generally given to us merely as a hard, level, and stable surface. For a woman in high-heeled shoes, it will be given more specifically as, say, an object of concrete, asphalt, wood, or metal grating. To a driver, it is merely the beginning of a dangerous and forbidden boundary. These various levels of specificity are not merely meanings but are the objects themselves.

An analysis of freedom will allow us to appreciate, first, the complexity, inexhaustibility, and ambiguous organization of an individual's metastructures, and, second, the way that the "centrifugal" power of the subject-side balances the "centripetal contact" of every situation.

My freedom . . . does not necessitate that there is an obstacle here and a passage-way there, it only necessitates that there are some obstacles and passageways in general; it does not draw the particular figure of this world, it only lays down [*pose*] general structures in it. (*F*502)

Merleau-Ponty limits the use of the concept of freedom to acts which contain an element of personal choice; he does not make it synonymous with Existence or subjectivity. The above quotation states that freedom creates metastructures which, given our present field, will reveal objects and their properties that are relevant to our chosen purposes. The metastructures that result from free choice are many levels above our first-order structures, for they release other capacities which are, in fact, lower-level metastructures. For example, if I wish to climb a mountain, this desire will ready certain of my motor capacities and will correlatively reveal the practical properties of the entities facing me. Rocks will have the physical properties, large or straight only insofar as they have the meta-structural practical properties, manageable or unclimbable. The former properties can be given because we possess innate visual capacities to experience shape and size and the latter because we possess innate metastructural capacities to move our bodies. These structures are not, then, *created* by such a choice, but are sedimented structures that are made figural or focal by means of it. "Insofar as I have hands, feet, a body, I sustain around me intentions which are not dependent on my decisions" (*F*502). These "general intentions which potentially evaluate my environment . . . [indicate] a natural self . . . which constantly adumbrates absolute evaluations" (*F*502).

All our sedimented capacities, perceptual and metastructural, are potentially contained in our field. Yet things are not given to us with all their potential attributes plainly in view. Rather, the thing carries them in its inexhaustible horizons and their correlative prepersonal structures are selectively organized and revealed by our present interests. Notice, however, that this complex of situations need not be triggered by free choice, for there are certain biological and practical interests which are actualized spontaneously. For example, if I fall or stumble, my interest in self-preservation will release my capacities for motor recovery and perceptually disclose obstacles and dangers.

When I choose to act, I call on prereflective capabilities that are already sedimented as potential modes of behavior. The choice merely releases this system of behaviors, which will be particularized by the present field. Hence, there is no need to create and sustain our choices at every moment, as Descartes and Sartre claim, for once the decision is made it is carried on by the prepersonal body-subject. There is a possibility of personal choice because the subject necessarily maintains a distance from his present mode of inherence in a field. Yet freedom is merely the reverse of being involved in the world through many regions. Because of his infinite horizons of potential ways of structuring the world, the subject is never totally engaged in any one situation and is always capable of switching to another. The subject, then, is always literally "more than" or beyond his present actual situation. Therefore, subjectivity may be said to "trigger" the present field as much as does otherness; it resists, contacts, and presents a "texture" to otherness as well as the reverse. Contact between subjectivity and otherness is a double movement and comes into being through both poles of a present situation.

Our innate regions cannot all be activated to a high degree nor all our potential interests simultaneously deployed. We can see, then, that there must be a horizon of engagements surrounding any particular present mode of subjectivity. This subjective horizon is certainly distinct from the outer horizon which ties the entire world to our present field or focal object. For example, in a concert hall my interest may be auditory-aesthetic such that I do not notice the coughing that surrounds me or the poor repair of the hall. If I lose this interest, I shall find that the concerns that are nearest on its horizon will replace it. I take up a philosophical attitude by directing epistemological and critical questions to my perceptual milieu. Or perhaps my social consciousness is the next strongest region of concern or will follow the philosophical: I may, then, find the zest and intended meaning of Wagner's music deplorable, or I may meditate on the social injustice of a concert hall with limited and high-priced seating. What is noticeable here is that the hierarchy of these interests suggests a "personality," and reveals a sedimented order of interests that determines to some extent the subject's freedom to will different modes of attention. But Merleau-Ponty notes that such a pattern has only a probable force and that I am capable of calling up rare attitudes, although they will be more difficult to attain than the habitual. The above presents the standard horizons of my concert situation. But this overall pattern may entirely dissolve, as when we say we "cannot concentrate." At this point, curiosity takes over, and I wander irrationally from interest to interest and even from attitude to attitude. For example, my attention becomes riveted first on the breathing, scratching, and coughing that surrounds me, next on the conductor's movements, and then on the pomposity of the orchestra. Once my standard concert situation has broken down, another horizon of interests has to take its place, for if my present perceptual field lacked metastructuring, it would approach complete contingency and I would be close to absolute boredom and anxiety.

The above example reveals the vast complexity of metalevels. Not only do we have a cognitive, a practical, and an affective layer of metastructures, but above these we have systems of interests, such as the concert situation, which horizonally order these lower-level metastructures. Furthermore, as Heidegger has shown, our moods also metastructure our interests in a global way by excluding possible concerns and dictating the remainder's degree of specificity. Although all these structures form about a perceptual nucleus and can be found in our perceptual field, we can never fully describe them, for their layers are indeterminate and vaguely blend with one another (for example, consider the conflicts and equivocalness of being angry in a scientific situation). Yet it is just this ambiguity that leaves us room to freely create and choose new systems of metastructures. If any of these global situations were fully determinate and explicable, personal freedom would be inconceivable. (Schneider and other psychiatric patients whose phenomenological scope is greatly narrowed approach such a status.)

4. Temporality

For Merleau-Ponty temporality is the "structure of all structures," as Being is the "situation of all situations." An analysis of the form of temporality is, therefore, basic to any study of the logic of situations. Also, and equally important, the dynamic of temporality clearly discloses the essential properties of subjectivity and Being. In this section we shall be particularly concerned with furthering our understanding of Merleau-Ponty's notion of Being. Also, the examination of subjectivity in terms of temporality will be invaluable for the succeeding analyses of the phenomenologies of perception and cognition, for it will introduce the crucial notions of operational intentionality and transitional synthesis.

Almost from the beginning we have been aware of the close connection between these three major concepts: Being, temporality, and subjectivity. In the first chapter, we saw that Being must be grasped as the action of splitting, spreading, or division (*écart*), and as radically finite. We were able to acquaint ourselves with these two characteristics and their coincidence through the central movement of temporality, its *ekstase*. We concluded that Being temporalizes itself by constantly seeking to overcome the otherness that lies in an indefinite future, through ever-renewed attempts at self-coincidence in a present, while always maintaining and using those aspects of itself which were already determined in its past. It has also become clear from our analysis of the logic of situation that this movement, which is the same as that of the creative articulation and disclosure of otherness, and the acquisition of its determinations, gives us an essential definition of subjectivity. Being's *écart* is the coming to be of temporality and it is here that we find the sense and possibility of subjectivity. Thus our analysis has often made use of the fact that these three are interrelated, but only now are we in a position to clarify why this is the case.

A large number of the elements and problems we have encountered in our study of Being can be finally articulated through this study of temporality, and many of the problems resolved. It will explain how Being can be an endless thrust; how we can understand its finitude and otherness; how it can cohere with itself throughout its evolution; how its whole movement is to articulate itself and become conscious of itself; how its otherness can blend with its determinations; why it has been traditionally characterized as presence; how we can grasp its identity in spite of its radical alterity, and how it can be one yet many.

With this understanding of temporality, Being, and subjectivity, we shall have attained a sufficient grasp of Merleau-Ponty's metaphysics to move to a close examination of his central phenomenological studies of perception and cognition. Then in the last chapter we shall return to many of the metaphysical themes already touched upon, in the attempt to comprehend Merleau-Ponty's deepest descriptions of Being and its relationship to man. There we shall consider such questions as how Being can open itself and make itself visible by means of a subject; in what sense Being is perspectival and progressive; how there can be many subjects which are all equally manifestations of Being; how this plurality of subjects makes a social world and history possible; how social being (sociality) is as metaphysically significant as natural being; and how history can be understood as the concrete embodiment of the single temporality that is Being itself.

In opposition to an objective and analytic conception of time, Merleau-Ponty insists that time is not merely a uniform succession of nows or the following of one discrete and indivisible moment upon the previous moment, which was also exhaustively presented and in-itself. He counters this traditional model of time, which is the thematic and cognitive version of lived time, by showing that the present is not an instant but must be understood as our "field of presence" (416); that past, present, and future are three distinct dimensions of time; that the whole of time is contained in every present; and that time moves throughout its whole length, as it is essentially "lapse," "flux," or "*ekstase*." We can understand Merleau-Ponty's notion of temporality if we familiarize ourselves both with this field of presence, which contains the past and future as irremovable horizons, and with the phenomenon of lapse which is its essence.

The only distinctions Merleau-Ponty allows in time's "unique movement" (419) are those between the past, present, and future, for each is given to us in a different way. The future is not empty or nothing, but consists of protensions, or "lines of intentionality which trace out in advance at least the style of what is to come" (416). The past is given as retentions of previous presents. However, these two dimensions tend to collapse into the present, which we can define either as our present field with all its horizons or as the "point" which anchors the "system of retentions" (*F*479) which is putting forth the most up-to-date "system of protensions" (*F*479). We can begin to grasp how these three dimensions are distinct and yet essentially defined by one another if we consider the present as the figure or point of the otherness with which we are always in contact. In that case, the future consists in the inexhaustible, but ordered, system of possible determinations that are characteristic of any encounter with otherness. The past is constituted by our previous determinations of otherness, as well as the possible directions of further articulation that they imply. Our present is grounded in these past specifications of otherness and is the making explicit and bringing to realization of some of the directions they indicated.

Merleau-Ponty uses a version of Husserl's diagram to illustrate this unity of time, although he warns us that it can be very misleading if we reify the hypothetically separated series of presents (419 and *VI*195). The following diagram is an extension of Merleau-Ponty's, for his does not show the system of protensions (417). Husserl's diagram is briefer still.[31]

31. Husserl's diagram appears in *The Phenomenology of Internal Time Consciousness*, p. 49. In spite of the similarities, it should become clear that Merleau-Ponty's notions of retention and protension are very different from Husserl's. The source of this difference is Husserl's irrepressible tendency to understand the present in a phenomenalist or "sensationalist" manner; that is to say, as the only real and full moment and as one that arises from a passively received datum, content, or impression. Because the present is taken as the model of self-givenness, Husserl says occasionally that protensions are "completely empty" (e.g., *Experience and Judgement*, pp. 110-11) and that their meaning is derived solely from the broadest a priori categories of the object in general. In contrast, for Merleau-Ponty protensions present positively given phenomena with varying levels of determinacy, which are always achieved to some degree, for they are rooted in the structures of the past and in the subject's present grasp of his field. For the same reason, Husserl understands retention in terms of the traditional notion of the immediate past. Yet this notion is mistaken in that it implies that there is a privileged moment in the past when we still are affected by, coincide with, or passively receive an impression. On the basis of this hypothetical entity, one is able to explain away the original givenness of the past as a mere variation (e.g., a weakening) of "genuine" presence. Similarly this notion helps make possible Husserl's pure conception of the reduction, for it allows one to reflectively coincide with a *cogitatio*, which thereby has the possibility of being apodictic. Surprisingly, even Sartre occasionally depends on this notion of the immediate past to justify his phenomenological reflection (cf. *The Transcendence of the Ego*, p. 46, and *Being and Nothingness*, p. 157). Merleau-Ponty, of course, holds that reflection is inescapably corrigible because there must always be a temporal spread and epistemological distance between the act of reflection and the act on which it reflects.

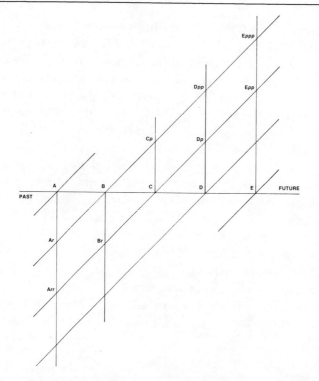

Let us label the presents *A, B, C, D,* and *E*. If *C* is taken as the present moment, then *B*, the immediate past, is given as a retention of *C* (labeled B_r). *A*, in turn, must be understood as a retention of *B* (labeled A_r). This means that *C*, which is our present, is the retention of *B* (B_r) and the retention of the retention of *A* (A_{rr}). The same will apply, *mutatis mutandis*, to the system of protensions which are *C*'s references to *D* and *E* (D_p, E_{pp}). This means that *C* must be more fully described as A_{rr} - B_r - D_p - E_{pp}. When one moment becomes the next, for example when *B* becomes *C*, time "moves throughout its length" and in "waves" (329), and we should understand this transition as equally A_r becoming A_{rr}, *B* becoming B_r, and C_p becoming *C*, etc. When *C* is the present field, it is the evolution of *B* which held it as C_p; equally, it is the transforming of *B* into B_r, which is a fulfillment, denial, alteration, or confirmation of the presence which was *B*. Thus one can view all of time as the stage-by-stage development of a single but continuous contact with otherness. One cannot argue that this conception of time entails an infinite regress, for the initiating present, which is primordial contact, already had a "prehistory" of thrown structures opening on to an otherness which demanded infinite specification.

Time maintains what it has brought into being, at the same moment that it chases it from being, because the new being was announced by the preceding as destined to be, and because it was the same thing for the latter to become present and to be destined to pass. (*F*480)

There is no need for a thetic synthesis of identification, or an explicit constitution of time, for there are no individual instants that require an act of relating or unification. On the contrary, for Merleau-Ponty time is the original "transitional synthesis" (419); it necessarily and naturally "uncoils" itself into a series of presents which "interlock" (422) and "issue one from the other" (419). Yet there is a transition because there is a "distancing" (*F*483) or splitting apart (*écart*) in time: it "takes time" for Being to constitute itself. The spread is between a past which structures and sets the essential conditions of this present and a future of perpetual demands for new and present articulations of the past. Time, as a "chain of fields of presence, has the essential characteristic of being able to actualize itself only little by little and by degree" (*F*483). This necessarily partial actualization of time by degrees points to the finitude of time and, thus, to the finitude of Being which it expresses. Similarly the necessity and "innateness" of the continual synthesis, or of time's "indivisible thrust and transition" (423), is the direct reflection of Being's own primordial action of *écart*.

We can make this finitude and spreading of time more explicit by analyzing the relationship between the past and the present. Although "each present reasserts the presence of the whole past" (420), it does so only partially and incompletely. The present preserves the past by carrying forward and creatively developing *some* of its protensions. These were only foreshadowed and their development could not have been deduced within the past. Naive or lived consciousness indeed experiences the present as transcending itself into the full past and future, but this does not mean that time is "eternal" or that we can attain a total and exhaustive grasp of it. It is instead the case that the field of presence has a "double horizon of original past and original future and the infinite openness of the evolved or possible fields of presence" (*F*484). My former field was the result of an attempt to achieve the maximum articulation of otherness. In necessarily failing to exhaust this presence, it revealed innumerable further possible determinations. My present field can be said to actively "differentiate" (419) itself from this past because it must take up and develop some of these suggestions and directions. However, in doing so, it cannot reproduce this previous hold and must leave it with its thisness (its unique organization and distinctive but inexhaustible horizons). We can always return to this past but never exhaustively comprehend it, for it has the denseness (*épaisseur*) of the inexhaustible inner and outer horizons through which Merleau-Ponty defines any real entity or presence (cf. chapter 3.2). My present, then, redevelops and reorientates the gestalt of the intentions of the preceding present. The result is that each present establishes its own unique sense but must also have a direct connection with this past and is thus "never without motivation" (*F*489).

If Being were not finite, even though it spread itself out into time it would be conceivable that, by constantly making itself present, it would eventually achieve a total and final determination of itself. However, we cannot postulate such an infinite Being, for the spread in temporality is given as unmistakably finite. There must always be a "distance" (*F*484) between presents, as the later cannot entirely gather together the earlier nor the earlier fully predict the later. One of Merleau-Ponty's best concise descriptions of time is that it is the "thrust" or "the power that holds events together by distancing them one from the other" (*F*483). The transitional synthesis moves haltingly forward, but the advances it makes must be offset by the continual but erratic loss of the distant past. The "confusion of what is far, a sort of shrinkage of the past of which the limit is the forgotten" (*F*483) gives us a striking illustration of the finitude of temporality and Being. This loss is partially a function of the present being able to select only some of the ambiguities of the past for determination while necessarily ignoring others. It refocuses this past field by concentrating on certain articulations and pushing others, which previouly may have been already highly determinate, into the background. A quite distant past may still be molded and completed by our present, but such a past is linked to our present through the original shape of each of the less distant pasts that succeeded it. Our present's bond to this distant past's own distinctive set of possibilities continually weakens.[32]

---

32. Herein lies Merleau-Ponty's interesting theory of repression. A repression gives to a past (a particular project or involvement) an inordinate importance such that it continues to have a strong horizonal presence. It refuses to fade, or be dialectically subsumed, as does a normal past through its integration into the more recent concerns of the present. One becomes "fixated" on this past because one remains blind to the traumatic revelation given

We equally discover the finitude or spread of temporality in the otherness which is made obvious in every present. Our new present arose as soon as the otherness, which the previous present failed to encompass, became obtrusive. This new present puts forth a thesis or "posit" (427-28) which is meant to account for and make up the deficiencies of the previous. But in revealing a new determination and organization of this otherness, it also immediately reveals new inexhaustible horizons. This means that it is already fulfilling its own protensions and is hence becoming still another present. Thus the present, "as soon as it comes into existence, begins to lose its substance" (F477). The present has pulled the past further, but in becoming a present it is, in turn, pulled in a new direction itself and subsequently it becomes a posited and sedimented past. This movement is the lapse or *ekstase* of time which never stops or achieves itself. It accounts for the constant tremor in our world or "the slipperiness [*glissement*] of the soil under our feet" (EM92F). Every present is in this fashion contingent, corrigible, and general, in the sense that our grasp of its particularity must remain forever incomplete. Similarly, our past and future are horizons that are directly accessible to us but opaque and "slippery [*glissantes*]" (F398). Therefore, the temporal spread between any two presents is only another expression of the initial stretching beyond itself of Being.

Merleau-Ponty repeatedly states that subjectivity *is* temporality (422, 432). He demonstrates that the lapse we have discovered to be the essence of time must be explicated as a thrust or drive into otherness, as the "cohesion of a life" (421, VI98, VI112), and as the birth of a consciousness. Where the three dimensions of time intertwine or where temporality lapses beyond its present hold on itself and thus transcends itself, we discover the deepest meaning of subjectivity. By analyzing these characteristics of lapse, we shall deepen our understanding of both temporality and subjectivity with the result that we shall be able to see clearly that temporality and subjectivity are equivalent to Merleau-Ponty's description of Being as division (*écart*). We shall then be in a position to see how he solves

---

in that moment that certain closely held desires, values, and certainties are unrealizable and insupportable. As a result, they become a perpetual task and a "complex" that subsequent presents must continue to pursue without the possibility of satisfaction (83 ff.).

the problem of maintaining that Being (time and subjectivity) can be both one and many.

> We are saying that time is someone, or that temporal dimensions, inasmuch as they perpetually overlap, confirm one another and ever confine themselves to making explicit what was implied in each, all express a single bursting forth [*éclatement*] or a single thrust [*poussée*] that is subjectivity itself. (*F*482)

This thrust has been variously referred to as transcendence, spontaneity, projection, and Existence. We have come to understand it as the innate drive of subjectivity to articulate, interpret, or specify itself. In our discussion of articulation earlier in the chapter, we saw that what was articulated was the highly general openness of our thrown modes of being-in-the-world or, correlatively, the broad regions of otherness which perpetually demand our attention. We can now see that this drive to explicate otherness is so comprehensive because, as the essential movement of temporality, it is the structure of all structures:

> It is necessary that consciousness be a global project . . . of time and the world which, in order to appear to itself, in order to become explicitly what it is implicitly, that is to say consciousness, needs to develop itself into multiplicity. (*F*485)

This quotation demonstrates how close Merleau-Ponty is to Hegel's understanding of the coming to be of subjectivity, temporality, and Being. Here he equates the three by defining consciousness as a global project of both time and the world. Therefore, when one characterizes consciousness essentially as that which must make itself appear to itself, or explicate itself, one is not only giving the condition of a subject's consciousness but also that of Being's or temporality's own self-consciousness (or, better, that of the global thrust in general). Being becomes "consciousness" (*VI*118) in unrolling itself into a multiplicity of presents and is essentially the coming to be of consciousness or "making visible" (*F*487). Merleau-Ponty agrees with Hegel that Being is an "undivided thrust" (*VI*104) that seeks to know itself by unfolding itself in time and by spreading itself into multiplicity. The entire process must be understood as a progressive explication of Being's originally given, implicit hold on itself. We have come to understand this process by seeing that every present or creative articulation of otherness is the making explicit of our general, implicit, and pregiven contact with otherness. Therefore, each present carries on as far as it is able the work of all the previous. Like Hegel, Merleau-Ponty holds that it is in this perpetual lapse of presence, or in becoming, that we discover the birth of subjectivity or self-consciousness, and that consciousness can only comprehend itself in the otherness that it continually delimits, articulates, or makes present.

Merleau-Ponty makes this multiplicity concrete by referring it to the subject's lived experiences (*Erlebnisse*), articulations, actions, decisions, or generally to the subject's meaningful and authentic presents, which are those that count for it (and do not merely "tick by"). "All consciousness, as a global project, outlines itself [*se profile*] or manifests itself to itself in acts, experiences, or 'psychic facts' where it recognizes itself" (*F*486). This Husserlian or Jamesian sounding language should not mislead us into thinking that for Merleau-Ponty the primary constituents of time are *cogitationes* (and, thus, that time has the characteristics of a "stream of consciousness"). On the contrary, "consciousness ensconces itself in being and in time by taking up a situation" (*F*485) with all its externality and publicity. This "empirical self" is not different from subjectivity taken as a continuous and singular thrust, for we saw that time, as *ekstase* and lapse, is a unified movement which expresses itself in the transition of one present to the next.[33] Subjectivity's present actions and experiences are the "distinct manifestations" of its "indivisible power [*puissance*]," and both constitute "the movement of temporalization itself" (*F*485).

> The original flux . . . not only *is*. . . . It is essential to time . . . to know itself; for the explosion or dehiscence of the present toward the future is the archetype of the *relation of self to self* and sketches out an interiority or ipseity. (*F*487)

The subject thus gains awareness of itself in the movement that pulls it out of its narrow present or anchorage in a field. Just as it is necessary for consciousness to posit itself in a present, it must also always be beyond this present in order that it may grasp it against the background of its entire history and inexhaustible future. (The expansion of this "scope" of oneself or of one's field of presence allows one to approach a limiting ideal of pure authenticity, as well as what Hegel calls absolute knowledge.) Each present is a gathering

33. Some critics have mistakenly maintained that Merleau-Ponty is unable to unite the empirical self with the personal, free, or creative self.

together of the past, which consists of thrown and subsequently articulated structures, in a new attempt to totally determine, and thus fully comprehend, itself and otherness. In doing so, time gains some hold on itself. But if this hold were exhaustive, time would stop, Being would become a pure plenitude or motionless self-identity, and subjectivity would be inconceivable. In the same present wherein time grasps itself, it must also find that it remains beyond itself and is dragged into a new view of otherness which demands explication. Temporality, *qua* singular and global thrust, is always there as the background for each present, and each present must, therefore, represent only a slippery and obscure grasp of this global something. Similarly, the subject's (and Being's) self-disclosure in a present is equally the revelation that it has not captured itself and is still "ahead of itself" in an otherness that remains to be determined. (As Heidegger insists, revealment and concealment, or truth and error, must be equally basic.)

Merleau-Ponty describes this thrust and spreading of temporality and subjectivity as "auto-positing [*autoposition*]" (*F*487). The process is one continuous attempt to grasp or articulate itself (the "self" which is articulated is the presence of both its primitively given past and its future, which perpetually escape every such attempt). Temporality must be a system of transitionally posited presents and a continuous attempt to capture itself, because, from the first, it was a general and indeterminate presence to itself and was thus primordially ahead of any specific grasp it could get of itself. In order to understand lapse, we must understand the condition under which temporality can be "present to itself," in the two senses of being a momentary determination of itself and being with itself throughout its length. Understanding presence as the unity of these two senses is possible only if we understand Being as *écart*. Being possesses itself to some degree, but it is also removed from itself, for it is finite, and thus other than itself. The *écart* implies that Being remains one with itself but is equally and essentially many (differentiation and division from itself). If each and every such division of Being (which can be taken as a present articulation of it) must necessarily fail to articulate itself exhaustively, and yet if in spite of that Being is to remain one with itself, Being must leap outside of this particular *écart* and posit a new one in the same action by which it posited the first. It is in this way that *écart* coincides with lapse, flux, or *ekstase*. Given Being's finitude, it gives rise to a temporal unity which is just Being's endless spreading of itself into a transitional multiplicity. If Being were to give rise to a pure "moment" or "now" (and thus "stop" its *ekstase*), it would no longer be unified and *one* but would become a mere multiplicity.

We can now see why Merleau-Ponty says that "there is a temporal style of the world" (422) and of every form of existence. We discover this style within subjectivity as the "cohesion of life"[34] which is an ecstatic being outside of itself which is thereby characteristic of every modality of subjectivity. The "outside of itself" then becomes the "constant style" (*VI*146) of every kind of situation, and provides a comprehensive formula for Being itself. We can understand this notion concretely by studying its appearance in subjectivity as a cohesion of life and *ekstase*.

Subjectivity is "a single experience inseparable from itself, a single 'cohesion of life,' a single temporality that progressively explicates itself from its birth and confirms its singularity in each present" (*F*466). We have seen that this need to articulate otherness is an irremovable characteristic of our thrownness and is equally primordial with our primordial contact with otherness. We can now see that this cohesion and equal primordiality are "given with its [temporality's] *ek-stase*" (*F*481), or that facticity is directly derived from the essential characteristics of temporality. Strictly speaking, the subject does not reflect temporality nor is it founded on temporality; rather it *is* temporality. As Merleau-Ponty insists, subjectivity explains and clarifies time as much as time does subjectivity. "Time remains the same [constant and unified] because . . . there is at the core of time a gaze [*regard*] or . . . someone" (422). And, conversely, no synthesis of the empirical self or the multiple world is needed (and thus no transcendental self) because this "synopsis" (*F*320) is "given" (*F*481) along with temporality itself.

Therefore, the cohesion of life—time itself—is just the movement of the perpetual specification of new presents which are grounded in the general and more indeterminate past and are explications of it.

34. When using this expression on pages 466 and 481 of the *Phénoménologie de la perception,* Merleau-Ponty refers to Heidegger's expression *Zusammenhang des Lebens,* citing respectively pages 388 and 373 of *Sein und Zeit.* (In fact, the phrase that occurs on page 388 is *"Zusammenhang" des Daseins.*) (See also *VI*98 and *VI*112.)

We can begin to comprehend how such a metastable Being can remain one with itself (how it coincides with its own otherness) by describing the "first present" or the "absolute past." It is possible to conceive of such a limiting point by examining the commencement of a particular concrete duration, as Merleau-Ponty has done in a number of places: notably in his studies of the evolution of relatively self-contained styles and phases of literary, artistic, and philosophical expression in *The Prose of the World*, the genesis of interpersonal relationships in *The Child's Relations with Others*, and the development of Swann's love (425). The initiating present must protend, and actually contain in a vague manner, every present that will follow, for every subsequent present will be the working out of this project or original presence. This most general something is the implicit presence of all that will explicitly evolve from it. It is in the ontological relationship between the general and the specific that we comprehend how our thrown regions and the "prehistorical" world can contain all that they will ever disclose themselves to be; how the three dimensions of time must interrelate and through their dependence give rise to meaning; and how Being can be other than itself and still coincide with this otherness and be singular or one. Being's otherness is just its general, and thus indeterminate and unspecified, contact with itself, and Being remains other than itself only insofar as it is equally a drive to overcome this generality by making itself determinate (that is, by the action of making present). "Presence" must always have this double sense of being a general given and of being that which still remains to be determined. Once this is understood, we are already part way to conceiving how Being can be both one and many. As Merleau-Ponty says, as soon as we recognize indeterminacy, the problematic dichotomy between "multiplicity" and "synthesis" can be abandoned (*F*316). Just as we saw that the world is an open individual which is necessarily incomplete and indeterminate (chapter 2.1), we can now see that every existent also must be a "determinate-indeterminate," a "delimited negativity," or a "general particular," because these are in fact key descriptions of Being itself.

Time "is nothing else than a general flight outside of Self, the unique law of these centrifugal movements, or again, as Heidegger said, an '*ek-stase*' " (*F*479-80). The "movements" to which Merleau-Ponty is referring are all the possible protensions and retentions that radiate from a field of presence. Yet, it is important to realize that this implies that for Merleau-Ponty *ekstase* is the "law" of every possible type of subjective act (426). We have just seen that this law of temporality gives us the form of every type of articulation, contact, and synthesis, from the synthesis of the empirical self and its states of mind to that of the world and perception.[35] We have come to understand the movement of temporality through studying these essential dimensions of subjectivity. However, at the same time in this section we have transcended the individual descriptions of such phenomena as articulation, intentionality, and spontaneity and have come to see temporality as the common or general law of all of them. Thus, in grasping temporality, we comprehend subjectivity or Existence as a unity and find its "meaning [*Sinn*]" (410). But, further, we have found that this *ekstase* "is nothing else than a general flight outside of Self" (479). Thereby we are brought once again to the most essential characteristic of Being, of which temporality is the expression—the *écart* or outside of itself.

In the remainder of this section we shall examine in detail Merleau-Ponty's solution to the problem of the one and the many. The solution is very similar to the one that Hegel summed up in his notion of the Concept (*Begriff*), and it will give us a crucial comprehension of Being. It is interesting to establish that Merleau-Ponty agrees with Hegel on such an essential matter, for it implies strongly that Merleau-Ponty's existentialist vision is close to Hegel's and therefore, that he sympathizes to a large extent with that privileged metaphysical intuition which Hegel calls absolute knowledge.

In an important footnote to the *Phenomenolgy of Perception*, (*F*319-20), Merleau-Ponty criticizes Bergson for making the unifying activity of subjectivity or temporality a "real operation" (*F*319) that affects and encounters an objectivity or multiplicity that is also independently real. Although Kant gives us a better understanding of the unity of the subject and the world by making the function of subjectivity transcendental, both he and Husserl are also criticized for taking as real the multiplicity that is outside consciousness. For

---

35. Merleau-Ponty has defined operative intentionality in these terms and has related it to Heidegger's notion of transcendence (418); therefore he has made it the general form of every type of practical-motor and interpersonal mode of behavior as well.

Merleau-Ponty the unity of time, space, and the world is "a flux" which "dominates diversity" through a "synopsis" which "does not . . . indicate an explicit positing of diversity" (*F*320). Similarly, space must not be seen either as an "irreducible multiplicity" or a "unique and indivisible" unity (*F*282).

> We must avoid treating as real or distinct either the indivisible thrust or its distinct manifestations; consciousness is not one or the other; it is one and the other, it is the movement itself of temporalization. (*F*485–86)

Like Hegel, he holds that unity and multiplicity are dialectical extremes, and that at this ultimate level the subject-side and the object-side are together within a higher-order unity. This latter, second-order "one" above both unity and diversity results from that "turning" of the relationship of the one and the many into but one term of the higher-order relationship that is Being itself or the Concept for Hegel.[36] For Merleau-Ponty, it is a way to understand the self-identity and uniformity of Being in spite of its essentially changeable and metastable character.

In order to explain the *cogito* and the basic experience of our own unity and self-identity, Merleau-Ponty instructs us to understand "the for itself as itself an incontestable, but derived, characteristic: it is the culmination of separation [*écart*] in *differentiation*—Presence to self *is* presence to a differentiated world" (*VI*245F). In other words, Being splits off from and folds over itself, giving rise to *Dasein*, which is equally the production of a self and a world as a field of multiplicity. As Hegel has demonstrated, the subject is a unity only insofar as it exists in opposition to the many, and it constantly seeks its unity through the action of diversifying itself by differentiating the world. The one and the many arise simultaneously and are fully interdependent; thus their source and overall unity is the oneness of Being itself. Activity and passivity, like the for-itself and in-itself, are abstract sides of Being's primordial separation and are mere descriptions of, or "derived" (*VI*245F) from, the singular movement of *écart*.

We have already seen that this *écart* can best be characterized as *ekstase* and as that which is "wholly outside of itself" (*VI*180F). Hegel's idea of the Concept reveals the fluidity of these notions and

36. Compare especially Hegel's chapter entitled "Understanding" in *The Phenomenology of Mind*.

the way in which one can conceive of Being which is one as well as outside of itself. Following Hegel, let us show how this dialectic works. We begin by taking the one as the subject or as that point of Being which shows the action of thrusting or transcending beyond itself (or, as Merleau-Ponty often refers to it, the action of "dehiscence" or "inherence"). The many can then be taken as the otherness or outside wherein Being "is in the process of manifesting itself" (*VI*127*F*), or as the world where the subject seeks its articulation. Merleau-Ponty refers to the dialectical movement of the many to the one as, for example, "this concentration of the visibles about one of them," and to the correlative and reverse movement of the one to the many as "this bursting forth of the mass of the body towards things" (*VI*146). Furthermore, he understands the two sides of this dialectic as equivalent and inseparable.

By following Hegel's outline of the dynamics of the Concept and the terminology he uses to describe it, we can establish how each side is related to the other. From the point of view of Being *qua* one, multiplicity is the otherness it perpetually seeks to conquer and that wherein it attempts to articulate itself through differentiation and diversification. The many is indeed other, for it is inexhaustible; that is, its multiple articulations do not give the one the whole of itself at the instant of the one's *ekstase* or posit. Hence the place where the one explicitly discovers itself remains foreign and strange to it, and Being is thus alienated from itself. However, we can now see that Being is *outside of itself* just because it does not possess its unified and whole self in the many. In other words, in Hegelian fashion, the movement of the one to the many has reversed itself: it now appears that what is other than (foreign to) Being is its full possession of itself as a purely unified existence. We have, therefore, arrived dialectically at the other side, where Being comprehends itself in terms of the many and, as Hegel says, "yearns" for its unity. From this point of view (the many), its initiating movement of thrust and transcendence is now incomprehensible and other. Therefore, its oneness and *ekstase* is now characterized as what is outside of itself.

To this Being that exists in multiplicity, Being *qua* one is strange and alien and is what it seeks to achieve (i.e., the unification of its diverse articulations) in order fully to comprehend and make itself explicit. Both Being and subjectivity are "a flux . . . which gathers itself together" (*F*320) and a "never-ending integration" (*F*270). As was to be expected, this dialectic presents us with the general structure of the movement of temporality and subjectivity—a movement that differentiates and diversifies itself in a present, and then, on this ground taken as a past, lunges after a unity which results in still further diversification. "The act which gathers together takes away and holds at a distance; I only touch myself in fleeing from myself" (*F*467). Thus, like Hegel, Merleau-Ponty "turns" the relationship between the one and the many, by demonstrating, first, that the entire dialectic is the *single* movement of *ekstase, écart,* self-estrangement, or being outside of itself, and, second, that this higher-order oneness of Being is just the *dynamic* movement between the two ideal moments of identity and diversity (which can, if one wishes, be equivalently taken as a higher-order "many"). The dialectic is, as Merleau-Ponty says referring explicitly to Hegel, "*a movement which creates its own course and returns to itself...,* which retakes itself (*se reprend*) little by little and launches itself anew through the mystery of rationality."[37]

Again, for both Merleau-Ponty and Hegel, Being is most fundamentally a "coming to be of consciousness" and a "making visible"; it is "Self-manifestation, unveiling, in the process of making itself" (*VI*125F and *VI*127F). But for Merleau-Ponty this dialectic is a never-ending process which cannot arrive at the complete and exhaustive differentiation of the world that Hegel envisions in his notion of absolute knowledge. Hegel held that the multiplicity of Being had become, in his time, totally determined and articulated; and that the contingency that gives sense to the continuance of time was to be found only on the side of the individual subject who unified this multiplicity and made it cohere. Merleau-Ponty, on the contrary, insists that the contingency, or finitude, of Being is radical and cannot be compromised because the multiplicity that represents the articulation of Being's significance is essentially indeterminate, vague, and partial. To name Being *Concept* is, of course, unacceptable to Merleau-Ponty, as it is a central purpose of his to make it clear that Being does not possess the clarity, coherence, and precision of the conceptual. However, in the Hegelian mode, Being could well be named *Situation* ("situational being" [*VI*93]), for the logic of the situational is founded by, and thereby reflects and manifests, the

37. *La prose du monde,* p. 120.

logos of Being which we have come to understand through the study of temporality.

The above explication of Being as one and many should establish finally that the notion of otherness is a *primitive* for Merleau-Ponty's understanding of Being. When we analyze the metaphysics of the social world and the relationship between history and Being in chapter 5, we shall see that in these areas as well Merleau-Ponty consciously carries forward some of Hegel's essential claims.

3 Perception

The topics of the next two chapters require a general introduction. The content of these chapters is more phenomenological and epistemological than that of the previous two, which was predominantly metaphysical, and the form of our treatment—its style and structure—will be altered to accommodate this new content. There is thus a significant change of direction in our discussion as a whole at this point, which calls for some explanation.

By relying upon Merleau-Ponty's major phenomenological discoveries in the preceding analysis of his ontology, we have become familiar with most of them. However, we still need to examine them because up to now they have been presented somewhat dogmatically, and only in a general way. Our frequent references to the texts attempted to show that Merleau-Ponty held these positions, but, in the context of his metaphysics, we were unable to see how he developed them and whether he was justified in holding them. Also, our selection of and comprehension of these texts were the result of an overall interpretation. Since, no doubt, there are some who would quarrel with this interpretation, it is necessary to justify it, and the only way this can be done is by means of a detailed explication of Merleau-Ponty's phenomenology.

We have decided to concentrate on perception and cognition, rather than on the other possible areas of Merleau-Ponty's phenomenology, for several reasons: they are the main areas of traditional philosophy and phenomenology; Merleau-Ponty is best known for his contribution to the phenomenology of perception; and many people have been baffled by, and at odds with, his phenomenology of cognition. Furthermore, since a central aim of the succeeding chapters will be to demonstrate the effectiveness of situational analysis, we have selected the topics that present the greatest challenge to Merleau-Ponty's metaphysics. The epistemological issues raised by the philosophy of vision and cognition are crucial tests of the conclusions reached in the previous chapters, for they appear, at first glance, to put into question the viability of Merleau-Ponty's monism and realism, or his anti-Cartesianism and nonintellectualism.[1]

There is as well a need to discuss the other two regions of Existence if our treatment of his philosophy is to be comprehensive and complete. We shall reserve the discussion of sociality for the chapter 5 discussion of Being, for it allows us to come to grips with the key issues of Merleau-Ponty's deepest metaphysics, to demonstrate the metaphysical relevance of society and history, and to understand how sociality metastructures and entwines with nature at this metaphysical level. We shall analyze perception, and especially vision, in terms of its mundane and concrete structures, that is to say, in enough depth to demonstrate precisely how, for example, vision and its correlative qualities of shape, size, and color follow a general situational logic and how each manifests primordial contact in its own distinctive manner. By means of such an investigation, we shall be able to give an effective analysis of the region of motility as well. This is best accomplished by merging the study of motility with the study of perception for the following reasons: First, it allows us to examine the motility and motor intentionality of the body-subject in concrete and standard perceptual situations. Secondly, the way it permeates the perceptual region gives us another excellent illustration of the intertwining and intertranslatability of regions, on which Merleau-Ponty bases his definition of Existence.[2] Finally, although there is a need for this type of study of motility, a general explication of gross motility cannot be justified in the context of

1. Even excellent commentators like De Waelhens and A. Lingis have slipped into dualist explanations of Merleau-Ponty's notions, implying that he affirms that there is a thing-in-itself. See De Waelhens, *Une philosophie de l'ambiguité*, p. 388, and Lingis's preface to his translation of *The Visible and the Invisible*, p. lv.

2. Because Kwant has missed this most important theme, he spends much of his critical chapter (*The Phenomenological Philosophy of Merleau-Ponty*, chapter 13) arguing that Merleau-Ponty has neither analyzed nor explained freedom or spirit (or Existence). We shall frequently in the next three chapters discuss how the four regions always interrelate.

contemporary Merleau-Ponty scholarship, for it has been carried out frequently and well by other commentators.

In the present context it is necessary to explicate Merleau-Ponty's phenomenological studies of cognition, not only because cognition is a major region of Existence, but also because its characteristics appear to be the least amenable to situational analysis, which may seem to have been primarily designed to account for our prereflective capacities. Furthermore, such a study is needed because many of Merleau-Ponty's conclusions about cognition which we found to be vital to the development of his metaphysics seemed, as undefended assertions, to be the most radical and least defensible of all his phenomenological premises. There are a number of loose ends regarding cognition that must be tied up if we are to convey the full cogency and strength of Merleau-Ponty's philosophy. We shall have to explicate his views of truth, evidence, and certainty (which were left incomplete at the end of chapter 2.1); of cognition's distinctive manner of articulating the world and the way that it specifies and articulates its own structures (which were obviously missing from chapter 2.2); of cognition's facticity and its mode of intertwining with the other regions (which were relied upon in chapter 1); and, in general, his views of the extreme limitations of the rational and cognitive point of view (which were applied throughout). These were questions important enough to occupy Merleau-Ponty even in his latest discussions. This region is more accurately referred to as the "cognitive-linguistic," for we shall see that our language capacities are essential to the concrete embodiment of cognition. Therefore, our study of cognition will necessarily include a study of language. This explication will be limited to aspects of language directly relevant to cognition, for, as is the case with motility, there are numerous and adequate general accounts of Merleau-Ponty's theory of language, and such an account is not essential to our concerns.

We have often stated that Merleau-Ponty's metaphysics pre-supposes his phenomenology and that the source of most of his metaphysics and logic of situation is to be found in the study of perception. It might seem, therefore, that the best approach would be to begin with his phenomenology of perception. However, we could not have hoped to have been able to present a total *interpretation* and explication of Merleau-Ponty by starting from the beginning using the method of introductions and by assuming that the reader had no knowledge of Merleau-Ponty's philosophy. If one must rely on a knowledge of Merleau-Ponty, it is far safer to presume a knowledge of his phenomenology and his theory of perception. Furthermore, it is a major aim of this work to make Merleau-Ponty's metaphysical perspective apparent, something which we believe has not been done in contemporary scholarship. Another fallacious assumption of beginning with the phenomenology is the belief that Merleau-Ponty's metaphysics is a generalization and clear derivation from his epistemology (the reverse, that the epistemology can be deduced from the metaphysics, is equally misguided). This is incorrect, at least insofar as the existentialist's metaphysical intuitions of Being, time, man, nature, and history have sources independent of mundane phenomenological studies—studies not dominant within the history of existentialist thought—and insofar as these existentialist insights give guidance to the phenomenology and supply it with a badly needed ontological ground. We have encountered the circle formed by these two types of investigation often enough to realize that, although they depend on and contribute greatly to one another, neither can be considered to have an inherent methodological priority.

Another advantage of starting with the metaphysics is that the study of the epistemology is aided immensely by a familiarity with Merleau-Ponty's major concepts. We can give a complete and "pure" explication of perception and cognition without the serious encumbrance of having to explain terminology and concepts introduced by Merleau-Ponty in other contexts. And this kind of explication is obviously necessary, for Merleau-Ponty's (and his commentators') work has still not yielded a clear presentation of his theories of perception and cognition. Yet it is understandable that pure descriptions of these regions have not been given previously, for, unless the notions that are necessary to explain them are already available, one is forced to fragment the analysis by explaining them as they occur. Merleau-Ponty himself has this problem, for although he centers his philosophy around perception, he does not believe that he can begin there directly, and he delays its study until midway through the *Phenomenology of Perception* (the study of cognition is delayed almost to the end).

Finally, we must warn the reader that because of the above aims the following analyses will be thorough, detailed, complex, and often difficult. We have selected these areas precisely because their difficulty and frequent abstruseness allows us to test Merleau-Ponty's situational analysis and metaphysics and our interpretation of them (as well as of his main phenomenological insights). For this reason, and because we must give a full justification of the phenomenological premises upon which we have relied so heavily, the succeeding studies must be primarily phenomenological explications of the kind that will present a change from the argumentative and summary structure of the previous chapters. We shall accommodate these requirements by basing most of our discussion on key, and not generally understood, passages from Merleau-Ponty, our main purpose being to give a consistent, unified, and complete interpretation of them. It is tempting to discuss his descriptions of perception and cognition in the context of the standard problems and positions of contemporary epistemology. But if we were to organize our investigations around such standard problems, we would "level" Merleau-Ponty's descriptions, thus failing to reveal their depth, completeness, and coherence. Therefore we shall refer to other positions only when it serves our understanding of Merleau-Ponty without distracting us from his descriptions.

1. The Constancy of Shape and Size

It is necessary to note before we begin, first, why our study of vision is sufficient by itself for grasping Merleau-Ponty's entire theory of perception, and, secondly, why his full description of vision can be presented by concentrating on the constancy of an object and its properties. Once we have answered these questions, we shall give a broad summary of the chapter's organization and central themes.

Most epistemologists would agree with Merleau-Ponty's choice of vision as the main area of analysis: they all recognize that since it is the major source, by far, of perceptual knowledge, and since its complex capacities are the most challenging and interesting to philosophy's general concerns, it is the most important sense and its analysis the test of any epistemology (or metaphysics). We shall see that the study of vision also best suits Merleau-Ponty's own distinctive purposes; for, as the study progresses, it shall become clear how his phenomenology of vision is at the source of all of his phenomenological studies and reveals, without difficulty, the main notions of his philosophy. It thus demonstrates by itself the "primacy of perception"—that it is the "archetype of the originating encounter, imitated and renewed" (*VI*158) by other regions—and justifies to a large extent the phenomenological premises of his metaphysics. He does, of course, consider the other senses, especially touch (which we briefly considered in chapter 2.3), whose structures and logic, that of the primordial contact of the perceptual region, are closely tied to those of vision.

It may seem surprising that Merleau-Ponty makes constancy the main issue in the study of perception, since it is considered by most contemporary epistemologists to be a side-issue. However, since we shall see that he gives a constant and strong criticism of all forms of phenomenalism, he cannot build his theory around an analysis of appearances or sense-data, as others do. Rather than making appearances the basic unit of investigation, he treats their analysis as secondary to that of the thing and its constant properties, and their ontological status as minor in comparison. His style of epistemology is much closer to Husserl's, which is also concerned with the way we structure and constitute the perceptual world. But, as we shall see, he parts company with Husserl when he criticizes "intellectualist" theories of perception by rejecting the operations of thetic intentionality, as well as the thematic syntheses, and cognitive categories, of rationalist constitutional theories. It will be another ongoing concern of ours to show how he demonstrates that the logic of the body-subject (or, in general, of situation) is superior to that of such pure transcendental theories. Besides presenting Merleau-Ponty's non-intellectualist constitutional theory of perception, the following will present in detail his noncausal and nondualist realist theory, which, as a form of realism, must make central the possibility and analysis of the constancy of properties and objects.

The chapter will begin with an analysis of shape and size, to enable us to become familiar with the issues, concepts, and principles that are relevant to the study of constancy (these will then be applicable to Merleau-Ponty's more difficult and radically original study of color constancy). The section that follows will generalize on the previous by discussing "proximity" (*F*302), or the epistemic situation wherein the object and its constant properties are constituted and where they can be given, whenever encountered, with *évidence*.[3] By means of these first two sections, we shall comprehend the following: the main principles and characteristics of constancy, proximity, and objectivity; the mode of existence of appearances or perspectives and their dependence on constants; the relation of constant properties to the object (and, thus, Merleau-Ponty's answer to the problem what is a thing or real object); the way that situational analysis can be applied to these issues; and how motility or motor intentionality is essential to vision and perception. Thus the first two sections will give us an invaluable preparation for the study of color in the remaining three sections, which will develop all of these points and follow a similar pattern of investigation, allowing us to include further important descriptions, such as the coming to be of depth and space.

We shall begin this section with a general outline of Merleau-Ponty's understanding of appearances and their relationship to constants. We can then attain an initial grasp of his characterization of constancy by considering his refutation of the empiricists' handling of this problem. The bulk of this section will consist of detailed discussions of Merleau-Ponty's descriptions of appearances, of the criteria for epistemic proximity, and of the relation of motility to the perception of shape and size.[4]

It is, Merleau-Ponty claims, a phenomenological fact that

a thing has primarily *its* own size and shape under the perspective variations which are only apparent. We do not attribute these appearances [perspective variations] to the object; they are an accident of our relations with it, they are of no account to it. (*F*345)

Merleau-Ponty refutes most traditional empiricist and intellectualist theories by insisting that there is a category difference between appearances, on the one hand, and objects and their constant properties, on the other, or that the latter are of a different "order" (232 and 233) from the former.[5] Furthermore, he reverses their

3. Henceforth whenever *evidence* or its cognates occur, we shall be using it in the sense that corresponds to the French *évidence* or German *Evidenz*.

4. Since these two aspects of extension invariably occur together, we shall follow Merleau-Ponty in not dividing the study of shape and size.

5. Therefore he would agree with Ryle to a large extent (see *The Concept of Mind*, pp. 17 and 197-98).

procedure of taking appearances as primary, and thus making constants constructions from them or privileged members of the class of appearances. The originality of his theory is most obvious when he transcends all phenomenalism by establishing that appearances are ontologically dependent on constant properties, and that even these sense constants are not the basic givens of perceptual experience but are parasitic on, or abstractions from, the full experience of the object itself. We can get a preliminary view of the main points to be clarified in this chapter if we sketch those characteristics of constants and appearances which show their categorical or logical difference (as well as their relation). Merleau-Ponty will demonstrate that constants are the actual properties of things, that things are constituted in a peculiar sense by their constants, and that these constants thus have an objectivity that appearances lack. Ultimately, we shall understand them as the noema of our concretized sense structures and see that this explains why they are the norms or "intentional objects" to which every appearance must refer. Appearances will be described as the contingent presentation or manifestation (which is nondeterminate and nonobjective) of a constant. We shall see that they are given to us only as a "lack" or "deformation" of the constant, or as a "blurring" or "tension" between constants of the same type. They will finally be understood as the otherness that escapes every actualized sense structure. However, they do disclose our present relationship to the object and its properties (our "epistemic situation"), even if they do not disclose anything about the properties themselves, and thus this blurring or deformation of our constants points us to their proximal epistemic situations, where they are achieved and given with evidence.

When the empiricist claims that an object's constant size and shape is distinguishable from any other possible perspective merely on the basis of convention or statistical frequency, he is presupposing what must be explained. We can learn much about constants by clarifying this difficult argument of Merleau-Ponty's (299 ff.). Once we have done so, we shall apply it to Hume's concerns about constancy. Then, before turning to a detailed explication of Merleau-Ponty's description of appearances and constants, we shall give a preliminary and general analysis of perspectives and appearances (paralleling the following analysis of constancy).

The empiricist presupposes implicitly that perspectives or appearances are in themselves already determinate, characterizable, or have significance. If he were to ask initially how there can be, for example, "determinate sizes and shapes" (299), he would begin to understand constancy; for he would see that the constant is the possibility of appearances having any determination or significance. Merleau-Ponty states that this question leads ultimately to the question "how can there be objectivity" (300), for the only way an appearance can be determinate is to be recognized or identified as an object or as "something." Now it follows that unless the empiricist accepts that a constant's ontological status is different from that of an appearance (rather than being merely the result of an "arbitrary" selection from a set of appearances), he will be caught in an infinite regress. The regress is generated by the fact that the only way that something can be made an object is to become the focus of one's attention. We have learned that, when this occurs, a structure is created or reproduced which makes it possible to comprehend or articulate the entity. Although in lived perception we are normally directed toward things such that only the constant properties count for us while the apparent are ignored, we can no doubt focus on a perspective or appearance of a thing. When this occurs, the thing becomes our entire perceptual field or background and the appearance gains the status of object or figure. However, given that we can experience the paradigmatic objectified and determinate appearance which belongs to this analytic attitude, this appearance must still have the same logic as any concrete object; that is, it will have an inner horizon of ways of approaching it and, like any perceptual object, be inexhaustively specifiable.[6] In other words, if an appearance is objectified or reified, there must be a new set of second-order appearances of this first-order objectified appearance. The phenomenalist will no doubt deny that there can be appearances of appearances, but how can he? He has maintained from the beginning that objectivity can only be obtained by selecting (on whatever principle) from among a set of appearances which are our basic givens or particulars. Thus, he cannot but argue that one of these second-order appearances (whatever his principle of selection) is just

6. It might seem that there is an equivocation on the word *object* in this argument, but Merleau-Ponty's theory of objects, which will be discussed in the next section, establishes that these uses of the term are uniform.

the object, that is, the determinate first-order appearance, and so on *ad infinitum*. Thus Merleau-Ponty can conclude that the only way to escape this regress is to deny that a constant is merely a privileged appearance, and to affirm that a constant must have a different logic from appearances and be prior to them.

Since it was Hume's empiricist study of constancy that set the problems with which most epistemologists are still grappling, we can make Merleau-Ponty's argument more concrete, and broaden our understanding of what he means by "constant" by comparing his argument to Hume's. Hume's concern revolves about the question of how we can know that something is the same thing (reidentify it) when it is experienced again after an interruption. The question falls under Merleau-Ponty's criticism because Hume presupposes that we do know the entity (what it is) while it is being experienced. If he had asked how this knowledge is possible or how the entity can be given to us as a determinate "something" in the first place, he would have found the answer to his question. It is implied in the way that we determine an entity (with acquired structures, or, in more Husserlian terms, by constituting it or possessing it as an intentional object) that we can also reidentify it (and for Merleau-Ponty we must do so, as its structure is triggered by otherness). In other words, we are able to identify or recognize something as such and such on a particular occasion only if we are able to reidentify it as such and such whenever it presents itself. Hume concluded that because we in fact posit constant properties in an object beyond their diverse appearances, we must just *assume* that there is a function that allows us to do so. As Kant first demonstrated, this function is a transcendental one. However, Merleau-Ponty now wishes to demonstrate that it is the *noncognitive* function, being open to the world only by means of the structures of the body-subject.

We can obtain a preliminary grasp of Merleau-Ponty's theory of appearances by examining some of his examples of the perception of apparent size and shape. "When I look at a road which sweeps before me toward the horizon, I must not say either that the sides of the road are given to me as convergent or that they are given to me as parallel: they are *parallel in depth*" (*F*302). In lived perception, I do not experience the road's shape as a two-dimensional perspective or, for example, as a geometric projection on the retina. But neither does my visual experience present me with the idealist's determinate shape, which would be the road seen ubiquitously as from above and which is merely a "limiting idea" (204). "The perspective appearance is not posited but neither is the parallelism. I belong to the road itself, through its virtual deformation, and depth is this intention itself which posits neither" (*F*302). Rather than positing my present perspective, I go "through [*à travers*]" (*F*302) it and arrive at the road itself with its own constant shape. Yet my perceptual position, which is the noesis of the perspective, has some status, for the constant is given as a deformation. Merleau-Ponty relies heavily on this use of *through*. He means, "I pass by without stopping to perform a possible act of attention" (this possible attention is indicated by the present distorted manifestation of the constant). It is a "virtual" (*F*302) distorted shape, because an analytic phenomenalist stance is a possibility of my perceptual behavior. But if I did give it attention, I would not reach the road itself with its own shape but would have been misled and distracted along the way. When one is dealing with the thing itself, one has traversed the numerous ways of taking it (its inner horizon); for the thing is just the unified style that retains all its possible manifestations. The fact that the appearances of shapes and sizes are always given as three-dimensional (except when abstractly reified) was perhaps what motivated giving them the status of primary ("real" or "substantial") qualities; for when this fact is taken seriously, one must be pushed toward a realism. This follows because having a shape in depth implies having it at a distance and thus experiencing the entity as a basic constituent of space. Therefore, given this fact, one cannot affirm the degree of separation between appearance and reality that is essential to a phenomenalist position. Merleau-Ponty's demonstration (see chapter 3.4) that even the appearances of color are essentially spatial (for they ground depth) is thus extremely important. It shows that the so-called secondary qualities are as objective, material, or substantial as the primary qualities.

Let us now examine, in detail, what an *appearance* is as such. This study will reveal any appearance's essential dependence on a constant or structure and show that the only way it can be given, or have any status, is as a "blurring" or obscuring of a constant. Once we have established why constants are only available through the interference and inadequacy of appearances, we shall have to explain how the body-subject's look can be aware of this inadequacy and, more precisely, how it recognizes a constant property without thetically identifying it or thematically constituting it. We shall describe subsequently how distance is given by means of the appearance of the constant, and why a constant must be taken as the norm of any appearance.

The "virtual deformation" (F302), or the appearance that is traversed, is strictly presented to us as a "lack" in our present grasp and not at all as an objectified given (i.e., a pure positivity). This *lack* of achievement which accompanies every constant is just its present appearance. Let us examine why this is the case.

For me the perceiver, the object at a hundred paces is not present and real in the same sense as it is at ten paces, and I identify the object in all its positions, at all its distances, under all its appearances, insofar as all the perspectives converge toward the perception that I obtain for a certain typical distance and orientation. . . . At a shorter or greater distance we have only a perception blurred [*confuse*] through excess or deficiency. (F348)

The diversity of points of view is only hinted at by an imperceptible shifting [*glissement*], a certain "blurring" [*bougé*] of the appearance. (F380)

Although I perceive the thing itself with its own constant properties when it is either too far or too near, it is not given to me as evident or fulfilled but as vague and lacking the required determinateness. This "blurring" is what appearance *is, qua* appearance.[7] Yet this notion only makes sense if the appearance is a "confusing" *of* something. This something that is partially manifest is just the constant shape or size. But this is strictly a noematic statement. Noetically, there is a "typical" (F348) orientation of, and distance from, the body which is none other than a general structure of shape or size. In other words, a constant shape or size is the noematic expression of a visual structure. When a shape is given as blurred, its correlative structure is strained and does not fulfill the present demands of otherness. Depth carries "a level of distances and sizes that define the near and far, and large and small" (F308). Similarly, a shape is "recognizable and distinguishable from every other shape by its . . . physiognomy, and not by any of its properties" (F317), because it is also part of a level. With this in mind, we can see that

7. This is Merleau-Ponty's answer to Hegel's (and his own) criticism of Kant: that one of Kant's main weaknesses was that he did not understand or analyze appearances *qua* appearances.

when an entity triggers a visual structure of shape, it selects the most appropriate species of shape that is available within the level. Blurring and deformation indicate that this species of shape is not as clearly differentiated from the other types of shape that constitute the level as it would be in its most favorable epistemic situation. The shape is vague because the given tends to center itself through one specified shape but also fades into other possible shapes. It fits none fully, but indicates some, perhaps favoring one. Hence, to say that the thing itself or the constant property is only given "through" the apparent, normally means that our present situational bond to the world uses structures that are correlative to the thing itself but not optimally concretized. When we concentrate on the appearance and objectify it, we are further specifying our constant structures. We are acquiring a new species that accommodates the tension in our old. As Merleau-Ponty frequently insists, perspectives are very highly specified structures which are grounded in, or are specifications of, our more general structures, which correspond to constant properties. Again, it must be noted that it is always possible for us to focus on appearances by making our perceptual field more specific. But we do so only when our interests and concerns require this reflective perception of the analytic attitude. Ordinarily, we experience and live appearances noematically as blurred constants, and noetically as a strained hold on otherness.

It is necessary to explain how the look can be *prereflectively* aware that its present triggered structure is inadequate; for if it were not we would always, in the naive realist manner, coincide with the thing-in-itself and not approach it through the apparent. The purpose of the following description of how we recognize or identify a constant is to present this process strictly in terms of the logic of the body-subject or by means of situational analysis (an aim that will be pursued throughout the chapter). We shall thus attempt to demonstrate that such an account is possible without relying upon any intellectualist devices (e.g., cognitive syntheses, meanings, or posits) or any empiricist techniques (e.g., association or causal action).

We can begin by noting that the look must grasp the given by means of vision's available structures. We saw that sedimented structures must either be creatively acquired in commerce with otherness or innate and thrown. The structures of constants, being high-level specifications, are creatively acquired and, hence, are attained when the subject articulates a certain presence. Therefore, the structures (and the resulting constants) which articulate the thing itself must be developed when the thing is maximally present to the subject. Hence, secondly, our structures are ordinarily limited to those obtained through the evidence of the thing. When the thing is not fully present, the look must use these same sedimented structures. Therefore, at one and the same time, vision encounters the thing itself and yet "knows" that its grasp is not an exact duplication of its originating experience of this entity (that it "is not real and present in the same sense" [F348]). Finally, no experience will ever exactly reproduce the original, because what was retained from the creative event was a general comprehension of it (cf. chapter 2.3). Even when one claims that the thing is evident and its structure fulfilled, one has it through an appearance, for this appearance is precisely what distinguishes this present from the originating present. There is, then, a proximity where we merge with our present by creatively articulating it, and a secondary proximity which results from the generality of the acquired structure and which is repeatable whenever we meet a similar entity (or the same entity if the structure has been specified sufficiently to individualize it). It is to the second that all perspectives and appearances are intentionally directed.

We saw in a previous quotation that "depth is the intention itself" (F302) which does not posit perspectives. Hence, when Merleau-Ponty says we "identify the object" (F348), he must be contrasting his own theory with Husserl's "act of identification." If one wishes, one can say that what is affirmed in an appearance is its constant. But this is not a posit or a thetic judgment, for the optimal constant is not given with the clarity and determinateness of a *cogitatum*. We cannot help but identify the thing itself, because the only way we can have it given to us or recognize it is by means of the sedimented structures which have it as noema. We do not *judge* a given to belong to a certain species; for there can be no given apart from that which is disclosed by means of a structure, and otherness has triggered, actualized, or called forth the specific structure most appropriate to it. We have seen that the structures of size and shape are specifications of depth, which is a thrown perceptual structure. Our visual primordial contact is articulated by these constants and is a distinctive type of operative intentionality.

When we see an entity from a great distance, we do not make a judgment about this distance using a description of the small apparent image as our premise. We do not have, for example, the apparent image of a man to measure or compare to a standard size. It is, instead, the case that

> *he is the same man seen from farther away.* One can only say that the man two hundred paces away is a much less articulated figure, that it offers my look less numerous and precise holds . . . , that it does not offer a configuration rich enough to absorb my power of clear vision. (*F*302)

It is no doubt true that, from an analytic standpoint, the figure would be smaller, but this is an abstraction from our lived perception. Ordinary language makes this plain, for when we say that a man becomes smaller as he gets farther away, *smaller* does not modify the subject in the same way as it does when we say "he is a small man." It is a category mistake or an equivocation to say that the man's own constant size has the same status as the size of the objectified apparent image of him at different distances. Furthermore, we need not *infer* that the thing itself which we have is distant rather than close. The distance is given as a phenomenon before it can be thematized. "The distance from me to the object is not a magnitude that increases or decreases, but a tension which oscillates around a norm" (*F*349). Hence, simultaneously, both the apparent size and our distance from the thing are suggested by the "tension" of my present grasp or the inarticulateness, deformation, or blurring of the percept. Again, it is only to this extent that an appearance is given. The tension is given with the constant itself and this constant is the "norm" of our present perception. "This privileged perception ensures the unity of the perceptual process and gathers into it all the other appearances" (*F*348). The constant property can be called a norm (and its evident perception "privileged") because it is the object-side of a structure through which every appearance is related and determined.[8]

8. Merleau-Ponty can be considered to be successfully developing a theory that W. H. F. Barnes is just beginning to work out in "The Myth of Sense-Data." When we keep in mind Merleau-Ponty's contention that there is a "teleology" of truth and that truth has degrees, Barnes can be taken to be describing a "teleology" of appearances. He states that "in perceptual situations objects reveal more or less of their nature to us." In the latter case, such instances should be "regarded as their failing in differing degrees to appear to have the properties they do have, such failure being accounted for by the conditions under which they are perceived." In Ernest Nagel and Richard B. Brandt, eds., *Meaning and Knowledge*, quotations from pp. 593 and 590.

But, equally important, the word *norm* carries a connotation of value, for we have seen that such a specific structure is acquired because of the interests of the subject, and the differentiations we make in our standard levels are also, no doubt, culturally influenced. Hence this connotation is present when Merleau-Ponty says that, when I view a die obliquely, I give "to the acute or obtuse angles the value of right angles, to the distorted sides the value of a square" (264), and that it has a " 'natural' position that it 'should' occupy" (F292). Since all perceptual presentations must be structural, in a wide sense they are as much evaluative as descriptive. Let us finally note that although phenomenology is frequently accused of multiplying entities, Merleau-Ponty's theory of proximity conserves the number of entities that a subject is capable of recognizing. We can see that in comparison to Merleau-Ponty the phenomenalist excessively multiplies entities, for every possible appearance is objectified. For Merleau-Ponty, only constants are determinate and objectified in the form of sedimented structures. Although all degrees of fulfillment are potentially specifiable, we do not have reified perspectives corresponding to each. Our hierarchal system of structures does not flow smoothly like an exhaustive scale but has great leaps and gaps, under which, however, every intermediate given still falls.

Since the whole theory hinges on the way in which a structure is formed or triggered in the proximal epistemic situation, we must now turn to an initial discussion of how *proximity* is defined. Merleau-Ponty says that there are three criteria used for determining the proximal epistemic situation: "symmetry," "plenitude," and "determination" (F303). By analyzing the way these criteria function, we shall begin to comprehend proximity in its relationship to perceptual evidence and intentional fulfillment.

The following quotations will reveal the main elements of the theory, but they will show us as well how this irreplaceable epistemological situation corresponds to the main characteristics of Being discovered in the "limit situation" or in the key metaphysical situation:

I have visual objects because I have a visual field where richness and clarity are in inverse proportion . . . [and which] determine for the perceptual process a certain point of maturity and a maximum. (F367)

There is an optimal distance from which each object demands to be seen . . . , we tend toward the maximum of visibility . . . obtained by a certain equilibrium between inner and outer horizon. (F348)

Vision essentially strives for the greatest degree of articulation of its present field. The gaze achieves a unified grasp of itself and its world when it anchors its spatial levels (which are the present organization of all its potential situations). It does so in order to achieve a maximum balance of all its visual modes of being-in-the-world, given the present demands of otherness. These criteria and principles guide the body's attempt to achieve its fullest grasp, whether it be directed toward its entire field, a certain thing, or a constant property such as shape. We have learned that subjectivity, temporality, and Being are ultimately defined by this never-ending drive toward a unified and maximized grasp of themselves and otherness. Thus Merleau-Ponty states that, in order to comprehend Being, "we must return to this idea of proximity through distance ... or palpation in depth" (*VI*128). Therefore, once again, we find that Being can be understood through the phenomenological relationship between the body and the thing; but, inversely, once again we find that this same relationship (expressed in terms of proximity and maximization of grasp) is an ultimate premise of Merleau-Ponty's epistemology which can only be finally justified by his metaphysics.

Merleau-Ponty never gives precise analyses of the various norms of proximity, perhaps because they are interdependent and always occur together. We shall separate them as much as possible in the context of shape and size, but we shall not attempt to give an exact definition of each in isolation. Merleau-Ponty refers to plenitude and determination as "richness and clarity" (*F*367) and as "inner and outer horizon" (*F*348). He means by the latter term of each of these three pairs that a constant shape is given in its relation to all the other shapes within its field. If an entity is too close, it will occupy too much of our visual field. This results in our level of shapes being unable to determine the focal shape, for the level does not have a sufficient number of shapes within its field to anchor itself. In other words, as we have seen, entities are determined by their outer horizons because their constant structure is both part of a level and defined by its differentiation from other shapes within the field. On the other hand, when an entity is too close in terms of its outer horizon, we have a grasp of its inner horizon which is richer and more plentiful, such that I can make out the fine detail of a given when it greatly fills my visual field. Therefore, as we put the entity at a greater distance, we begin to lose our grasp of its inner horizon, which becomes less available, but we gain in its definition and clarity. We cannot say that at one point we have the greatest determinateness and at another the greatest plenitude, for both are responsible for our perception of a single shape. What we can say is that the proximal position simultaneously gives us, on the one hand, the most determinate field or the greatest outer horizon, which lets us hold the maximum number of entities in our field, and, on the other, the richest inner horizon, which gives us the greatest ability to examine the plenitude of our focal entity. When we reach this balance between the possibilities of our inner and outer horizons we have achieved an intentionally fulfilled grasp. As we move away from proximity, the entity is given as unfulfilled. "The variations of appearance are not changes in size of more or less, nor real distortions: it is simply that either its parts mingle and confuse themselves or they clearly articulate themselves in their interrelation [*l'une sur l'autre*] and unroll their wealth" (*F*349).

The third norm, symmetry, is closely bound up with the other two, for the orientation of the entity bears strongly on the degree to which it can be articulated. "The oblique orientation of the object in relation to me is not measured by the angle that it forms with the plane of my face, but experienced as a disequilibrium, as an unequal distribution of its influences on me" (*F*349). My body experiences a disequilibrium because it cannot implant its visual existence fully in its milieu. It cannot clearly encompass the otherness that faces it by means of one of its structures, and thus it cannot bring it to its maximum visibility. The object-side of this situation can be described as an unequal distribution of influences, because otherness is unable to precisely trigger and specify the one structure that would have accommodated it had it been proximal. The importance of this last criterion will become clearer with the study of the motor capabilities of vision that accompany the perception of shape and size.

By examining visual motility, we shall get a better understanding of how our sedimented structures are the norm of all appearances, and also of why the body-subject requires a particular stance (designated *proximity*) in order to reveal the maximum of its field. Through the study of vision's motility, it will be shown how the distinctive subjectivity of the body makes possible our creation and recognition of a constant size and shape. We shall particularly note that although Merleau-Ponty's discussion (*F*350) *prima facie* seems to reduce the noesis of our visual structures to physical movements of the eye, a close analysis of the key passages shows that this physical interpretation is not possible. Vision's use of motor intentionality and of its temporal form of synthesis will thus be established. In order to summarize and confirm the conclusions of this discussion, we shall explicate Merleau-Ponty's analysis of the recognition of a face.

Merleau-Ponty describes the level of sizes or the noetic series of a differentiation situation in the following way.[9] "The thing is large if my look is not able to envelop it, small if it does so easily, and the intermediate sizes are distinguished from each other, according as, at an equal distance, they more or less dilate [*dilatent*] my look [*regard*]" (*F*350). The entity's constant size is determined by its distance from the perceiver when it is optimally present. This distance is not physically defined, for we have seen that it is characterized by the maximum balance that the gaze can achieve between the inner and outer horizons. Physical distance, which is revealed through the analytic attitude, is a thetic refinement of our lived phenomenological distance, which is established by the criteria of proximity.[10] Therefore, when I have two entities (of not too great difference in size) that are visually evident or proximal ("at an equal distance"), I place them on my level of sizes, from large to small, by comparing and differentiating the way they modulate my visual grasp. My look must give more of its field to an entity whose real size is large. Noetically, its focus must be "enlarged" or "expanded" in order to range over the figure, and this is the sense of *dilate* that Merleau-Ponty desires.[11] For example, when two objects that are identical except for their size are placed at an equal distance (and they will have the same optimal distance if their sizes are not

9. Let us recall why we call this a level. Since every size is experienced in its differentiation from every other size on a single scale, the structure that is used for recognizing or identifying a size carries all other potential constant sizes as well, such that only one structure at any one time determines every different size in the entire field. This is just the definition of a level. We can begin to see (it will be made clear in our study of color levels) that for a size to be structured in one's field, there must be at least two differently sized entities available to anchor or actualize the level.

10. "This distance is not the contrary of this proximity, . . . it is synonymous with it" (*VI*135).

11. He uses *dilate* in the same sense on *F*168, where he refers to expanding the scope of our Existence or our phenomenological hold on the world.

radically different), the pattern of the gaze necessary for organizing their shape will be identical but require a greater temporal spread; or, noematically, the extent of the field that the gaze will be able to articulate while it focuses on each of these entities will differ. Little sense can be made of this passage if *dilate* is taken in an operational sense which refers exclusively to the opening of the pupil. Merleau-Ponty has given the sufficient condition for determining constant size, while dilation of the pupil is neither necessary nor sufficient. [12]

Merleau-Ponty also describes the motility of the gaze that corresponds to the perception of shape. "The object is circular if, all its sides being equally near me, it does not impose on the movement of my look any change in its curvature [*courbure*], or if those changes that are imposed on it are imputable to the oblique presentation" (*F*350). All the sides are equally near me when this object satisfies proximity's criterion of symmetry. In the privileged epistemic situation, the entity's objective shape will be determined as circular when the movements that are required to envelop it have a consistent "sweep." When otherness "imposes" (*F*350) an alteration in this pattern of movement, the constant shape (if recognized) will appear as unfulfilled, and this will be attributed to its oblique orientation to the subject. We must not take "curvature" (*F*350) as a physical characteristic. Merleau-Ponty is not making a claim about the physical movement of the eye but is referring to a *gesture* that organizes the visual world. This physical interpretation, like that applied to size, commits what James calls the "psychologist's fallacy *par excellence*,"[13] "which means that what we know to be in things themselves we immediately take as being in our consciousness of them" (5).

Recognition of the relevance of movement to vision is of immense importance, for it goes far to convince us of one of Merleau-Ponty's central claims: that motor intentionality is the essential form of

---

12. The English translator (303) accepts the physical interpretation of these passages and makes Merleau-Ponty read like a physiological behaviorist. But this is partly Merleau-Ponty's fault, as he often uses terms, such as the present *dilation* and *curvature of the gaze*, which belong to the technical vocabulary of opposing theories.

13. Aron Gurwitsch, *The Field of Consciousness*, p. 94. Roderick Firth ("Sense-data and the Percept Theory," in Robert J. Swartz, ed., *Perceiving, Sensing and Knowing*, pp. 237-38) also refers to this fallacy, which can be found in James's *The Principles of Psychology* vol. 1, pp. 196-97, and elsewhere.

every type of human capacity. Therefore, it will also make credible and concrete Merleau-Ponty's insistence that every structure is symbolized or expressed by (and hence grounded in) the body-subject. We have a tendency to attribute motor intentionality strictly to those gross movements of the body that project our practical world. The motility of the various senses will differ as much as the senses differ from one another, but all will share the logic of this type of intentionality. Merleau-Ponty has adequately demonstrated that a gross motor capability of the body cannot be defined by physical characteristics, such as a description of the exact muscles used and a cross section of their tensions and leverage. It is, instead, a potentiality that can be infinitely manifested by innumerable muscular movements and their combinations (138-39). Similarly, those of the eye's physical movements that occur at any one time in a particular combination are only concrete actualizations of a single motor capacity. The look can organize its field to yield a required circular shape under all sorts of physical conditions, for example, when only one eye or half a retina is functioning, or through half-closed lids or "out of the corner of the eye." Hence, no one set of physical movements can define a motor capacity of any sort. Temporality is as important to the motility of shape as it was to that of size: to recognize a shape, otherness must trigger a certain specific pattern of the look as well as modulate the time it takes the look to range over its field. It is noteworthy, but not surprising, that movement and time are similarly the transcendental conditions of touch, as motor intentionality is essentially temporal. All these capacities have the form of a transitional synthesis where the beginning and terminal points of a motor act are simultaneously given in the subject's field but have a temporal spread between them. Movement itself is just the actualization of these temporal routes and directions, and it is aware of itself, as is temporality, by making its future (its goal) present on the grounds of its past (its route and starting point) (see 110-11 and 116).

Merleau-Ponty's analysis of the recognition of a face confirms our interpretation of these passages. He shows that recognition of a constant shape is dependent on the shape having a certain orientation. Our spatial levels (particularly those of height and breadth) give us the general orientation of a field by adjusting the body-subject's potentialities, with the aim of being able to make use of the maximum number of structures that the demands of the present field will permit. When an entity is disorientated, the axes that determine its symmetry do not correspond to those of our present field's levels. If its orientation is radically different—for example, an "upside-down" face—it "is unrecognizable" (F291). But when the face's orientation falls between this critical range and the normal, we see it as if it were upright. The "upright" face, although it "enjoys no statistical preponderance, . . . is given to me more often than any other" (F292), because this is the constant shape that is correlative to the structure that is capable of recognizing it. Yet the constant shape we are given is not the intellectualist's idea or the law that gives us a constant relation between the variables of our milieu, for it cannot correct the disorientation beyond a certain point. But, most important, the constant shape is not given to me with the same evidence as its disorientation increases. Rather, it *appears* and becomes "deformed" and indeterminate, or, noetically, its structure becomes strained.

We must conclude that my gaze, which moves over the face and in doing so favors certain directions, does not recognize the face unless it comes up against its details in a certain irreversible order. . . . To see a face . . . is to take a certain hold upon it, to be able to follow on its surface a certain perceptual route. (F292)

We must not take this to mean that there is a point-by-point or "part by part" (11) tracing of the entity by the eye. On the contrary, it means that the entity need only present itself to the minimum degree that is necessary to separate or differentiate its structure from other similar species. "They exert an effect only to the extent of making possible a basic pattern" (11), and the level of generality of the structures that is required is determined by my metastructures, interests, or concerns (for example, I may only want to distinguish male from female or acquaintance from stranger). The look need only *sketch* the given because it has a limited number of shapes that it is capable of recognizing. If the gaze only passively received data, it would need the given in absolute detail, and we have already seen that perception is not the result of induction.[14]

---

14. It is interesting to note again the similarity of this theory to Chomsky's solution to the problem of forming behavioral hypotheses with inductively inadequate data and to his understanding of Peirce's notion of abduction. See *Language and Mind*, pp. 78-79.

2. Proximity, the Thing, and the Real

This section, which extends and broadens the discussion in the previous section, will be worked out in more detail in the remainder of the chapter. It is perhaps one of our most central analyses, for it gives all the essential themes of Merleau-Ponty's theory of perception and brings together many of the important notions that we have discussed throughout under the topic of the perceptual object. It will discuss what a thing is and how it can be given with evidence; how the whole motor body is involved in perception; Merleau-Ponty's nonthetic and nonthematic theory of constitution and intentionality; the precise relationship (epistemological and metaphysical) between the thing, its properties, and its modes of givenness (and thus between essence and existence, form and content, and sense and reference); and how Merleau-Ponty arrives at his final characterizations of reality and otherness through his phenomenology of perception.

We are beginning to understand the extent to which the body as a whole is involved in all perception. We have seen that visual motility, being the noesis of all visual situations, is an essential part of the phenomenon itself. But since all the regions of the body are expressions of a unified Existence, once one aspect is triggered the whole body is put into action. Therefore, we shall show first that the gross motility of the body is inherent in every perception; secondly, that epistemic proximity can occur only through a balance of all the body's regions; and, thirdly, that the thing is a "concrete essence" (*F*442).

When we move ourselves or manipulate an object in order better to perceive it, we are fulfilling our vague grasp of a constant. We can do so because every global motor attitude can be viewed as the "power of a certain spectacle, and because each spectacle is for me what it is in a certain kinaesthetic situation" (*F*349). Our epistemic situation corresponds to a particular bodily stance. Therefore, when I experience a deformed or blurred shape, I am able to account for this appearance through the consciousness that I have of my present bodily schema. The appearance is immediately given in its relation to its potentially optimal presentation, for it protends the motor attitudes that would bring it to achievement. The point is that vision itself is in such close alliance with the body-subject's gross (or overall) motor capacities that the gaze comprehends the lack of fulfillment of its present grasp in terms of these motor possibilities (which always show it the direction to and method of attaining proximity). It will help us to proceed if we examine Merleau-Ponty's frequent use of the word *kinaesthetic*, which is misleading and which he admits is a bad expression (94), for it has strong physiological connotations. He does not hold that we know the body, for example, through deep muscular sensations, an inner sense, or "introceptivity" (76). Rather, the body is self-given as the system of structures that is actualized within, and contained within, the present field, because "I am through this body at grips with [*en prise sur*] the world" (*F*349). One must not take this awareness of our bodily position as a variable for a calculation that cognitively corrects our inadequate perceptions; on the contrary, this bodily presence is part of what constitutes the given *qua* apparent and is an irremovable part of the natural or perceptual world. Merleau-Ponty uses the term *kinaesthetic* because it is useful to distinguish the global motor region from the other types of motility and from other regional capacities of the body-subject. Also, this use is another case of Merleau-Ponty's working out of one of Husserl's formulae.[15] His lengthy refutation of kinaesthetic sensations in "The Child's Relations with Others" and his entire study of motility in the *Phenomenology of Perception* (98 ff.) clearly show that he does not use this term in its technical sense (nor, of course, does Husserl).

Merleau-Ponty shows the essential interdependence of the body's overall motility and the given perceptual world by means of the following description, and in doing so he determines precisely what a perspective is.

And just as the perceptual attitudes are not known to me singly but implicitly given as stages in the gesture which leads to the optimum attitude, correlatively, the perspectives that correspond to them are not posited before me one after the other, and only offer themselves as some steps [*passages*] toward the thing itself with its size and shape. (*F*349)

15. Compare the first quotation in this paragraph to p. 161 of *The Crisis of European Sciences and Transcendental Phenomenology*, where Husserl says that perspectives "are related back to correlative multiplicities of cinesthetic processes having the peculiar character of the 'I do', 'I move' " and pp. 106–07 and 161–62, where Husserl argues that our perceptions protend the movements that will fulfill them.

We have already seen that a perspective is a reification of a constant's present manner of appearing. It now becomes clear that a perspective is the noema of an *evanescent* present bodily stance. Hence perspectives come into being through a double abstraction. First, the object-side is isolated from the situation. Secondly, by means of an instantaneous cross section which artificially halts the perceptual process and its transitional synthesis, one is finally able to focus on a discrete given. Merleau-Ponty has adequately demonstrated in his study of motility that the series of movements that constitute any motor act are not individually posited. Like temporality itself, each stage of a movement is inseparable from those that led up to it and from the goal at which it is directed. Like the present, the movement is an "interlocking of each with all of its horizon in the denseness of the following" (*F*307). We are perceptually aware of the noemata of our bodily movements (i.e., perspectives) in the same way. If perspectives are given at all, they are given simply as "yet to be achieved constants," and because they are correlative to motor attitudes the route for their achievement is a concrete part of the given phenomenon. Already we can conclude that, besides each sense having its own type of motility, the region of perception is interwoven with the gross motor body, and that, correlatively, the natural world and lived space are in part constituted by, and are thus material expressions of, our body's ability to move within the world (this will be discussed in greater detail below).

Let us now turn to a consideration of the main passages where Merleau-Ponty discusses the question: "What is an object?" We shall explicate these in detail as they are as difficult and misleading as they are important.

What I call the experience of the thing or of reality . . . is my full coexistence with the phenomenon, the moment when it is under all its relations, at its maximum articulation, and the "givens of the different senses" are orientated toward this unique pole, as my focusings through a microscope oscillate about a privileged focus [*visée*] . (*F*367-68)

The norm of each appearance is a constant which is correlative to our proximal epistemic situation. In our examination of the criteria that determine the maximum givenness of a shape or size, it may have seemed that when these criteria were fully satisfied vision would have necessarily determined its constants for a particular thing. If this were the case, sense constants would be logically prior to things.

However, Merleau-Ponty stresses that the thing itself is a constant for perception, and thus the demands of the body-subject as a whole mediate the criteria that determine the constants of each individual sense. This must be the case because the body seeks the "maximum articulation" (F368) of otherness, which implies that it uses all its regions to do so. Furthermore, since the thing is the only entity within the world that is capable of manifesting every primordial region, the world's articulation will be in terms of things. Hence the basic constant, or real, can only be a thing, while the constants of each sense must be the secondary expressions of this intersensory entity (and thus the existence of a property is secondary to that of its object). If the prime epistemic situation is that in which the body as a whole achieves a maximum grasp, if it is through this situation that constants are acquired, and if it is to this situation that all appearances refer, then appearances manifest those sense constants which are, in turn, derivatively constituted from the unitary state of our intersensory proximity to things.

"Things . . . are not significations offered to intelligence, but opaque structures, and . . . their ultimate sense is confused" (F384). Just as sense constants are the noemata of sedimented sense structures, the thing is a constant which is the noema of an object situation. Merleau-Ponty's analogy comparing the acquisition of a thing structure to the focusing of a microscope is helpful. The factors that have to be balanced and adjusted to achieve proximity are all the capabilities of the body-subject and, most directly, of our perceptual regions. It is obvious, for example, that the position of the body which is optimal for perceiving the shape of an object may radically differ from the one that is optimal for perceiving its color. Since "each appearing phenomenon attracts toward the field of existence the whole of my body as a system of perceptual powers" (F367), and since "sizes and shapes are only a modality of this global hold on the world" (F350), it will be necessary to mitigate the articulation of, for example, visual shape in order to achieve a high degree of articulation in the other senses. In other words, a constant of a sense must compromise its own clarity in order to accommodate the clarity of all the remaining types of perceptual constants. For example, the constant shape of a very large entity, such as a mountain, a building, or a tree, will not be the one that meets all the previously discussed criteria which determine the maximum grasp of shape. If it were, these entities would be too distant to enable us to have a similarly maximal grasp on their size, color, tactility, and sonority. Rather, the constant shape must be less articulated (in terms of the three criteria) than it would be if all the other kinds of perceptual constants were irrelevant when it was acquired. But the same considerations apply to the other types of constants and they will therefore be similarly deficient in order to accommodate this visual constant. The nonperceptual regions of our body will further compromise our sense constants by making their own claim on this one and only proximal situation. For example, the practical uses of these entities, which are correlative to gross motility, may well favor more exact constancy in one sense than in another. Their socio-cultural predicates, which may correspond to either our affective or our cognitive realm, will have a similar effect. (These factors will be discussed further below).

Merleau-Ponty describes the thing as follows:

The thing is the correlative of my body and more generally of my existence, of which my body is only the stabilized structure; it [the thing] constitutes itself in the hold of my body on it. . . . Its articulations are those of our very existence. (F369)

We must not conclude from this statement that the thing is no more than a gestalt of constant properties or, similarly, that Merleau-Ponty is defining the object as a "bundle" of properties; for he sees it as a singular irreducible structure which inheres in otherness. The above operations that arrive at the constant thing with its constant properties are not cognitive nor can one say that the body-subject exclusively constitutes or projects the thing. How can we understand that the thing "constitutes itself" (F369)? Proximity is achieved through a dialectic between the general capacities of the body-subject and the centripetal demands of otherness. It is in this sense that the thing is a "concrete essence." The object structure has its own unique system of constants, because otherness, in contact with the body's regional potentialities, dictated the single and unique epistemic situation wherein all of these constants were established. When the object structure was originally acquired, it was not constituted in the strict sense, but it came into being through the unique combination and intertwining of all its thrown openings to the world, which were brought together by the demands of a contingent and concrete present. Here again Merleau-Ponty must rely heavily on his concept of innate structures and their innate drive toward unity. The acquisition of the object structure was thus a "reconstitution" of otherness. Once acquired, the object structure with its own constants will be automatically *triggered* and the entity will *"reconstitute"* itself (F377, F247, and F249). Only if the thing as well as its constants were precise and clear, like cognitive meanings, would there be grounds for the traditional claim of transcendental philosophy that the thing is rationally constituted from these constants. "We shall see that things define themselves primarily by their 'comportment' and not by static 'properties'" (F318). Things "behave," in the sense that they distinctively modulate and exert a presence on all our regions of openness. Once again this shows that perceptual identification is nonthetic and nonthematic.

We are now in a position to explicate and thereby defend the major claims of Merleau-Ponty's theory of objects. These are radical and original enough to challenge, and be denied by, every other major philosophical position on sense qualities and objectivity.

The arrangement of the color on the thing . . . signifies by itself all the responses that it would have given to the interrogation of the other senses, because a thing would not be this color if it had not also this shape, these tactile properties, this sonority, this odor. (F368)

In other words, just as an appearance is a mode of givenness of a constant, the experience of any one sense is *of* the thing itself and, hence, *of* the constants of every other sense. The extent to which the thing is fulfilled will depend on which sense is activated and the degree to which its constant is achieved. The reason why the givens of each sense open on to the structures of the other senses is that the constant of that sense carries the limitations or compromises that had to be made with the other senses when it was acquired. This incompleteness of a particular constant refers and signifies because the norm which mediates the standard criteria of proximity is a definite object situation.

Merleau-Ponty finally characterizes the thing itself in this way:

The unity of the thing beyond all its fixed properties is not a substratum, an empty x, a subject of inhering properties, but this unique accent which discovers itself in each, this unique manner of existing of which they are the secondary expression. (F368)

This manner of existing is an object situation, for it is a global structure of all the regions that express Existence. Merleau-Ponty can

call the thing's being *accent*, because it exists solely in the intertwining of our perceptual regions and hence has the presence of a
"style" (39) that is shared between them. Yet, since this perceptual
existence is a primordial contact with otherness, this particular and
unique organization belongs as much to the ontological world as to
the body-subject. We can understand now why every appearance is
an experience of a thing and not of a sensation; for appearances
present constants and each constant carries the accent that *is* the
intersensory thing itself. It is essential to the plausibility of this
theory that we keep in mind that object situations exist at differing
levels of specification. Some senses and appearances may open only
on to very general things, such as the minimum objective modifications of tactile constants (cf. chapter 2.3), which may give us, for
example, merely surface, gaseous, or porous objectivity. But even
this is still "the most secret texture" of the thing (*F*265). Furthermore, we can be aware of a highly specific color and only very
generally aware of the object it qualifies (and, thus, by implication,
of its texture and odor). This could be the result of many factors,
such as our metastructures giving one sense a preference or merely
our taking an analytic and abstract interest in the color. In any case,
Merleau-Ponty insists (as we shall argue in detail in the following
sections on color) that the constants of the other senses must be
present at least very generally.

This theory of Merleau-Ponty's, which establishes that the object
qua multiplicity of properties is inseparably unified—an "organism"
(39)—, shows that he would favor a theory of "qualified particulars"
and has, in fact, thoroughly developed one.[16] When he states that the
thing "is not an envelope of *qualia*, but what is between the qualia, a
connective tissue of exterior and interior horizons" (*VI*173*F,n.*), he
means that the accent of the thing is contained in all its qualities and
is definable by the way they have been uniquely interrelated in the
proximal situation. Thus a particular is more than and prior to a
bundle of qualities, but it is not at all separate from its own constant
properties.

Finally we can see why in the previous section there was no need
to make a sharp distinction between sense constants and thing

---

16. Cf. D. C. Long, "Particulars and Their Qualities," in Michael J. Loux, ed., *Universals
and Particulars*, especially pp. 277-81.

constants (notice, for example, the discussion of criteria). Thus Merleau-Ponty refuses to distinguish between "sensing" and "perceiving," or sense- and object-directedness, for in lived perception they coincide.[17] It is, of course, possible to give attention to a sense constant or sensation and thus make it one's figure; but, as we have seen, this still involves a transcendent reference to the thing's inner horizon, while the thing becomes, and is retained as, the field. Hence, this process is not equivalent to what the phenomenalist means by *sensing*; nor does it give support even to the weak phenomenalist claim that there is a noncomparative sense of this term.[18]

The perceiver sees the die "in the world" and

does not see projections or even profiles of the die, but he sees the die itself either from here or from there, and those appearances that are not yet fixed communicate between themselves and pass into each other; they all radiate from a central *Würfelhaftigkeit* [cubeness given as a whole] (Scheler) which is their mystical bond. (*F*374-75)

This *Würfelhaftigkeit* is the closest that Merleau-Ponty comes to giving a concrete name to the accent which is a particular object situation, and the description of its experience suggests the essential aspects of the object as situation: the thing itself is given only through its concrete appearances; these appearances can in turn be presented only if there is a structure available to articulate them; and the structure can only come into being insofar as it is demanded by the thing. The bond between the die's diverse properties and perspectives is "mystical" because it cannot be posited or conceived in abstraction from its actual appearances. Yet we have seen that the thing "emanates" (*VI*161) from within its appearances. This follows because if the appearances are sufficiently fulfilled or "fixed" they refer us to a constant property which carries the accent of the thing itself. Even when these appearances are too vague to give us a particular thing, they still refer us *generally* to that which has triggered their confused presentation. Merleau-Ponty stresses that " 'subjectivity' and the 'object' are one sole whole, that the subjective 'lived experiences' count in the world . . . , that the object is nothing else than the *tuft* of these *Abschattungen* [profiles or

17. Cf. "The Primacy of Perception," in *The Primacy of Perception*, p. 42.
18. For example, cf. R. M. Chisholm's *Perceiving*, pp. 50 ff., and *Theory of Knowledge*, pp. 34 ff.

perspectives] " (*VI*185). Like a tuft of grass, all of the perspectives of a particular constant or all the different sense experiences of the thing are gathered together through a direction and intertwining that they share.

It will be valuable to complete this section with a discussion of the status of the thing and the real. We have seen that, because the thing is itself a constant, it has a sense or a meaning; but at the same time it is acquired and given through a contact with otherness. As a meaning, it has a non-sensory presence or is invisible, and Merleau-Ponty variably calls it an ideality, a concrete or carnal essence, and a material a priori. But since the thing is given through contact, it is also "insurpassable plenitude" (*F*373) and "inexhaustible" (*F*374). As in all situations, there is an inextricable blending of the in-itself and the for-itself, of existence and essence, of content and form, and of reference and sense. The following statements will help us to understand the way Merleau-Ponty deals with these standard philosophical dichotomies by applying his situational ontology to the phenomenological notion of evidence.

The sense itself of the thing constructs itself under our eyes . . . , a sense . . . which merges [*se confond*] with the exhibition of the thing in its evidence.(*F*373)

It is not behind the appearances . . . , it incarnates itself in the appearances with evidence. This is why we say that, in the perception, the thing is given to us "in person" or "in the flesh" [*en chair et en os*] . (*F*369)

The thing is acquired and experienced for the first time when all our senses are adjusted to their maximum epistemic proximity. Once this particular organization of our sense openings has been sedimented, every contact with a similar thing will call up this same pattern of sense constants. We have the thing we intend in evidence when one or more of these constants closely approximate their originating appearance, which was given in the thing's proximal situation. Therefore we experience the sense or accent of a thing originally, and subsequently, through the concrete contact that our senses make with otherness. Only by being engaged in the given, can we experience the ideality of the thing. It is not a matter of cognitively positing, projecting, or having the thing as an idea; rather, an operationally intentional act is possible (can be directed toward its object) only if its constitutive structures have been actualized by otherness. The thing itself is present only when it is enclosed in its correlative "subjective" experiences, and we are directed toward an object itself with any appearance we experience. "We now discover the core of reality: a thing is a thing because whatever it imparts to us is imparted by the organization itself of its sensible aspects" (F373). We saw that the only way the thing could be experienced was by manipulating the openness of our senses. We find reality in an intersensory organization because every sensory constant is compromised by every other while each is attempting to achieve its own maximum grasp on otherness. "The marvel of the real world is that in it sense makes itself one with existence . . . ; in it the sense profoundly invests and penetrates the matter" (F374). Essence and existence are one because the form or structure of the real thing is both constituted and reproduced in our inescapable inherence in otherness.

In summary, we have seen that the thing with its constant properties is the norm of all perceptual experience because it is the noema of perception's key epistemic situation. To this extent, Merleau-Ponty's concept of the perceptual object is very close to and performs many of the functions of Husserl's intentional object in the context of perception; but, unlike Husserl's conception, it is the object-side of a situation. This implies that we are not dealing with thetic and thematic constitution but with Merleau-Ponty's own understanding of contact, temporal synthesis, operative or motor intentionality, and reconstitution (some of which concepts he has taken from Husserl). The perceptual situation's means of recognition and reidentification are nonthetic because it does not deal in assertions or judgments but is operative in the sense that its structures are contacted (demanded, selected, or triggered) and can only be actualized by otherness. On the other hand, its organization and meaning are nonthematic for two reasons. First, its object is not synthesized by means of rational principles or cognitive devices but has the logic of the body-subject, of situations. Secondly, what is organized does not get its sense through the precise articulations of cognitive significations or linguistic predicates, for it uses the ambiguous and obscure categories and structures that are innate to, and prereflective developments of, the body itself.[19] Thus Merleau-Ponty

19. Merleau-Ponty goes far beyond Husserl's studies of passive synthesis in this regard, for Husserl never succeeded in describing operational intentionality in its own terms. For example, in *Experience and Judgement*, which represents his interesting attempt, he ultimately only reproduces, within the precognitive realm, a pale copy of distinctively cognitive modes of constitution.

says that it uses an "operative reason" (50), a "lived logic" (F61), and a "silent language" (48).

By returning to Merleau-Ponty's description of reality and objectivity, we shall be able to show finally how our characterizations of otherness, which were so important to chapter 1, are discoverable within Merleau-Ponty's phenomenology of perception and the thing. "The senses are apparatuses to form concretions of the inexhaustible, to form existent significations" (VI245F). "We will therefore have to recognize an ideality that is not alien to the flesh, that gives it its axes, its depth, its dimensions" (VI152). Although the senses are in primordial contact with otherness, they can deal with it only through structures or within generalizable situations. It is important to understand this "ideality" that permeates the natural world, for it is the given possibility of cognition and the reflective awareness that accompanies perception.

To show that "matter is 'pregnant' with its form,"[20] let us now reverse our order of presentation and explicate Merleau-Ponty's analysis of otherness as inexhaustible plenitude. We shall learn that its unconquerable presence is not that of an opaque and material being different from our own; it can only be comprehended in terms of structure and sense. "The real lends itself to infinite exploration, it is inexhaustible" (F374). Like Leibniz, Merleau-Ponty illustrates this infinite plenitude by noting that a stone can be perpetually fragmented but always remains as stone and existent. Contrary to a Cartesian or Sartrian dualism, this infinitude does not describe an extended substance that opposes itself to a "mental substance" or "nonbeing"; we are not faced with the stultifying impact of a foreign matter. Rather, otherness is infinitely explorable and determinable. It is that which *can* be structured and not that which is impenetrable to form. Nevertheless, we still say that it is beyond because it escapes our present articulation, and that it is foreign and alien because our body-subject as a system of structures is unable to encompass it absolutely. But it is not beyond our transcendence or our ability to specify it perpetually, and it is not alien to structurability and differentiation in general. Visibility and separation (écart) are its essence.

The secret of otherness or Being is that it is infinitely structurable.

20. *The Primacy of Perception*, p. 12.

Facts and essences are abstractions: what there is . . . [is] the impossibility of meaninglessness [*non-sens*] or ontological void, since space and time are not a sum of local and temporal individuals, but the presence and latency behind each of all the others, and behind these, still others, of which we do not know what they are but know at least that they are determinable in principle. (*VI*156-57*F*)

Otherness must have meaning from the beginning, for it is necessarily differentiated into the dimensions that are correlative to our original meaning-giving regions of Existence. It must also be inherently amenable to meaning because it is defined in terms of, and perpetually constituted by, the structures that result from the specification of these regions.[21] If we recall that our present field holds the entire world as its horizon and that all specific structures contain a reference to their parent hierarchy, we can make this inexhaustibility explicit. The givenness or appearance of a constant presents us with the otherness that presently actualizes it since the constant is a noema of a structure of our Existence. Beginning with the constant, we have seen that the experience of one sense constant refers to the constants of the other senses. Each of these constants is a specification and differentiation of its sensory region; hence, included in the meaning of its givenness is the negation of alternative specific constants, the affirmation of the genera that subsume it, and the protension of further potential specifications of this species. Furthermore, these constants put us in touch both with things which separate themselves from all other object structures, and, since they belong to levels, with fields which in turn are also defined by their difference from other fields. In other words, a constant is a manifestation of its own entire region of structures as well as of every other opening to the natural world. Hence, "there is a logic of the world which my whole body espouses . . . and of which the thing is only one of the possible concretions" (*F*377). Part of the inexhaustibility of every experience is its reference to every other potential structure. But we have seen that every actualized constant

21. It is in this sense that Being is "rational" (408) and it is what Merleau-Ponty means when he says that "flesh . . . is not contingency, chaos, but a texture that returns to itself and conforms to itself" (*VI*146), for he immediately ties it to "typical dimensions of visibility" and to "generality." Therefore, this passage cannot be understood in the way that Kwant wishes, in order to give weight to his thesis that there is a major change in the later Merleau-Ponty, that is, that he no longer stresses the notion of contingency. (see *From Phenomenology to Metaphysics*, pp. 78-79.)

appears or always resists a present structuring to some degree; thus every experience is also inexhaustible because it perpetually points to a further specification of the present grasp. "There is nothing to be seen beyond our horizons, but other horizons, and still other horizons, and nothing in the interior of the thing but other smaller things" (F384). The beyondness which characterizes presence refers us to the complexity and endless determinability of every experience. Complete concordance between our structures and that which concretizes them is impossible at every stage; for in the denseness (*épaisseur*) and profundity of every present appearance is contained a horizon of all our past sedimented structures as well as a horizon of endless future specifications. The inner horizon of the thing does not consist of unalterable and basic details, but of all the possible ways in which we can specify it (for example, scientifically, aesthetically, visually) and of the hierarchies of specifications that fall under each of these types. For example, it will not do to argue, as philosophers of science have, that either macroentities or microentities, but not both, are reality. We have seen that the proximal epistemic situation yields an object which, as a constant, can become the norm for an infinity of microscopic structurings. Hence the physicist's microparticles have no more of a claim to reality than the noema of any other type of structuring (for example, sensation or perspectives, and cognitive, practical, or affective givens). None is real in isolation from the others, for all are on the horizons of the others, and it is just the presentation of this "chiasm" of dimensions, or inextricable blending of possible and still-to-be-determined perspectives, that gives us reality. Finally, inexhaustible structurability reveals Being's finitude and not merely a human limitation, for as we have seen Merleau-Ponty defines Being as visibility, articulation, and separation. Hence the subject's inability fully to grasp otherness and his drive to do so are an expression of Being's essential incompleteness and a manifestation of its attempt to gather itself together. "It is thus essential to the thing and to the world to present themselves as 'open', to send us beyond their determinate manifestations, to always promise us 'something else to be seen' " (F384).

3. Color Constancy and Lighting

In the next three sections, I shall turn to the analysis of color constancy. We shall find that although explicating the constancy of an object's own color is much more difficult than explicating its shape and size, it follows the same logic and thus confirms and deepens our previous analyses. However, it is not a mere repetition; for proving that color is situational (i.e., that it is a type of primordial contact or material bond between the body-subject and the thing itself) will answer the stronger standard types of objection that the phenomenalist can raise against Merleau-Ponty, since the color patch has always been the paradigm for the discrete, self-subsistent, and private sense-datum or appearance. In particular, the present analysis will go beyond the previous ones in showing how the perception of color is, at one and the same time, the constitution of depth and space, and in showing in greater detail how the body's overall motility is tied to vision.

We have already seen that in order to investigate color constancy and its status as a sensation, we must understand its dependence on light. We must now deepen the analysis of chapter 2.3 by studying the structure "lighting and object illuminated," through which all colors are perceived. Thus lighting will be the main topic of the next two sections. In order to make Merleau-Ponty's very original and difficult theory as clear as possible, it is necessary to examine lighting with its contrary capabilities of being a level and a color, the modes in which colors must appear, and the inseparability of color constancy from objectivity.

We have already seen that since lighting is itself a member of the spectrum of colors, and since all colors are only given as differentiations from one another, the colors within a field will differentiate themselves from the color of any type of lighting in a uniform and constant manner, and thus every type of lighting will yield the same series of colors in a field. But lighting is a peculiar type of color; for every other visual given is mediated by lighting's direct contact with the eye. Lighting is only lighting proper "when it envelops us, when it becomes our milieu, when we establish ourselves there" (F358). The lighting sets a general tone for the gaze, such that all other visual structurings will be in terms of this prior *situation*. "My body is my general ability of inhabiting all the milieu of the world, the key to all the transpositions that keep the world constant" (F359). When the body adjusts to the dominant lighting of the field, the resistance of the colored entities in the field to this particular light will result in the standard series of constant colors. We have seen that this occurs because entities separate their color from that of light to the degree that they clash with it. A photometer gives us a physical sign of this resistance. It shows that a blue paper in gaslight and a brown paper in daylight send the same mixture of light rays to the eye (F354). If we used a screen or squint, we would see these colors as identical. But in normal perception they look, respectively, blue and brown. There is a difference between the photometer and lived perception because the gaze has taken the type of lighting into account. It must do so, for as we shall see the lighting situation is vision's initial openness and contact with the visual world. Colors, as in our example, that match their particular lighting identically clash with their own lighting to the same degree. Furthermore, since this point or degree is established by the dominant tone of the gaze (the lighting situation), and this tone is itself a member of the spectrum, the color will be placed in its constant position in the spectrum. Every other color will distinguish itself from the norm (the color of least resistance) to approximately the same degree that it does in the spectrum. Hence the blue paper is as different from, or as like, the color that matches gaslight as the brown paper is different from or like the color that matches daylight. Yet each object is seen with its own constant color in any lighting because the gaze's dominant structure—lighting—is correspondingly different.

It is necessary for us to see that, although the explication of the possibility of color constancy is highly complex, the actual process has the simplicity requisite for operations of the body-subject. In other words, we must be able to account for the phenomenological fact that we always encounter the object's own constant color under all types of lighting, without resorting either to cognitive, rationalist, or inferential methods for attaining consciousness of it, or alternately, to behavioral, empiricist, or physiological devices for explaining it. Once the eye has acquired the ability to see colors, it understands each color as, simultaneously, a differentiation from all other colors of the same species and a manner of existing or merging with the world. Hence the ability to perceive colors in a field (as differentiations of that field) and the ability to adjust to a lighting as a level (to merge with the color dimension of the field) are one and the same. Given the gestaltist fact that colors are individually determined in relation to those that surround them, it would be inexplicable, without the notion of light as a level, how an entity could sustain a constant color when it changed its background and also how the things behind me could fall into the same color series as those before me. But whenever an entity occurs in the same type of lighting it will always be assigned the same color. The background entities will affect the *appearance* of this constant but not change its *own* color, for the lighting acts as a uniform standard which the body carries with it to all relevant fields. Finally, each lighting is immediately transposable into every other lighting level, for the eye comprehends each in terms of its distinction from these other levels.

Just as colors cannot appear unless they are the specifications of a dominant lighting, they are also essentially dependent on various kinds of objectivity. A constant color will appear through the perspective of a lighting level and, as well, in a certain mode which at least refers it to a general type of object. "The weakness of both empiricism and intellectualism is in not recognizing colors other than the fixed qualities that appear in the reflective attitude, whereas the color of living perception is an introduction to the thing" (*F*352). Both empiricism, with its mechanisms of association and memory, and intellectualism, with its use of perceptual thetic judgments, must imply that colors *qua* properties are always perceived as fully determinate and as qualitatively identical, irrespective of the objects to which they are attributed. But this is no more true of our perception of color constants than it is of our perception of shape and size. We have shown thus far that although all levels distribute the same series of colors in their fields, each lighting varies the sharpness with which each of its colors differentiates itself. The color must appear, then, rather than be fully achieved or ideally given, for the lighting "blurs" and "deforms" the constant color, preventing a one-to-one correspondence between its presentation and its constant structure. When the reflective attitude claims that we perceive colors as *qualia* or properties in themselves (uninfluenced by the objects in the field or even the light), it is reducing all the possible "modes of appearance" of colors to one mode—colored areas, or that which the prism best exemplifies.

But these colored areas (*Flächenfarben*) are in reality only one of the possible structures of color, and already the color of a piece of paper or a surface color, (*Oberflächenfarbe*) no longer obey the same laws. The differential thresholds are lower in surface colors than in colored areas. (*F*353)

Hence two modes of appearance of the same color will be given differently because each will distinctively differentiate itself from the remaining colors of its color series. But we have just recalled that different types of lighting are also distinguishable by the degree of strictness with which they distribute their colors. Hence the gaze is aware both of its lighting level and of the type of objectivity that modifies that level through the way in which its color constant is blurred and deformed by the present given appearance.

How can we understand Merleau-Ponty's defining two separate modes of constancy in the same way? Or it is conceivable that these two influences on vision's grasp are able to intertwine to yield a single appearance? We can accommodate these two facts by using Hegel's insight that at a certain point quantitative change becomes qualitative. The following construction is technically speculative and only claims to show that Merleau-Ponty's descriptions are logically and empirically consistent.

Let us say that any two neighboring colors (e.g., red and orange) within the white light series are separated to the clearest degree (which we can designate as 100 degrees). Blue light, which is next to white on the spectrum, separates any two of its neighboring colors by 90 degrees. If we hold that there are ten major colors in the spectrum, and hence ten types of lighting (and we shall later see why we can be so arbitrary), each lighting will be distinguishable from the next by having 10 degrees greater or less clarity between any two neighboring members of its series (for example, the colors in white light are 10 degrees clearer than those in blue light). Within these 10 degrees there is room for the difference between the way in which the modes of appearance (the modifications due to the type of objectivity of the color) distinguish their member colors. Since Merleau-Ponty suggests that there are seven main modes and that one of these is the color of lighting, we can divide the 10 degrees into seven parts. We can then hypothesize that red and orange (or any two neighboring colors) in white light will differ (a) 100 degrees if they are themselves lights (for example, shadows or colored rays of light); (b) 98.67 degrees if they are area colors; (c) 97.24 degrees if they are surface colors, and so on (this series postulates that lights are clearer than areas and areas more distinguishable than surfaces). In the same way, an area color will be differentiated from its neighbor area color in blue light by 88.67 degrees and two surface colors by 87.24 degrees (80 degrees will be the beginning of a new level of lighting). This schema accommodates the fact that every color must appear in one mode or another. Furthermore, it shows how, in most cases, the look can grasp in the color's appearance its particular level of lighting as well as, and distinguished from, its particular mode of appearance. It does so because the degrees between each level of lighting are great enough for the eye to locate this level. Once this is accomplished the variations within the level's range (10 degrees) will be attributable to the modes of appearance (the modes, then, are a "species" of the lighting). This schema has the advantage of allowing for ambiguous and misleading appearances which might be specified by either of two lightings or two modes of appearance. It must be noted that whenever we have spoken of degrees, we have referred to degrees of difference. Hence these degrees must not be understood in a physical sense, but as evaluative, for they can all be translated as being better or worse than the next, our criterion being the clarity of differentiation.

Besides area and surface colors Merleau-Ponty lists:

the color of transparent bodies which occupy the three dimensions of space (*Raumfarbe*); gloss [*le reflet*] (*Glanz*); glow [*couleur ardante*] (*Glühen*); brightness [*couleur rayonnante*] (*Leuchten*), and in general the color of lighting. (*F*353)

Each of these modes of appearance reveals a certain general type of objectivity. We shall soon see that there cannot be lighting unless it structures itself through a mode of appearance. An appearance, by being specifiable in terms of its mode of appearance and level of lighting, intentionally directs us to a color constant. But simultaneously we are referred to the constant forms of objectivity that correspond to our modes of appearance. For example, surface colors adhere to hard objects, transparent colors to gases or to transparent entities like glass; glossy colors refer us to the genus of entities with reflecting surfaces, such as liquids and mirrors; and as we shall see area colors give us the thetic object in general of the analytic attitude.

After listing the various modes of appearance, Merleau-Ponty continues with a striking demonstration of how lighting as a level *is* strictly the series of colors that it distributes in the field or, equivalently, is given strictly in these colors. "The color of lighting . . . confuses itself so little with the light source that the painter is able to represent the former [the color of the lighting] by the distribution of light and shade on the objects without representing the latter [the source]" (*F*353). In other words, the painter is able to choose the internal lighting he wishes to present to the viewer by differentiating the colors in his painting to varying degrees. In the same context, Merleau-Ponty demonstrates how the colors of objects can be given only in their distinction from surrounding colors. "When a painter wants to depict some striking object, he does so less by applying a lively color to that object than by a suitable distribution of light and shade on the surrounding objects" (*F*360). Since the color which resists a level the most (or the least) will stand out under a certain lighting, the artist can make an object the center of his painting by choosing the lighting which serves this purpose; and this lighting can be conveyed merely by altering the shading of the colors that surround the key object. This technique must of course take account of the fact that certain colors are usually more aesthetically attractive than others. But the inherent capacity of lighting to be visible in the interaction of the colors in its field allows the painter to reorganize this attractiveness, hence making his selection of colors more flexible. For example, consider how some of the impressionist painters have made extremely pale colors, which would fade and be insignificant in most lighting, central and clear.

Therefore, a species of lighting (as a level) is given in the series of colors it lays out in the field, and as Merleau-Ponty says in his later works the level is to be found "between" its elements. Yet for a color to appear it must be triggered and concretized by otherness. We have provisionally separated these types of contact into the seven modes of appearance. Hence, to be given, colors must have the objectivity of one of these modes at least (it should be noted that, of course, a single level of colors will be manifest in the field by many modes of appearance). Hence, every constant appears minimally through a structure of the form, color x in lighting y of mode z. This is the highest level of generality that lived perception can use, but no doubt it does so rarely. We must distinguish, then, between two references of the phrase "constancy of color." The one in which we are most interested is that of an object's *own* color. Its own constant color will be much more specific than the above, for it will be adjusted by the intersensory requirements of the proximal epistemic situation. Thus far we have only arrived at a color constancy that discloses types of objectivity in general rather than things themselves. Although this general constancy also opens on to the other senses, it does so with an equally high degree of generality. We have only answered how it is possible that all entities constantly have one of the colors of our standard series, but not how things have their own colors, which are, as well, constant throughout all of their appearances. Before we can answer this question (see section 5), we must clarify the status of area colors in distinction from the other modes of appearance.

4. Area Colors, Sense-data, and Primordial Depth

Merleau-Ponty examines area colors by using standard psychological experiments that reduce the organization of a field. He considers the psychologist's reduction screen, light boxes containing a contrasting light and color, a cone of light in a dim room whose base is a revolving disk, and the artist's squint.

> This change of aspect is inseparable from a change of structure in the color: by the act of interposing a screen between our eye and the spectacle, or by squinting, we free the colors from the objectivity of bodily surfaces and restore to them the simple condition of areas of light. (F354)

It seems from this quotation that an area color is not a mode of appearance of lighting but is lighting itself. If the area colors are freed from objectivity, why did he insist previously on calling them modes and separating them from the "color of lighting" (F353)? Furthermore, if they are identical, we were in error to state that constancy, experienced even most generally, had to have a mode of appearance. This issue is of great importance since, if it is possible to experience the colors of a light level for themselves, we would have a case of an absolute and apodictic sensation that did not refer beyond itself, and even this degree of phenomenalism would be too much for Merleau-Ponty. By making area color a mode, Merleau-Ponty is not supplying us with a merely verbal solution but is stating that the experience of such color is situational. Hence it too is a case of otherness triggering a structure of perception with the result that our grasp of the area color is inexhaustible and infinitely specifiable (rather than being given fully and completely). The confusion arises because the screen and box give us a single color that constitutes our entire visual field such that the constant and the light thoroughly blend. But we do not then have one self-identical given; for lighting by itself is invisible unless it reveals, and color by itself is impossible without light. In other words, an area color is still due to otherness modulating our color level in a particular manner. This is made clearer when there is more than one color present. For example, in the case of the artist's squint or beams of light (or pathological cases like Schneider's), the field may consist simply of many different patches of color. But this field is also situational, for the lighting still distributes itself as a level and the particular manifestations of its colors are necessarily triggered by otherness's resistance to this level. The objectivity of particular bodily surfaces is indeed reduced and leveled in area colors, but all objectivity or otherness does not disappear and we are not left with a pure datum of sensation.

We no longer see real bodies, the wall, the paper, with a determinate color and at their place in the world; we see some colored patches which are all vaguely situated on one and the same "fictional" plane [a reference to Gelb] . (F354)

Since we shall place a lot of stress on this statement, it is important to note that Merleau-Ponty uses almost identical phrasing at another point in the *Phenomenology of Perception* (F262). The quotation is important because it gives us a concrete case of cognitive perception, explains the key experience of phenomenalism, and locates sense-data. Merleau-Ponty has repeatedly criticized the analytic or reflective attitude for abstracting from our lived perception by reducing all modes to that of area colors.[22] We can now see that this abstraction is not reflective in the sense that it is strictly a cognitive operation, for being able to perceive area colors is a genuine perceptual capacity that is used in lived perception. Yet it is a case of "reflective perception," for our cognitive concerns have metastructured our primordial perceptual openness. The cognitive realm is concerned with the thetic and most determinate color and thus reduces and levels all modes of appearance to the most precise type of color, area color. The analytic attitude does not deal with the world from within the total privacy of a realm of thought (sense-data thus are not mental entities as some phenomenalists have claimed), but it modifies one's actual perceptual being-in-the-world. Perception and cognition are always interwoven to some extent but here their equilibrium is in favor of cognition or of analytic interests to an extreme. Merleau-Ponty shows that the phenomenalist's sense-data are not

22. The following argument is close to Toulmin's position (compare p. 107 in his *The Place of Reason in Ethics*).

merely theoretical constructs because they are genuine experiences of which perception is capable. However, he shows at the same time that sense-data are not pure givens but are situated. Area colors have an object-side with a factor of otherness which escapes the structured grasp of perception. In other words, a phenomenalist situation has a noematic side that is actualized by otherness.

Since area colors make the lighting and its mode indistinguishable, we can understand why philosophy has had such a difficult time locating sense-data and deciding whether they are mental or physical. They are actual, but their existence for lived perception approaches the status of the phantoms and is on a different plane than our world of things. The other modes of appearance directly refer us to things, involve all the senses, and, as we shall see, give us a three-dimensional world. Hence, the plane on which the thetic objects of the analytic attitude exist is two-dimensional, but not strictly "fictional," as Gelb stated.

For the structure lighting and object-lit to be given, at least two surfaces of different reflecting ability are needed. (F355)

The screen puts out of action [jeu] . . . the articulation of the whole of the field, the richness and subtlety of the structures which it carries. (F355)

Merleau-Ponty means that when lighting is unable to distribute a series of colors and, more exactly, a system of objects, it merges with area colors and no longer functions as a level. Lighting "hides itself in making the object visible" (EM167), for it presents us with a constant property and not its own color. Yet we saw that this constant must have an appearance and it was here that the lighting indicated itself. The constant's appearance or the degree to which it is articulated is dependent on its degree of differentiation from another constant. Lighting only functions as such in the "distance" or "tension" it creates between two constants. Hence we are intentionally directed to constants *through* their differentiation or appearance, which is just the lighting *qua* level. The lighting and the constant then separate themselves and hence stop being an area color when the field becomes multiple. At this point, we can say analogically that the lighting becomes invisible and that the constant is given "under the appearances, as the ground persists under the figure . . . in a nonsensory presence" (F352).

This analysis prevents a misunderstanding that might have arisen from our earlier analysis. We originally saw that lighting revealed through differentiation a constant set of colors because it itself was a color with which they clashed. Yet this seemed to imply that lighting could disclose a single and isolated objective color, and even a color that filled an entire field of a homogeneous type of objectivity. We can now understand that we are not in fact given a constant color at its place within the world in such circumstances because we do not have lighting but an area of color (for example, the cone of light). What is important to understand here is that lighting allows us to place the colors of things in their relation to an entire set of color constants, even though our present field does not exemplify every one of these constants; but at the same time lighting is powerless unless there is more than one entity or substance within this present field.

This conclusion has two important consequences. First, it not only shows that property constants are dependent on the things they manifest, but that a field is given prior to the individual entities within it. The structures that articulate the world are not primarily property structures or even object structures; they are field structures (i.e., levels). We already approached this conclusion when we studied differentiation situations. But we have now seen in a concrete way that no property can be given unless it modulates an already-assumed sense level. (In the case of a full object, it modulates a spatial level that is a balance of all the possible types of levels that constitute the field.) Thus we are again brought back to Merleau-Ponty's central claim that the constancy of properties is dependent on that of things themselves, which is in turn grounded in the constancy of the world.

Secondly, the fact that the articulation of our milieu is due to the level of our present body-subject means that one cannot give a realist-gestaltist interpretation of Merleau-Ponty's theory that all givens exist only in differentiation from other givens. For example, when Merleau-Ponty explains the cone of light experiment, he gives a strictly objective description of the way the parts of our present field influence each other to form a gestalt. Yet throughout he is careful to qualify this description by saying that it is "as if" each thing altered the perceiver's grasp through "a kind of reciprocal action" (312). He is cautioning us against a gestaltist interpretation, according to which elements in themselves affect one another so that our total grasp of the milieu is strictly determined by the actual entities that face us. (He uses the same argument to show that spatial levels are not dictated by their contents.) On the contrary, he has made clear that "the colours of the visual field . . . form an ordered system round a dominant which is the lighting taken as a level" (313). It is the body-subject itself that mediates every part of the field and allows each to have an influence on the other.[23] Only when the gaze assumes a level of lighting will colors be able to superimpose themselves on each other, even on all the potential colors that are not actualized at present.

Merleau-Ponty gives us a rough outline of the logical priority of lighting to things and their shapes when he describes the synthesis of our spatial field:

With the structure lighting and object-lit, there can be planes; with the appearance of the thing, there can finally be univocal forms and positions. The system of appearances, the prespatial field, anchors itself and becomes fully a space. (F373)

We made use of this quotation earlier to show the role of levels, but only now are we in a position to see why lighting is the ground of our visual world, spatiality, and depth. Because of the originality and comprehensiveness of this claim, we shall examine it in some detail.

Merleau-Ponty's explications of shading, of shadows, and of the experiment with the cone of light on a disk will allow us to gain an understanding of how lighting is the coming-to-be of depth. "If in a brightly lit room, we observe a white disk placed in a shady corner, the constancy of the white is imperfect. It improves when we approach the shady zone containing the disk. It becomes perfect when we enter it" (310-11). Besides showing us that constancy is dependent on the epistemic situation of the body, this experiment reveals that the transformation of a colored area (the shadow) into lighting can be gradual and progress ambiguously. We can carry a dominant level while being aware of other possible lightings in our milieu. Furthermore, these other lightings are already beginning to distribute the colors they encompass. Hence the entities within a shaded area of our present field will have a slightly altered logic of

23. This point is a concrete example of one of Merleau-Ponty's major criticisms of gestalt theory, that is, that a gestalt is not just another thing-in-itself or self-subsistent entity within the world, and thus that it does not have a *causal* relation to the subject. This objection is strong enough to make gestaltist interpretations of Merleau-Ponty incorrect or at least extremely misleading.

differentiation compared to those under our present dominant. In the cone of light experiment, "the disk appears, like the rest of the room, faintly lit" (308). When the disk rotates and the beam of light exactly matches its circumference, we do not have the minimum two modes of appearance. Therefore, the light beam appears as an area color within our dominant, and the disk distributes its color under our present level and not under that of the light shining on it. When a piece of paper (a second mode of appearance or color) is inserted into the beam, it changes it into lighting, so that it no longer appears as a semisolid cone. Correlatively, the disk and the paper now take on an appearance which is mediated by the beam (as well as the present dominant). This experiment dramatically proves that we can have another lighting within our dominant level that has a vague status between lighting and area color. Like any indeterminate given, it carries the logic of the two species between which it falls: thus, ambiguously and at the same time, it reveals colors as do lightings, and it is enclosed within another lighting, as are area colors.[24]

Since the body-subject settles on its phenomenal location by adopting a certain lighting as its level, the dimensions and organization of its visual clearing (field of disclosure) closely correspond to the physical direction and power of this lighting. (The lighting is a necessary but not sufficient condition of the scope and profundity of our visual field.) But Merleau-Ponty is stating much more than the truism that we cannot see without light. He is maintaining, instead, that because lighting merges with the gaze at the same time that it contains the elements of the field, it is the material expression (as is the spatial depth that results from it) of the way in which the subject is a being-outside-itself, a spatializing, and, most astonishingly, a flesh or substance of which the external world actually consists. Hence objects further away from the source of light will not clash with the lighting to the same degree as the closer. Constancy is "attenuated at a great distance" (308), but at all distances the constant's visibility or appearance will be slightly altered from its norm color. We can conclude, then, that the constant's appearance will motivate our grasp of the object's distance.

24. Our previous references to the ability of a painter to create an internal lighting for his painting, which is viewed under the gallery's own lighting, by varying the "light and shade" (306 and 312) show us that this mixture of lightings under one dominant is not at all rare.

It is also important that *lighting allows us to see three-dimensionally* and, as Merleau-Ponty frequently states, it allows us to begin to "see around" entities and in a sense to "see what they would see." When an entity is shaded from the source of light by another, its color is being structured through another type of lighting. This shading will segregate, and create strong distinctions within, the field, at least making closer areas of the milieu not reveal themselves in the same way as the farther areas. It is these distinctions which are responsible for motivating visual depth and which give lighting a *sens*, allowing it to act as a "guide" (310) to our vision. If we look at the two cases that arise from an object being shaded, we shall see how a third dimension is integrated with the planes (of distance) that lighting establishes. First, if there is another source of light in our milieu that gives the shadowed zone whatever light it has, then, as in the cone of light experiment, the entities within this zone will distribute their colors in a way that blends with but is different from those clearly under the dominant. Hence our eye will be guided from two directions and will "see around" objects. Secondly, if no other light source is present, these shaded entities will be responding to the light which is reflected by the neighboring entities that are within the dominant's range. In this case, there will also be a different type of lighting present (or at least a serious alteration and blurring of the dominant species), for the surfaces from which it reflects will change its direction and its logic. Since the surrounding entities (some more than others) become the source, we shall be seeing what these entities "see" of these shaded objects.[25]

For example, the shadow of a hand seen in Rembrandt's *The Night Watch* gives this hand "simultaneously in profile. The spatiality of the captain lies at the meeting place of two lines of sight which are incompossible and yet together" (*EM*167). Lighting "guides" us, as another person would, for it allows us to see the environment not only from our own position, but immediately from that of the light source and to a lesser extent from the perspective of other objects. We can see now that the light analogy that existentialists favor for describing Existence and its field has much ontological truth and is not as ill-chosen as many commentators make it out to be. (Both

---

25. Recent psychological research on the perception of space, lighting, and constancy continues to confirm Merleau-Ponty's descriptions. (See Alan L. Gilchrist, "The Perception of Surface Blacks and Whites," in *Scientific American* 240 [March 1979]: 112-24.)

Merleau-Ponty and Heidegger warn against following the analogy too closely, for like all analogies it eventually deceives.) Of course, our phenomenal and situational use of the term *light* is not that of ordinary usage; but neither is the use of *light* by the physicist when he states that "light travels in straight lines."[26] Both uses are slight modifications that do not deny our ordinary understanding of the term.

Let us return to Merleau-Ponty's statement that lighting is prior to things and space. We noted previously that he does not say that a synthesis has discrete stages, but that each stage blends into the one that logically follows; therefore, he calls it a transitional synthesis. In the same context, Merleau-Ponty approves of Cézanne's statement: "When color is at its richest, the form is at its most complete" (*F*373). Hence, at one and the same time that the colors of the field begin to appear, shapes and positions begin to differentiate themselves. At this point, we are already experiencing intersensory things and thus centering our spatial level. Color constancy immediately intertwines with the constancy of shapes and sizes, which, as we have seen, refers us to constant things.

Before continuing the analysis of how color constancy intends the thing itself, we can draw some important insights from the present analysis. First, one of the greatest problems with Merleau-Ponty's theory of spatial levels arises from the fact that these levels result from an adjustment of the body's present being-in-space to the contents of the field. We can now understand how these contents can be prior to a spatial level but need not be conceived—as they cannot in the context of Merleau-Ponty's philosophy—as passively received sense-data or things-in-themselves. These contents, in which the body's spatial level (i.e.,the level of object structures) will be anchored, are given with the constants of color or, if vision is not actualized, with the constants of another sense. Prior to having a spatial field, one has a colored entrance to this field through the contact of light levels. Merleau-Ponty calls the field at this stage a prespatial field because it precedes the lived spatial field that is structured by things in their interrelation. It is the noema of our primordial contact with the world into which we are thrown through the senses. It is the experience of the individuality and openness of

26. Stephen Toulmin, *The Philosophy of Science,* p. 21.

worldhood before we organize a "world" or field of objects. Finally, it shows us the primordial or natural space that precedes even lived space (293-94). This is one of Merleau-Ponty's most difficult notions, but we can intuit this primordial space through the primordial depth that is given with lighting. It is the ground of lived space's dimension of depth which gives us the maximum articulation of the field for our present bodily stance. And, since this final articulation is in terms of things, our field grasp, or "the certitude of the world" (*F*361), precedes our experience of things with their constant properties.

5. Color Proximity and Motility

Thus far we have discovered only how there can be a constant series of colors in general. We must now examine the constancy of a thing's *own* color. In doing so, we shall find, as with shape and size, that the maximum possible articulation of color is modified by the epistemic situation which presents the thing itself. We shall thus be able to conclude that the perception of an object's color takes us to the object itself (and even to its nonvisual properties). By proving this in the case of color, which no doubt provides the greatest test and challenge to the reliability of the theory, we shall be able confidently to affirm the general proposition that the appearance of any constant property intends the thing itself. We shall see that this theory solves the important epistemological perplexities that arise from the dichotomy of appearance and reality and from the phenomenological fact that we visually perceive nonvisual properties. We shall then be in a position to examine motility's relation to color vision, which will reveal to us the full significance of the interdependence of these two regions of Existence. This section will conclude our study of perception as it completes the investigation of the themes and concepts that account for the originality and importance of Merleau-Ponty's theory.

We have noted that lighting, as a primordial opening to a field, precedes the perception of things. On the other hand, the thing's *own* constant color is secondary to the givenness of the object situation of which it is part. This distinction is the same as that which we noted previously between colors as an identical *series* in all lightings and all modes and colors as the constant visual *properties* that are given to us in all perceptions of the same entity. This distinction is not paradoxical; there is a continuity between our previous and present studies because a particular object's own constant color is a very highly specified version of the initially given general constants of lighting.

Let us begin by noting that color constants are not given as self-sufficient particulars or as independent of the objects they modify. "The color of living perception is an introduction to the thing. . . . As Scheler puts it, perception goes straight to the thing without passing by the colors" (*F352*). Merleau-Ponty gives us the following facts to support Scheler's view that a thing's constant color must be abstracted from the object's global and intersensory presentation. He states that painters agree that there are few colors in nature that are not structured as things. Secondly, "the perception of colors develops late in children" (*F352*), after the world of things is already acquired (Merleau-Ponty, as we shall see, is here referring to a particular culture's color-distribution and not to the primordial and innate capacity to distinguish light and shade). Thirdly, different civilizations may have different series of colors: for example, the Maoris have three thousand color names because they fail to see as identical, colors that adhere to structurally different things. In other words, their object structures actually disrupt them and prevent them from isolating a limited number of color constants (or even a manageable number of modes of appearances). It is because of the particular way in which the Maoris have previously structured their world of objects that they are subsequently unable to abstract colors to the same high degree of generality that we do.

The dependence of colors on things can be better grasped if we look at the criteria and norm situations for color constancy just as we did with shape and size. We shall see that the appearance of an object's constant color refers us to the epistemic situation wherein this constant was constituted and thus intends as well the object which is the noematic correlate of the situation. It is no doubt true that clear or white light is the standard lighting (or ideal proximal situation) to which our color constants conform. This type of lighting gives us the clearest spread between colors (and thus that maximum grasp of them which we saw was the "law" of perception), perhaps because it contains all colors to the same degree (as a prism shows). However, we do not choose this form of lighting as the norm of all other lighting either because we experience it most frequently in daylight or because it physically produces a uniform spectrum. We choose it rather because it gives us the other aspects of visual perception (shape and size) in their maximum articulation (richness, clarity, and symmetry). If, like a scientist or an artist, one brackets one's existential concern to be alongside things with their own shapes and sizes, then a different lighting can be taken as one's standard (for example, the chemist's preferred lighting may best distinguish the modes of appearance of fluids and gases). The colors that are given in all other lightings are appearances that intentionally direct us to those constants that are given in our norm lighting. But, of course, this does not mean that constants in this privileged lighting do not have appearances or are perfectly sensed; even these constants appear through at least one mode.

Our next step is to indicate what mode of appearance yields the best differentiation between color constants. No doubt colored areas best satisfy this criterion; for the competition for proximity by the other sense constants (and also by the conditions that give us a maximum grasp of shape and size) will not be present and thereby affect this mode and interfere with it to the same extent they do in the case of the other modes. We have seen that we rarely experience area colors in lived perception. Hence most frequently the lived constants that appear in the other modes *interfere* with our "preferred" mode of grasp. In other words, just as a nonstandard lighting *appears in* the given constant because it resists or obstructs our way *through* to the constant, our nonstandard modes contribute to the constant's way of appearing because the objectivity which defines this mode is interfering with the maximum presentation. Therefore, objectivity modifies and, along with the other criteria, mediates our maximum grasp of color. Finally, the highly general structure, color x under lighting y with mode z, is very rarely given in perception, for it further appears *through* the epistemic situation that best gives us the particular thing itself. And as we have seen, proximity compromises each constant in order to accommodate the thing as a global intersensory structure.

"There is a total logic of the painting or spectacle, an experienced coherence of the colors, of the spacial shapes and of the sense of the object" (361). Even in the visual realm by itself one can see that an object's constant color will not be the one that satisfies the criterion for maximum color grasp: the epistemic situation which best gives us an object's color will be adjusted to, and compromised by, that which gives us its clearest shape and size. Furthermore, depending on the object's "sense" (which results from our practical, cognitive, and social concerns) the optimal epistemic situation might favor one of these constancies or perhaps make another sense's constant privileged. "It is impossible completely to describe the color of the carpet without saying it is a carpet, a carpet made of wool, and without implying in this color a certain tactile value, a certain weight, a certain resistence to sound" (F373 and F10). Each constant depends on every other and hence our grasp of each refers us to the remainder and to their common accent. "The complete definition of one of its attributes demands that of the subject in its entirety" (F373). As we saw with size and shape, it is in the way a thing's own constant color differs from the norm color (for a particular lighting and mode of appearance) that we find our intentional reference to the thing itself. The deepest significance of color constants is that they "manifest on the outside the interior structure of the thing. The brilliance of gold palpably holds out to us its homogeneous composition. . . . One sees the hardness and brittleness of glass" (F265). But even in the case of an auditory given, which does not have the high level of articulation of a visual given, "it is at least certain that it offers us beyond the sounds in space something that 'murmers' and, through this, it communicates with the other senses" (F266).[27]

Merleau-Ponty has proven that every appearance has some degree of objectivity and, most important, he has clearly and fully demonstrated Husserl's major assertion that the appearance takes us to the thing itself, or that we are given the thing itself through its appearances.[28] Similarly he has resolved the epistemological dichotomy between appearance and reality by showing the essential relation between the object as it appears and the object as it *is* with its constant properties. He thus refutes all forms of epistemology that claim either that the object is a thing-in-itself that is "behind"

27. Merleau-Ponty, therefore, directly opposes Strawson's thesis that sounds are nonspatial and not parasitic on objects (see "Sounds," in *Individuals*).

28. But he has done so without the Husserlian paraphernalia of multiple phenomenalist entities uniformly intending (unifying themselves) or meaning an object (which is their unity).

appearances or that the object is nothing more than a sum of, or construction from, discrete appearances. In doing so, he has also accounted for one of epistemology's most perplexing phenomenological facts; that is, he has solved the problem of how it is conceivable that we *see*, in the strict sense, hardness, coldness, noisiness, and so forth (and, as we shall learn, anger, love, and agility as well). No other epistemologist has been able to answer this question so well.[29]

We have a thrown capacity to perceive color, but at the same time the articulation of this given into specific structures is a function of the contingencies of our cultural milieu and creativity. Let us make clear how our culture and our freedom permeate even our sensations of color. Since our innate visual opening is to color in general, the child distinguishes light from dark as soon as its body is able. It begins to acquire color perception proper by learning to specify the light-dark structure into different types of lighting. Progressive blindness or other injuries such as Schneider's show us the progress made in color specification, for they result in a regression to an earlier color system or in the loss of "the power to receive either surface color or lighting . . . , [because it is] a special and highly organized type of constancy" (F354,n.). The learning of a single series of colors gives, simultaneously, the different light levels for entering the visual world and the type of color constants that can be discovered there. It is here that the child's culture will influence the particular series and classifications of its colors and the standard modes in which they are actualized. Hence the Maoris, the Eskimos (with their grasp of eleven types of snow and whiteness), or the Navahos (with their two species of black and single species of grey and brown) can have different distributions of color constants than we do.[30] Nevertheless, we cannot attribute our color series to an absolute cultural determinism. One is always capable of learning

29. Firth's Husserlian attempt to solve these same problems is not convincing, for it is simply a broadening of the sensory core theory to include the presence at the same time of all sensory predicates in the given. It thus retains the same unbridgeable gulf between the apparent and the real and between the given and the interpreted (with all nonsensory predicates still being made *by fiat* unperceivable). Firth has himself impressively demonstrated that these difficulties account for the inadequacy of the sensory core theory and are inherent to any sense-data theory. Cf. Firth in Robert J. Swartz, ed., *Perceiving, Sensing and Knowing*, pp. 204-71.

30. Paul Henle, *Language, Thought and Culture*, p. 7.

different patterns of color. Our color grasp of otherness is infinitely specifiable and orientated to our concerns. Even the individuals within one culture will have various systems of color constants, as the artists's and scientist's expertise illustrates. Therefore, when we previously outlined the types of lighting, color constants, and modes of appearance, we were justified in doing so provisionally and loosely. For the same reasons, Merleau-Ponty feels no need to delineate an exact number of colors or modes of appearance for any of the senses.

The final aim of our study of color is to understand its motility.

Perception presupposes in us an apparatus capable of responding to the solicitations of light. . . . This apparatus is the look, in other words the natural correlations of appearances and our kinaesthetic unfoldings . . . , lived as the engagement of our body in the typical structures of a world. (F358)

It is more difficult to isolate the subject-side of color vision than it was to discover the motor conduct that gave us the constant structures of shape and size. To do so, Merleau-Ponty examines some well-known psychological data on the correspondence of motor behavior to color perception, concentrating particularly on pathological cases of abduction and adduction (F242-49). He shows that abduction (which tenses the body, makes it gregarious, and draws it away from its most balanced stance) and adduction (which is the opposite action of withdrawing from its anchorage in the world and reposing in itself) are neither separate from nor caused by the sensation of color. He shows empiricism to be wrong in its belief that they are behavioral responses to visual stimuli by alluding to the fact that different wavelengths which are perceived as the same color have the same "motor physiognomy" (F243). Intellectualist psychology is equally mistaken when it claims that movement is caused by a *cogitatio* or the conscious awareness of a sensation; for colors have this "vital significance" (F244) prior to the perceiver's awareness of them (as experiments with subliminal perception demonstrate). Rather, these movements are the expressions of the presently actualized body-subject as the noesis of the color situation, just as the colors as properties of things are the situation's present noematic expression.

In studying the motility of shape and size, we saw that vision had a specific form of motility. Now we can begin to see that the logic of visual motility differs very little from the gross motor capabilities of the body-subject.

The motor significance of colors is only comprehensible . . . if they achieve in me a certain general setting through which I adapt myself to the world, if they are an invitation to a new manner of evaluating the world, and if on the other hand motility . . . becomes the function which at each moment establishes . . . the variable scope of my being-in-the-world. (F243)

If we keep in mind that lighting is our first contact with the world of color and that the acquisition of its different types is culturally and individually influenced, we can again see why visual structures can be labeled evaluative. Yet, more important, because lighting has priority in the perceptual synthesis, we can view it as a general attitude that makes ready the body as a whole for a global grasp of its present milieu. The experiments which clearly establish abduction and adduction use field colors or colored areas: for example, colors are flashed on a screen in a darkened room or, by covering one eye with a colored paper, the total visual field is made to take on its tone. Hence these experiments establish more directly the motility correlative to lighting than to a particular thing's own specific color (of course, as we have seen, these are only ideally separable). Abduction and adduction are not two discrete and contrary movements of the body; but, like different lightings, they are vague terms that describe a position on a scale or within a certain range. Just as lighting *is* the distribution of a series of colors and can only be found in the differentiation of the colors from one another, this global motility is describable at any one time as a particular *balance* or organization of all the body's standard motor capabilities. But this equilibrium, which being correlative to lighting even precedes our concrete anchorage in an objective field, is better described in more general terms as our "rhythm of existence" (F247). It is so highly general because we have not yet achieved the stage of a determinate, actualized, and present body-subject with its distinctive hierarchy and pattern of specific structures, actualized and potential.

Sensation is intentional because I find in the sensible the proposal for a certain rhythm of existence—abduction or adduction—and that, pursuing this proposal, and stealing into the form of existence which has thus suggested itself to me, I relate myself to an exterior being, whether this be in order to open myself or close myself to it. (F247)

Like lighting, the correlative movements are triggered, "proposed," or "suggested" by otherness and this highly general degree of openness is unclosable. In other words, lighting and these general movements express our primordial visual contact, and because of this thrown bond with the visual world we are intentionally related to something beyond us. (It is a case of the *il y a quelque chose*.) Furthermore, sensing is intentional because, given this inescapable contact, a process of specification or achievement is set in motion in order to determine this general grasp. But notice that Merleau-Ponty points out that it is only after the initial contact that we have a choice of, opening or closing ourselves to the further triggering of our specific structures.

This existential rhythm has a wider reference than just the visual region, for it describes the most general existential action of externalization and withdrawal, which is precisely being-in-the-world or temporality. In this context, the balance and scope of our being may roughly be understood in terms of the stress that our momentary existence puts either on the latter part of being-in-the-world (world) or on the former (being-in). We have seen that the subject-side of this structure can be taken as the self, which asserts its reality through being a "faculty of withdrawal," while the world or object-side establishes its otherness by attracting and captivating the subject. This equilibrium also coincides with that of authenticity and inauthenticity when they are taken as determined by the particular "distance" that the self keeps from the world. In both cases, one must not take these vague terms as the extreme limits of the structure of being-in-the-world. Similarly, abduction and inauthenticity suggest a movement away from the most balanced state of being-in-the-world (resulting from too much concentration on the self as well as on the world), while adduction and authenticity suggest the movement back toward the most balanced state. This homeostasis, which is dynamic and precarious, is never able to establish a perfectly stable present, and hence there will be a constant rhythm back and forth.

This "pulse of my existence" (285) is so general that one may even think of it in biological terms as the "systole and diastole" (285) of the body. Yet, it should be clear from our previous caveat against the use of the word *kinaesthetic* that we are speaking of the general motor intentionality of the body-subject and not of its contingent physical manifestations in an objective body. Hanly makes this error when he claims that Merleau-Ponty grounds the natural givenness of temporality in the physical rhythm of the body and its organs.[31] Moreover, even in the case of sleep (when the only realm of materiality our dreams can express is that of the body), the "rising and falling" or the directions of our dream space do not manifest our heartbeat or pulse, but our need either to broaden the scope of our grasp or to escape from whatever may be impinging on us.

The general motility of light can, as we have seen, be developed or articulated to yield the specific experience of a color. But this need not be the case, for we may "place" this initial contact in another region of the body (that is, articulate it through the structures of a nonvisual region). For example, the correspondence between affectivity and colors is well known—perceiving red is a way of living violently and green, peacefully—(211). Furthermore, Merleau-Ponty traces the possibility of synaesthesia and the normal synergy of the senses to this motor intentionality. "Movement understood not as objective movement and transference in space, but as a project towards movement or 'potential movement' forms the basis for the unity of the senses" (234).

Now that we have seen the interrelation of general motility and vision, we can complete this examination by describing the transposibility of the specific motor gestures of our gross motor region and of visual experiences. Since vision so thoroughly counts on the motor body for the productive specification of its own distinctive phenomena, we should no longer be astonished that we can directly experience the motility of another body visually. The above theory provides an unshakable foundation for the possibility of directly perceiving other persons and their gestures. Merleau-Ponty shows that we visually recognize the gestures of others by implicitly "imitating" those gestures in our own body. However, we shall see in chapter 5 that it is not an imitation by design or analogy, but as Merleau-Ponty says a *mimesis (CO)* or an imitation by identification, absorption, and syncretism. The "reversibility" of these regions allows Merleau-Ponty to go even further; for he can maintain in addition that vision can teach us to reproduce previously unacquired gestures. "Our perceptions provoke in us a reorganization of motor

---

31. C. M. T. Hanly, "Phenomenology, Consciousness and Freedom," *Dialogue* (Winter 1966): 342.

conduct even without our having already learnt the gestures in question" (*CO*50-51*F*). What transpires in these cases is that the motor-gestural body is used by the perceptual region to guide its structuring of the *active* entity that it witnesses, for example, another person. There is a dialectic between our gestural and visual body when we perceive the gestures of others. Our visual structures will immediately call up general gestural structures, which in turn will suggest the essential aspects that the gaze should anticipate in its object. Since perception is transitional or temporal, it will be able to keep ahead of its synthesis of an active phenomenon by means of the "predictions" it can make from its own motor capabilities. The gaze will then verify and correct the initial gestural interpretation, specifying it until it has grasped it. Unless there was this intertranslation between gestures and vision, it would be difficult to understand how the gaze would be able to anchor itself or clearly structure a field containing persons or even moving entities. The other is not a highly indeterminate percept and his minute gestures are accurately and easily perceived because the gaze carries the logic of such action and gestures through the probing of its own gestural body. Therefore, an organic entity is not merely intersensory, as are natural things, but is at least sensory-gestural. In the same way, Merleau-Ponty shows that when we read or hear a sentence we do not simply grasp it through one of our senses; rather we use our linguistic-motor capabilities to lead these senses away from the inessential (for example, nonlinguistic sounds or marks) and to protend what may follow.

4 Cognition

1. Sublimation as the Function of Cognition

In this chapter, we shall complete our phenomenological analysis by examining cognition as one of our given regions of being-in-the-world. Merleau-Ponty states that one of the main purposes of his situational analysis is to locate the cognitive realm and to make "reflection appear as one of the possibilities of my being" (*F*378-79). We shall see that although this region intertwines with the others, it is parasitic on perception or, more generally, on our natural contact with the world. Our previous discussions of cognition as a meta-structuring and of the way the analytic attitude objectifies our perceived world will be completed and deepened. But the main purpose of this chapter will be to examine the opposite movement, whereby cognition's structures or "ideas" originate through the *sublimation* of lived structures or of perceptual ideality. Not only is cognition dependent on the body for the creation of its own structures, but, as with all regions, the preservation and activation of these structures are materially based in the body-subject. Since motility in general and more particularly gestural and linguistic capacities are presupposed by all cognitive operations, it will be necessary to show the close relationship between language and cognition (sections 1 and 2). As Merleau-Ponty makes clear in *The Primacy of Perception* (pp. 21 ff.), in order to establish the role of cognition it is necessary to study the problems of the *cogito*. Early in this chapter, we shall begin examining the most obvious and epistemologically significant type of cognitive abstraction, showing how the epistemological status of a "thought of perception" is strictly derivative from that of perception itself. Following our study of cognition as a region and its relationship to language and Existence, we shall examine spontaneous or authentic thought, which will be seen to be both genetically grounded in prereflective existence and materially dependent on symbolic behavior. These studies will be completed by an extensive discussion of the concepts of evidence, certainty, and truth in the last two sections.

We shall discover throughout this chapter that cognition's own distinctive function can be revealed only by studying its relationship to our noncognitive existence and, most centrally, to perception. Merleau-Ponty characterizes this relationship (a type of reversibility) as *sublimation*, and comprehending this notion will be the main purpose of the first section and an aim throughout the chapter. We shall begin by noting the characteristics of cognitive processes and the way they alter the other regions to which they are directed. The study of the "thought of perception," Husserl's "essences," and Descartes's "verbal *cogito*" should give us a firm enough grasp of this notion (and thereby of the operation of cognition) to enable us to turn to more subtle and detailed examinations of creative and inauthentic thought and language (4.2), cognitive and noncognitive evidence and truth (4.3), and the phenomenology of belief and reflection (4.4). Following our usual method, the discussions of the first three topics in the opening section will give us an outline of and introduction to Merleau-Ponty's main claims and views, while the remainder of the chapter will deepen, defend, and support the preliminary studies.

It is important to note that Merleau-Ponty's theory of cognition does not change in his later works. Although *sublimation* only becomes an important and familiar technical term in his later works, we are able to explicate it with the help of his earlier studies, where it occurs both frequently and centrally (10, 41, 126, and 394). For example, he says in the *Phenomenology of Perception* that "visual contents are ... sublimated to the level of thought" (127) and he goes on to explain this through the important notion of *Fundierung* (127 and 394). He shows that to sublimate, or to cognitively understand and possess knowledge, is to "translate into disposable significances a meaning first held captive in the thing and in the world itself" (*VI*36) and "to preserve and continue our perceptual life even while transforming it".[1] Merleau-Ponty uses this term so as to allow connotations from its use both in psychoanalysis and in chemistry. Thus, when we reflect on a lived situation, we "distill" or "refine" its cognitive sense from the primordial contact with otherness that is essential to our prereflective "openness upon the world" (*VI*35). The analogy with distillation is an instructive one, for what we are left with is pure cognitive signification, which is characterized by an extremely fine articulation and unique clarity of the thetic and thematic.

However, it is equally important to keep the Freudian use in mind, for Merleau-Ponty agrees that sublimation not only refines but reconstitutes and rebuilds the "substance" on which it is grounded, redirecting or reinterpreting this given presence into a totally different mode of understanding. Thus sublimation also carries the important connotation that there is a repression of our lived contact and a fleeing from our thrownness and contingency. In summary, sublimation refines and represses our being-in-the-world by replacing it with a cognitive distillate, translation, or sketch, which, although preserving the founding term to some extent, reverses itself on it and gives it a new and specialized articulation.

> Our thesis is that this *there is* by inherence is necessary, and our problem to show that thought, in the restrictive sense (pure signification, thought of seeing and of feeling), is comprehensible only as the accomplishment by other means of the will of the *there is*, by sublimation of the *there is* and realization of an invisible. (*VI*145, *n.*)

In other words, we must comprehend the paradoxical status of cognition, which makes it an essential region of, and contributor to, our primordial contact with Being and, at one and the same time, a repression of our prereflective drive to articulate and understand Being. Cognition, like perception, is a means of achieving a maximum articulation of the world and it will help accomplish this articulatory drive in a new way. Its mode of articulation is distinctive because it is the "effort towards internal adequation, the enterprise to reconquer explicitly all that we are and do implicitly" (*VI*33). Although all the body's capacities symbolize and express the world, the linguistic

---

1. "An Unpublished Text," *The Primacy of Perception*, p. 7.

structures that constitute cognition are privileged: they give us the clearest and most precise means for determining our Existence. Hence the cognitive is synonymous with the thetic and thematic. Because this form of articulation is the most exact, it first appears that intellectualism is correct in holding that only rationality (in the narrow sense) can give us the truth of Being and that our prereflective modes of structuring have no ontological or epistemological relevance. But if we look more closely at the way our existential regions differ, we shall see that this is not the case.

We can compare cognition to perception in the same way that Merleau-Ponty compares the visual to the tactile: "Visual experience . . . pushes objectification further than tactile experience" (*F*365). Vision will maximize our grasp of an entity to a much higher degree, for when we move from a tactile to a visual exploration of an entity its inner and outer horizons are greatly expanded. Yet we also leave much behind, for the visual cannot reproduce the unique aspect of the world that is revealed by the distinctive capacities of touch. In the same way, cognition refines and clarifies our perceptual openness, but it uses its own distinctive type of structuring and cannot duplicate perception's disclosure of Being. There is, however, a much sharper difference between cognition and perception than between the senses. Although the constant structures of the senses are closely interwoven, each sense has a distinctive mode of directly contacting the world. Cognition is a metastructure and is thus parasitic on other regions. It has its own given character for producing structures, yet it is powerless to structure otherness unless it can "recapture and rectify" (*VI*152) those structures that have already been formed through perceptual contact. "The 'pure' ideality [the cognitive structure] already streams forth along the articulations of the aesthesiological body [noncognitive structures], along the contours of the sensible things, and, however new it is, it slips through ways it has not traced, transfigures horizons it did not open" (*VI*152). Here Merleau-Ponty means that cognition creatively acquires its specific structures by applying its *logos* primarily to preexistent perceptual situations. When they are acquired they become sedimented within our basically natural world or, correlatively, exist as secondary modifications of the structures the body-subject already possesses (they are merely an "optional expression" [35]). We may call them "extreme articulations," for their purpose is to isolate those aspects of our life that can be thetically and thematically stated. However, these extreme articulations are metastructures or are the result of specifying our reflective grasp of our prereflective life. In other words, what is further specified are not the perceptual structures which they sublimate but only cognition's own thrown opening upon the perceptual region.[2] We can agree, then, that reflective rationality or thought has a privilege but it is no more profound than that which any sense or region has in relation to the others. It cannot be taken as the pinnacle of our articulatory capabilities, for what it has gained in clarity it has lost in contact.

Merleau-Ponty criticizes all reflective philosophies (under which he includes both intellectualisms and phenomenalism) for limiting our understanding of all types of phenomena to the way they appear to the reflective ego or strictly within the region of cognition. By examining his analysis of these philosophies, we can discover the main characteristics of the region of cognition (this will provide an outline of what we shall discuss in detail in sections 3 and 4). The following passage contains the core of Merleau-Ponty's criticism:

> To say that perception is and has always been an "inspection of the mind" is to define it not by what it gives us, but by what in it *resists* the hypothesis of *inex-istence* . . . ; it is to require of the innocent the proof of his non-culpability, and to reduce in advance our contact with Being to the discursive operations with which we defend ourselves against illusion, to reduce the true to the credible [*vraisemblable*], the real to the probable. (*VI62F*)[3]

When we reduce lived perception to what can be known of it cognitively, we refine the opacity and indeterminateness of its bond with otherness. Since we have seen that the perceptually evident (or "real") object is defined by its inherence in otherness or as the inexhaustible focus of all our regions and of our present horizon, it is the evident and unchallengeable existence of the perceptual world that is "left behind" or is inaccessible to reflection. Reflective philosophies understand perception as an "inspection of the mind"

2. We shall continue to use perception as the region from which to take our main examples of prereflective structures. However, cognition performs the same operations on the structures of every other region and, as we shall see (particularly in chapter 4.4), even on its own.

3. Although the English translator renders the French *inexistence* throughout this portion of *The Visible and the Invisible* as *inexistence* (cf. *VI57F* ff. and *VI35* ff.), he misleadingly translates it in this passage as *nonexistence*.

because they grasp our lived perceptual experiences and situations as *cogitationes*. When cognition sublimates these situations, it is left merely with the "idea and its ideate" (*VI*39), for it has "denounced the bond between my vision and the world" (*F*262) and has thus translated our lived situations into that type of entity and significance that can be discursively and propositionally manipulated. By making the evident act and object of perception, which have their own distinctive form of subjectivity and self-consciousness, into mere objects of reflection (and thus into members of an immanent or private realm of consciousness), they transform our primordial experience of the "true" or "real" into the reflective awareness and appraisal of a "credible" or "probable" belief (*VI*62F and XVI).

When the perceptually evident is reduced to its cognitive version or to a noema of reflective consciousness, it becomes "guilty," for every *cogitatio* has the same ontological status. At this point, we must appeal to "discursive operations . . . , criteriological control" (*VI*62F), or conditions of "justification" (17) to differentiate the real and the true from other types of *cogitationes* such as those of imagination, opinion, memory, and so forth. But Merleau-Ponty says that to do so is to attempt to reproduce the "positivity" (*VI*51) of our perceptual existence and our world "with a negation of a negation" (*VI*62F), which is merely a secondarily instituted "resistance to doubt" (*VI*50).[4] Cognition negates perception's thrownness and the particular operational character of the latter's own intentionality, and now cognition must negate this leveling and the resulting uniformity of all its constituent objects in order to distinguish the real amongst all the remainder. Merleau-Ponty insists that, on the contrary, there are "two 'orders' [the cognitive and the perceptual] . . . which are set up within us before acts of discrimination which intervene only in equivocal cases, and in which what we live comes to settle of itself" (*VI*62F). In most cases, there is no need for the perceiver to decide whether the percept is a mere object of thought or a thing itself; for the former is experienced as the

---

4. H. P. Grice uses a similar argument when he states that I should "reject any demand that I should justify my claim until specific grounds for doubting it have been indicated. It is essential to the sceptic to assume that any perceptual claim may, without preliminaries, be put on trial and that innocence, not guilt, has to be proved; but this assumption is mistaken." "The Causal Theory of Perception," in Ernest Nagel and Richard B. Brandt, eds., *Meaning and Knowledge*, p. 602.

exercising or expressing of a cognitive structure, while the latter is given as a triggering of our perceptual capacities.

There are, no doubt, equivocal cases of perception where our discursive acts and principles can aid us (if our concerns and interests require it) in separating the real and the fictional. However, what must be noted is that perception only uses cognition's techniques in *crisis situations* and that its discriminatory powers do not guarantee a solution. I take up an analytic attitude "when I am afraid of being mistaken" (*F*262), because that aspect of the given which can be cognitively presented may fit one of my inductive principles assuring me, to some degree of credibility, that my perception is accurate. The justification conditions of our perceptual knowledge-claims can only deal with that limited part of our experience that is thematizable. Hence, the conclusions it draws concern a select sector of our experience; at the most they yield inductive evidence for the status of the whole; and they are never able to present us with the object as it gives itself in evidence.[5] The analytic epistemologist is concerned correctly with principles of justification and ought to favor some form of induction; but what he must realize is that his rules do not allow him to infer from the status of "inner" *cogitationes* a world that exists in itself and "outside."[6] It is instead the case that his inductions proceed from a part to the whole and at best only give probable information about the activities of the perceptual regions of our body. Therefore, epistemology can never hope to find criteria that would be infallible, or that would match even the certainty that is given to us with perceptual opinion. To make up for what is left behind by, or inaccessible to, reflection, a truth condition must always be added to the analyst's other jointly

---

5. When we wish to signify the dominant English sense of the word *evidence*, we shall use the phrase *inductive evidence* (taking *inductive* in a correspondingly broad manner) and we shall continue to use *evidence* as equivalent to the French, *évidence*. The difference between these two uses of *evidence* is apparent in their syntax. *Evidence* is a sortal or particularizing noun, while (inductive) evidence is a mass noun. Thus one can pluralize the former (evidents and evidences) and speak of "one evidence" or "an evidence"; but one must speak of the latter in terms of "pieces of evidence" or "some evidence" ("an evidence" in this sense is extremely awkward, and "some evidences" grammatically incorrect). In the inductive sense, one can use properly "an evident . . . ," but then it is an adjective and not a noun.

6. Cf. R. M. Chisholm's excellent attempt to explicate such principles in *Theory of Knowledge*.

sufficient conditions of "perception" and "knowledge." But for Merleau-Ponty lived perception has its own operative form of belief which he calls opinion or faith and which is, during the affirmation itself, justified by the inseparable evidence of this act and its object. There is no need for a truth condition, for evidence is the experience of "being in truth" (*VI*12) and only comes into being through a contact with Being. Hence, for example, Chisholm's attempts to discover cognitive principles that would account for the evident must fail (cf. Chapter 4.4). Furthermore, cognition's suppression of our lived perceptual contact also explains the analytic philosopher's need to make sensation into a cognitive presentation which may then lead to the hypothesizing of sense-data. Similarly, he makes "sensing" into a discrete and isolatable condition of "perception," which is then understood as completely distinct from perceptual belief, truth, and justification. As we shall see below (chapter 4.3), Merleau-Ponty rejects the whole analytic endeavor to give pragmatic definitions (clearly enumerating necessary and sufficient conditions) to "perception" or "knowledge," for this assumes incorrectly that the intrinsic character of these types of consciousness can be exhaustively articulated by reflection and in its own terms. The notion of hyletic data is attractive similarly, for by postulating a "real concrete content" (*F*278) within the cognitive realm (the only one open to reflection), it means to preserve the phenomenologically inescapable fact that our perceptual experience inheres in otherness.

We can learn more about the process of sublimation by studying Merleau-Ponty's analysis of the relation between actual perception and the "thought of perception." Most dualist epistemologies put great stress on the distinction between the two. They intend to show that the latter is always certain and incorrigible while the former is always open to doubt, hoping thereby to prove that the latter is independent of and prior to perceptual claims about the world. Although we shall examine the certainty and "direct" evidence of the "thought of perception" in great detail in sections 3 and 4, we can now improve our understanding of the cognitive region's relation to perception by explaining Merleau-Ponty's criticism of the claim that the "thought of perception" is prior to actual perception, in the case of two possible senses of "thought of perception": first, as the cognitive realm's version of lived perception and, secondly, as awareness of the cognitive constitution of the external world.

If "thought of perception" is the cognitive realm's version of lived perception, "in the restricted sense of alleged [*prétendue*] vision or the 'impression of seeing', then we will have the certitude of a possible or probable" which implies that we had a "genuine" perception to which this "bears a resemblance and in which the certainty of the thing was, on those occasions, involved" (*F*430). Merleau-Ponty agrees with Husserl that when we reflect on experience or live within the cognitive realm we "decompose the bond . . . between my self and my vision," for we "break its structuration," "interrogate," "surprise," and "describe" (*F*264) the look.[7] Instead of the ego naturally living in the perceptual region, our "existential current" runs through the cognitive realm, with the result that we "distance" (*F*457) ourselves as far as possible from our perceptual thrownness. The most favorable reading we can give to this "thought" (which makes the strongest case for its actually giving us some information about lived perception) is that our object becomes the subject-side of perception, beyondness is reduced, and our perceptual structures are given to us from a cognitive point of view. The thought of a particular perception is, then, "a possible" in two interconnected senses: it is the potentiality of an infinitude of concrete and actual situations which are all named by the same "thought"; it is "probable" rather than real, for its actual inherence in otherness has been omitted, and thus its horizonal and indeterminate references are lost to this clear thought.

> The certainty of a possibility is no more than the possibility of a certainty, the thought of seeing is only a vision in idea [*en idée*] and we could not have it unless we had on other occasions vision in reality [*en réalité*]. (*F*430)

We are certain of these particular thoughts only because they refer to possible future and past perceptions. We know that they are possible because we acquired our present cognitive grasp of them by sublimating a particular concrete perceptual experience or situation. They are thus the possibility of a certainty because the foundational experience of certainty is given with the evidence of a perceptual situation (cf. chapter 4.3), and this situation can be given only if it is triggered by otherness. Merleau-Ponty says here in the strongest terms that the thought's certainty is derivative from and parasitic on the primary certainty we attain with the activation of one of our

7. *Ideas: General Introduction to Pure Phenomenology*, pp. 124-25.

lived structures or when we encounter the thing itself. Cognition would not have, at the level of specification it desires, instantiated constant structures from which it could abstract if these structures had not been activated or clearly differentiated by an actual contact with otherness. Merleau-Ponty frequently uses the distinction between entities "in idea" and "entities in reality or act," for he always insists on the difference between cognition and perception. More exactly, he is stating that some of the structures which operationally exist in act can be sublimated, giving rise to cognitive equivalents whose essential characteristic is to be presented in idea. "The world in idea [*en idée*] . . . [is] only an abstract construction, and not a concrete consciousness, of the world" (*F*431).

In the second sense, which is intellectualist—where "thought of perception" is understood as awareness of the cognitive constitution of the external world—it is claimed that a "thought of perception" is the "consciousness we have of our constituting power" (*F*430). If our perception were entirely constituted by cognitive structures, perception would indeed give us apodictic certainty. But then, as in an "absolute realism," (*F*430) we would totally coincide with our object, which would be equally certain. Hence, "transcendental idealism" (*F*430) does not prove that the thought and its certainty are independent from, and primary to, the given object, but that thought "is only certain if actual vision is equally so" (*F*431).

Merleau-Ponty's denial of the total constitution of the world can best be grasped through his understanding of Husserl's eidetic reduction. He states that Husserl makes a self-contradictory assertion when he holds that "the world is constituted by me and that out of the constitutive operation, I can grasp no more than the outline [*dessin*] and the essential structures" (*F*430-31). He agrees that essences or cognitive objects are only a shadow or sketch of our full lived experiences, and he asserts that Husserl should have become aware of the implications of this "when he concedes that any transcendental reduction is at the same time an eidetic one" (*F*430, n., and *VI*45). Merleau-Ponty's interpretation of this famous formula implies that a full reduction is impossible and must break down: our thematization of the given quickly reaches a point where it can make no further progress but where it is still far short of delineating or capturing the richness of the full concrete phenomenon. Every ideation and its resulting essence "is formed in a space of existence, under the guarantee of my duration" (*VI*111). In other words, I must keep a hold on the experience that inheres in the world in order to "guide" (36) the acquisition of its cognitive derivative. Throughout the stages of the imaginative variation, I am assured that I am directed to a *single* experience, first because this experience has a prereflective identity or constancy that is an essential feature of perception (chapter 3.2), and, secondly, because my constant switching between focusing on this entity and cognitively manipulating it coheres through the opaque temporal unity of my Existence (*VI*37-38).

We reach the solidity or "essentiality of the essence" (*VI*111) through our power to vary the contingent circumstances that adhere to a type of experience. But "total variation" (*VI*111) is impossible, for it would mean that every motive must be transparent, or that all the horizons of possible experiences that are interconnected with the focus, as well as all aspects of its present field, must be made perfectly explicit. As we have learned, a concrete essence is given only insofar as it is actualized within the world or is totally bound to the gestalt of structures that constitute this world. Therefore, a "pure essence" (*VI*111) is impossible and, as Merleau-Ponty frequently reminds us, this explains why Husserl never arrived at final essences but always altered their descriptions (*VI*116). We have enough imaginative capacity to be able often to pick out inessential features of a type of experience, but we never attain a guarantee that what remains is "necessary" (*VI*112). "In order to affirm that [the necessity] I should have to soar over my field . . . which . . . would deprive me of that very cohesion in depth [*en épaisseur*] of the world and of Being without which the essence is subjective folly and arrogance" (*VI*112). In fact, if we could isolate and explicate all of these motives and horizons, we would find that they were all equally essential or, alternately, all equally inessential. (In the first case, the world would become the purely constituted noema of the reflective-cognitive ego, and, in the second, ideation would always be left empty-handed and cognition would have no function in Existence.) Unless the perceptual experience in its lived form was retained throughout the variation and in the resulting essence, there would be nothing to direct or control it. Like all cognitive structures, essences can never lose their reference to the prereflective experiences on which they were founded and, thus, contrary to what Husserl claims in the *Ideas*, the essence does not control the variation. For example, Merleau-Ponty describes in detail that what guides the geometer's deliberations, inspires his demonstrations, and accounts for their necessity is not a reflective grasp on a pure geometric essence but the "intuitive" (384) grasp of a prereflective motor-perceptual structure of lived bodily space (383-87).[8] The essence is a result of a cognitive manner of approaching the experience itself, which as a first-order unified existential situation is *beyond* this thematic activity. Our cognitive structures, like our perceptual structures, are situationally related to an otherness that transcends them. But the otherness of our cognitive experiences is the prereflective level of our own Existence. One does have an "incontestable power . . . to disengage the possible from the real," but this does not mean "that the real is a simple variant of the possible" (*VI*112). On the contrary, "the world is that reality of which the necessary and the possible are merely provinces" (398).

We are now in a position to understand Merleau-Ponty's criticism of Descartes's *cogito ergo sum*.

> I am not a constituting thought and my "I think" is not an "I am" unless I am able through thought to equal the concrete richness of the world and reabsorb facticity. (*F*431, *n*.)

> It is not the "I am" which is preeminently contained in the "I think" . . . but conversely the "I think" which is re-integrated into the transcending process of the "I am" and consciousness in existence. (383)

The "I think" is exclusively the formula for the cognitive realm. Hence to say that it always accompanies perception as Kant does is merely to say that there is always the capacity of thought to abstract to some extent from the "opacity of existence" (*F*430, n.). For Merleau-Ponty, this Kantian principle says no more than that the cognitive realm is part of our unified being-in-the-world and has the power to disclose, sublimate, or put into its own terms aspects of the structures of the other regions. We shall see that such a claim is not of special interest, for sublimation is an instance of the intertranslatability or reversibility that holds between all regions. Since the "I am" is the formula for our total Existence, the "I think," which is

---

8. "The concrete essence of the triangle . . . is not an ensemble of objective 'properties', but the formula of an attitude, a certain modality of my hold on the world, a structure" (*F*442).

but one part, cannot imply it. We are not able by means of what we have available to us cognitively to infer the richness, complexity, and infinite interdeterminations that give us the single thrust of Existence and define our primordial contact with the world. We shall soon note that cognition is even incapable of reabsorbing its own facticity (its distinctive mode of operational intentionality) through its thematic structures.

It is "not my existence that is brought down to the consciousness which I have of it" (384), but just the reverse. This and the above quotations are meant to remind us of the dialectic between sexuality and Existence (and objective economics and history) on which Merleau-Ponty spends much time (158 ff.). Like sexuality, cognition is a major region of Existence. Since Existence is found in the interweaving of these primordial regions, Existence without cognition is as inconceivable as cognition without Existence. We have sufficiently noted that it is false to claim that "all Existence is cognitive,"[9] but we must understand that it is equally false to hold that cognition can be reduced to Existence: cogniton, like sexuality, rather expresses (159) or manifests Existence.

By means of Merleau-Ponty's later notion of total parts, we can understand how cognition permeates our entire world—as does sexuality—without exhausting its depth, and thus how it can be symbolic or expressive of the whole. Each of our senses is an example of a total part of the world, for we saw that each of their levels covers or sets the boundaries of the total perceptual field. But we saw that, equally, they are only incomplete parts, for the structures of each are ontologically dependent on their interrelation with the others. In discussing the intertwining or "overlapping" (*enterlacs*) of two major regions—for example, perception and gross motility—Merleau-Ponty says: "In principle all my changes of place figure in a corner of my landscape; they are recorded on the map of the visible. . . . Each of the two maps is complete. The visible world and the world of my motor projects are each total parts of the same Being" (*EM*162). This map analogy can mislead one into thinking that these two regions only blend when they are both, but separate-

---

9. This is the position that is held by intellectualists who reduce all types of existential structuring to what reason and cognition can make of them. It is strictly parallel to Freudian reductionism, which claims that all Existence is sexuality.

ly, actualized in the world (like the transparencies of a geographer). However, we have learned that the body is synergic and that all regions are intertwined. All of these regions not only share the same perceptual-natural nucleus and use the modes of structuring of the other regions as models for their own creative structurings, but they "compromise" one another (cf. chapter 3), with the result that any structure within one region indicates structures in all the others. This reversibility—which we are in the process of analyzing for cognition and perception—we have discussed in detail for perception and motility in chapter 3 and will discuss for perception and sociality in chapter 5. As with every region, then, the activation of a cognitive structure will "echo" throughout our Existence and thus can, with varying degrees of clarity, be generally symbolic of it.

His study of the effects of Schneider's existential problems on his language shows that Merleau-Ponty would also hold that, like sexuality, language (understood as speech and not merely as the language of cognition and belief) manifests the total state and general structures of Existence (171-77). Thus Merleau-Ponty can explain and justify the success that ordinary language philosophy has had in dealing with the general problems of philosophy. However, ordinary language is not the only source of truth about Existence, just as sexuality (Freud) and economics (Marx) cannot exhaust all of its dimensions. Therefore, this type of analysis cannot arrive at an adequate description of all aspects of our Existence, and its proclamation that its limits coincide with those of philosophy itself is as dogmatic as Freud's and Marx's claims.

To complete our discussion in this section, it is necessary to show that cognition, like all regions of the body-subject, is an "anonymous function" (134), and that although its reflection on itself presents a clear ego (a verbal *cogito*), it "makes use of powers obscure to me" (*VI*38), as do all types of thrownness. Descartes, when trying to present the *cogito* to us,

(turns to his own life, fixes it, objectifies it, and "characterizes" it as indubitable) . . . , [but] does not attain his goal, since a part of our existence, that which is occupied in conceptually fixing our life and thinking of it as indubitable, escapes the fixation and the thought. (*F*460)

To untangle this apparent circle, one need only recall that life or Existence is our general thrust of being-in-the-world. The cognitive realm, even when reflecting on itself, must present its object as a thetic and determinate essence. As with any other aspect of our Existence on which it focuses, it accomplishes its reflection by sublimating the indeterminate facticity of the cognitive region. The reflective act which fixates and objectifies always escapes its own thematic perspective. Similarly, if one reflects on the first-order act of reflection, the source and possibility of the second-order act will be missed. Thought is doomed to grasping only what gives itself as clear and adequate, so much so that its "map," even when applied to itself, can only grasp this partial character of itself. The facticity of cognition is like that of any innate region, for its power and ability is out of its own control (it also needs a primordial faith) and it cannot be understood by its own structures. We shall finally comprehend this "thinking nature" (374) only when we have examined, in section 4, belief's own form of operative intentionality and the logic of cognition's reflection on itself.

In the same way that all of our visual structures are motor capacities of the body-subject which center about the gaze, our cognitive structures are retained by the body-subject, especially through our linguistic motor capabilities. It is the extreme articulatory powers of speech that make possible cognition's acquisition of precise structures. Therefore, when I reflect, "I have seized my thought and my existence only through the medium of language" (F459). The clarified ego at which one arrives through reflection is, then, "merely a verbal cogito [cogito sur parole] . . . and the true formula of this cogito should be: 'one [on] thinks, one is' " (F459). It is "that of all reflecting men" and not only of our own or of Descartes's own Existence. Like the "one" of the natural self or the senses, this ego is universally shared by all men, because language in general is a cultural system that is public and intersubjective and it founds every cognitive structure we may acquire. Furthermore, our cognitive-linguistic structures level individuality because everything in our Existence which cannot be made transparent escapes their hold. It is equally important to see that this "one" is also that of an impersonal region of the body-subject. Merleau-Ponty follows Saussure in insisting that language as a specific cultural system must be comprehended as an abstraction from the primary phenomenon of speech. Hence, he variably labels this universal cognito as a "speaking cogito [cogito sur parole]" (F459), "spoken cogito [cogito parlé]" (F460), and as a "read cogito [cogito lu]" (F460). In other words, the "one" refers to linguistic capabilities that are part of the given operational gestures of the body. These can be manifest verbally, auditorily, visually, and so forth (just as motor capabilities can be variously manifest). But what must be understood is that language is necessarily embodied in one material form or another and that the body's potentiality for speech has the same mystery as all our thrown potentialities. "What one calls an idea is necessarily bound to an act of expression and owes to it its appearance of autonomy" (F447). Therefore, cognitive structures are attached to our lived existence not only through their sublimation of its prereflective situations, but also through the use of the linguistic motor capacities of the body-subject. This does not mean that they have an "inferior" ontological status to those of our perceptual structures which directly inhere in otherness, for as we have shown the contingency of the world and the facticity of the body-subject are ultimately one and the same.

Therefore, as Merleau-Ponty repeatedly states, the analytic attitude and reflective philosophy can understand themselves only if they recognize the prereflective. This is implied not only by the fact that there are other regions of Existence beside cognition or that it acquires its structures through their sublimation, but also by the fact that reflection is itself an existential act.

2. Language and Cognition

By studying creative thought, we shall again see that cognition's operations do not allow us to posit an immanent realm which has a privileged evidence and is separable from our lived Existence. Since all of cognition's processes use our linguistic capacities, if we are to comprehend the former we must have an understanding of Merleau-Ponty's phenomenology of language. Although we shall not be able to give a full explication of his theory of language, an examination of authentic language's relation to thought and its status as an icon will give us a good indication of the core of his theory and will be sufficient for the purposes of this chapter. This section will consist of three basic studies. The first will demonstrate how in general cognitive-linguistic structures belong to the body-subject and thus, like all situations, inhere in otherness. This argument will be supported by showing that all such structures remain attached to their originating experiences wherein they were acquired through a creative articulation of otherness, and that their inherent inexhaustibility or contingency results from their membership in a gestalt of cognitive structures such that, when any one is actualized, all of the remainder are maintained and made present on its horizons. Since the acquisition of a language structure is the central phenomenon for Merleau-Ponty's theory, the second study will examine one of his concrete studies which reveals the logic of language acquisition and specification in detail. The third study will examine how such structures can be public and, particularly, how they are able to be communicated to others and to be symbolic of all the other regions of Existence. As part of this, we shall show how even acts of imagination depend on the body and our natural bond to the world. These analyses will prepare the way for Merleau-Ponty's more difficult theories of evidence and truth.

The importance of the notion of authentic language to Merleau-Ponty's total theory of language is made plain by the first chapter of *The Prose of the World*. Under the title of "The Illusion [*fantôme*] of a Pure Language," he refutes the sign theory of language by constantly stressing that it cannot account for the primitive fact of creative language (see, for example, pp. 10, 13, and 14). This traditional theory holds that language consists of a system of conventional signs which merely denote cognitive significances (or states of affairs) that are essentially independent of the language in which they are expressed. Thus an ideal-language position maintains that speech is just one symbolic system among many, all of which are able to represent preexistent concepts. Merleau-Ponty holds, to the contrary, that all mathematical-scientific systems must be based on speech, for it is "the organ and resonator of all the other regions of signification and consequently coextensive with the thinkable" (*VI*118). Anything that may be thought must be "speakable" or potentially "public," for all cognition uses our everyday system of speech.

> The possession of self or the coincidence with self is not the definition of thought; thought is, on the contrary, a result of expression, and is always an illusion insofar as the clarity of the acquired rests on a fundamentally obscure operation. (*F*446)

Once cognitive-linguistic structures have been acquired, they can be used by inauthentic speech or thought, which limits expression strictly to those meanings that are already known or sedimented. When we use this stock of structures to say or think something standard and unoriginal, these meanings appear to us as perfectly clear and transparent. But if we stop ourselves in order to examine these structures or if we use them for an authentic expression, we find that they are not totally given to us but have a beyond or contingency like our perceptual structures.[10] We are satisfied to experience the world only to the extent that it fulfills our preexistent structures and, hence, miss the "nonhuman" that concretizes them. To understand, then, why sedimented thought, which Merleau-Ponty calls a "humming with words," does not coincide with itself, it is necessary to ask how all our cognitive structures have a factor of beyondness. This question directs us, in turn, to consider the creative acquisition of such structures.

At first glance, spontaneous thought would seem to have a total and apodictic hold on itself, for it appears that it already grasps a meaning and only struggles to find the most effective public expression of it. Yet, if this were the case, "one would not see thought, even solitary thought, seeking expression with such perseverance" (*F*445), for it would find its own private grasp adequate. (Merleau-Ponty's phenomenology is not alone in making this "natural tendency towards expression" fundamental to any theory of language.[11]) Cognition does not possess a spontaneous thought before it expresses it, nor does it fully capture it even when it becomes sedimented. Since we have learned that cognition sublimates an ideality when it acquires a new structure, the meaning which it seeks to make cognitively apparent is a lived situation in which one or more of the body's prereflective regions are involved. We have also seen that it fails to capture this sense, because it must be presented through the *logos* of the cognitive realm, which refines the fullness of the prereflective. Hence the body does hold a meaning, but it is obscure both to itself and to cognition. All

10. There is an exact parallel in perception to this illusion of adequacy. We experience things in a sedimented way when we merely have them as ready to hand. In this case, we are not concerned with the otherness that has triggered them or with their corrigibility and infinite specifiability, but merely with that degree of generality that is relevant to our present purposes.

11. See, for example, Max Black, *The Labyrinth of Language*, p. 135.

cognitive significances follow the logic of sublimation and extreme articulation because every new structure uses linguistic structures that have already been sedimented. Authentic thought "transcends itself" (F445) by articulating the prereflective, and "speech is just the act by which it eternalizes itself in truth" (F445). The "ideality" or "cultural entities" for which thought strives are captured and given concrete existence in language, hence becoming part of the intersubjective and thetic region of truth. Since language and cognition have the same logic of specification as our lived structures, a new meaning is acquired by differentiation from or reorganization of already sedimented linguistic structures. Since these structures are general, and the new is given in their terms (as a tension between them), the process of authentic thought is prevented from coinciding with or totally exhausting the sense it seeks. When this sense has been sufficiently specified or linguistically articulated, it will always carry a reference to the originating experience which it has necessarily failed to conquer but which has motivated and guided its formation. It is necessary to add the qualification that all cognitive specifications need not be direct sublimations of our prereflective Existence, for they may be "narcissistic" and "internal" to the language system. In such a case, specification will result from a need to clarify the relations between already sedimented structures. Accordingly, language's power to speak about itself can give rise to special languages and logico-mathematical systems.

A cognitive-linguistic structure is dense (épais) not only because of its initial originating experience. As Merleau-Ponty notes, authentic language is a "paradoxical operation" (F445) because it uses given meanings to capture an intention that transcends them, while at the same time it "fixes" (F445) these sedimented structures and "recasts them all" (178) by using them in a new context. "It is by having been employed in different contexts that the word little by little charges itself with a sense which it is impossible to fix absolutely" (F445). Whenever a sedimented structure is used in the articulation of a new structure, the former's position in the "hierarchy" must change. It will find its sense either by differentiating itself from the new structure (as it did by locating itself in terms of the old), or by taking on a new way of combining with other sedimented structures. This gestalt of language can be roughly represented by the following example: a particular noun gets its sense by separating itself from every other noun of the same category. This category is then defined by its differentiation from every other category of noun (determined by their "depth grammar"). Finally, every noun and every category is determined by the way it may combine with all the other "parts of speech." Merleau-Ponty agrees with ordinary language philosophy that linguistic meaning is not self-subsistent, and that if it can be found anywhere it is to be found in language's use. With the later members of this school, he shows that, as in any kind of situation, one cannot clearly define and exhaustively establish such a "rule of use." These sediments that adhere to every linguistic meaning show us why they must always escape our grasp and why the speaker or thinker can always "find in his own words more than he thought he put there" (F445). It is only because their meaning is beyond what the speaker knows that conversations, self-dialogue, or mere self-expression can suggest new meanings and ideas; that they can drag their participants along with them, much as does the perceptual world; and that "consciousness can learn something" (178). It is important explicitly to conclude that every cognitive-linguistic structure gets its sense from every other such structure since they all form the gestalt that articulates the present cognitive realm. This also implies (as we shall see in chapter 4.4 in detail) that an actualized cognitive structure holds and keeps present all the other structures on its horizon.

Since it is essential to Merleau-Ponty's theory that all newly originated meanings presuppose a sedimented language system, he must explain how the first acquisitions of language are possible. His theory of innate structures, with which we are well acquainted, allows him to do this without difficulty. Like Chomsky, he believes we have what is in Merleau-Ponty's language called a "thrown capacity" for language acquisition. In "The Child's Relations with Others," he shows that we have a natural sympathy toward the gestures of others or a power of mimesis that allows us to absorb them, and that the child acquires "chunks" of language through imitating sets of phonemes and morphemes which are then given their standard sense through his lived experiences. This learning will follow the logic of the specification of differentiation levels where a group, or series, of species will simultaneously be acquired. And, of course, the child's capacity to sublimate from the lived to the cognitive is given: it is an instance of Existence's natural unity and intertranslatability.

In this same lecture, Merleau-Ponty's study of jealousy illustrates the way that important existential (temporal) and linguistic structures are acquired through the emotional breakdown of the central structures in a child's interhuman world. This study is of importance to us, first, because it gives us a case of cognition's sublimation of a structure of sociality; secondly, because it shows us how such a basic existential structure is manifest in a number of regions; thirdly, because it allows us to deepen our previous explication of the logic of creative specification (cf. chapter 2.2); and, finally, because it shows us precisely how a founded cognitive-linguistic structure intertwines with its founding region, even to the extent where it radically alters the constitution of this region's own structures.

The emotion of jealousy is extreme and critical when the youngest child's role in the family is usurped by that of a newborn sibling. Up to this point, the child's position in his family was his means for entering the human world; the loss of this role breaks the child's relation to this world. [12] Since this emotion results from the threat to a global grasp of the world, it is traumatic. Or, like anxiety, but to a lesser extent, it presents a "limit situation" which reduces his comfortable and secure involvements in the world. [13] The child's jealousy "is essentially a refusal to change his situation" and "consists in a rigid attachment to his present" (*CO*110). In this experience, the child encounters a dangerous present which disproves the absolute and static form of his being with others. Since it demonstrates the inadequacy of his structures and the corruption of his interpersonal world, the experience can be harmful unless the child can overcome it (*CO*112). The solution to this frustration is for the child to create a structure that will help him to understand that the roles in the family are interchangeable or, more generally, that

12. Hence, although the object of the jealousy is the newborn child and the role that it occupies, this intentional object acts more as a symbol than is usually the case when the intentional object is an actual determinant of the emotion itself (as, for example, are the objects of envy and hate).

13. Merleau-Ponty's theory of trauma and repression is clearly stated on pp. 82-85 of the *Phenomenology* and is entirely consistent with this later study.

social attitudes are replaceable and historical. It "is overcome thanks to the constitution of a schema of past-present-future" (*CO*110).

For the subject, the situation of jealousy will be the occasion of restructuring his relationship with others in the milieu in which he lives, and at the same time of acquiring new dimensions of existence (past, present, future) with a supple play between these different dimensions. (*CO*15F)

It is a whole usage of language as well as a way of perceiving the world. (*CO* 113)

The aspect of language that the child learns to use is the imperfect of the past and future. Previous to this new acquisition, the child was acquainted with the more general structures of past, present, and future, for he could use the past and future definite. Now he is able to interrelate these different dimensions, for his use of the imperfect shows that he can comprehend a "present that is past" and a "present that is futural." Yet the acquisition of this linguistic structure is secondary and parasitic on that of the lived structure which will be essential to the child's understanding of history and society. The child acquires the structure "somewhat like this: I *have been* the youngest, but I *am* the youngest no longer, and I *will become* the biggest" (*CO*110). The child is not creating totally new structures but is specifying his general grasp of the different temporal dimensions. But these dimensions are still incomplete: for example, the pluperfect does not appear and the imperfect is used selectively. It may well be the case here that, rather than becoming more specific, there is an addition of a new species (the imperfect) to other species (the definite) at the same level of specification.

"The acquisition of modes of expression always represents a sort of crisis, in which a whole realm of expression is annexed in a single stroke" (*CO*17F). There are cases of progress without "apparent emotion" but they are always "interrupted," "unstable," or "discontinuous" (*CO*17F). The child will only acquire such structures when it becomes clear to him that his present sedimented situations are not sufficient to accommodate his milieu, thus, even when acquiring mundane modes of behavior, the child will be traumatized. Unless he experiences the breakdown of his situation and the way in which newly absorbed attitudes correct this deficiency, his new structures will not be anchored in the past (the acquired system of structures) nor will they express a new mode of being-in-the-world.[14]

We have said that this form of language-acquisition is parasitic because a language structure can only become meaningful if it is founded on the lived meaning of an actual situation. "The acquisition of this temporal structure . . . gives a meaning to the corresponding linguistic instruments" (*CO*110). We have also learned that all ideas or pure significances sublimate or refine a concrete ideality that already exists in the prereflective or nonthetic realm. However, there are many cases where we possess the linguistic instruments (as well as all kinds of gestures) before we have the lived experiences from which they will get their sense. The child who speaks possesses many linguistic groupings which he does not yet understand. He can have linguistic instruments which are still meaningless to him, because he is already using his phonetic capacities and has the power of imitating all types of human gestures. These areas of language (verbal tenses in our example) exist as a question for the child until his lived experiences can disclose their meaning. Therefore, one must not conclude that there is a realm of pure ideas for whose expression the child could arbitrarily create linguistic tools. Just the opposite is the case, for an experience has a certain ideational or cognitive form because of the preexistent means of its linguistic expression. We can now see that cognitive meanings are determined by the language of the child's culture as well as being founded in lived structures. But, like all founded structures, they exert a counterinfluence on the founding structures. Since the cognitive structure is given a clue about how to articulate itself by the preexistent linguistic instruments, and since the cognitive-linguistic and lived structures come into existence simultaneously, and, finally, since cognitive labeling will help the retention and reapplication of a lived structure, we can conclude that a culture's language system will also have an important influence on the way in which lived experiences are finally structured.

---

14. They will only be continuous with the past system of structures if they modify them because of a felt deficiency in the system, otherwise the system will not expand temporally (or historically) as it must (cf. chapter 2.4).

In order to understand how we can comprehend the speech of another and how this conversation can communicate authentic structures, it will be necessary to study the "icon" as the physical expression of operative intentions. In speaking of the structures correlative to any perception, Merleau-Ponty writes:

> Things have an internal equivalent in me; they arouse in me a carnal formula of their presence. Why shouldn't these[the formulae or structures] in their turn give rise to some trace, yet visible, where any other look will rediscover the motifs that support its own inspection of the world? Thus, there appears a visible of the second power, a carnal essence or icon of the first. (*EM*164)

Merleau-Ponty calls our potential structures carnal formulae, for they are the bodily principles or capabilities that pattern and organize our lived situations. Our study of sublimation has given us a concrete example of the way in which the structures of lived situations can be assimilated to the *logos* of our cognitive region. Parallel to this intertranslation, it is possible, through the use of the productive imagination, to create equivalent structures in any one region for the structures that naturally belong to another. For example, physical language is a visual or auditory icon of a cognitive structure, for it is the expression of these cognitive capabilities in perceptual terms. Similarly, the gesture that I witness in another person is the visual icon of that person's present phenomenal orientation toward the world. But as Merleau-Ponty shows in "The Eye and the Mind" and in *The Prose of the World*, we can attain a better understanding of verbal expression if we put it within the context of expression in general and particularly that of the plastic arts.

The icon or carnal essence is not identical to a concretely existing situation (the concrete essence proper) or to the carnal formula which denotes the abstract structure or subject-side of a situation. On the contrary, it appears to correspond to the object-side, especially in the case of painting. There we see that a painter produces a visual icon for a sensible entity, which expresses this entity by triggering its correlative structures. Yet obviously the painting does not give us the same otherness that is present to our natural perception. Merleau-Ponty says that the imaginary in general gives a "quasi-presence and immanent visibility" (*EM*24F) and that, in the painting, "significance precedes existence and clothes itself in only the minimum of matter necessary for its communication" (323). In the case of the real, we saw that essence and existence merged in its inexhaustibility and infinite structurability. In a painting we have a "matter" that triggers our visual structures in much the same way as does the real but without its beyondness. In other words, we may say that the painting as an icon gives us the object-side of a visual situation in isolation from otherness.

How are we to conceive of an object-side in isolation, for our first principle was that a situation can only be given and actualized when it inheres in otherness? The icon is the closest Merleau-Ponty gets to the noema taken as an intentional object that is immanent or inexistent to the act. We can arrive at this "pure noema" through the imaginative reproduction of our lived structures. But just as we could not find a pure cognitive act that coincided with itself, even purely fictional imagination cannot create new structures *ex nihilo* but can only manipulate or translate the structures that are already held by the body-subject's facticity.[15] "The world has at least once emblazoned in him [the painter] the ciphers of the visible" (*EM*166). Returning to the description of the painting, Merleau-Ponty says: "It is more accurate to say that I see according to it, or with it, than that I see it" (*EM*164). "Neither the design nor the painting belongs to the in-itself any more than the image does. They are the inside of the outside and the outside of the inside" (*EM*164). Just as we could not say "where" a sense-datum or colored area was located, except that it occurred on a uniform fictional plane, the painting is not a constitutive part of our natural space (chapter 3.4). An icon triggers the exact structure of which it is the correlate, while the real is given through an appearance which refers to its inexhaustible inner and outer horizons. Merleau-Ponty accepts Sartre's theory of imagination, which shows that the image is distinguishable from the real because it is always given to us as fulfilled. "The hallucinatory phenomenon is no part of the world, that is to say, it is not *accessible*, there is no definite path leading from it to all the remaining experiences of the deluded subject. . . . It lacks the fullness, the inner articulation which makes the real thing reside 'in itself' and act and exist by itself" (339). The painting has the same status as the hallucination and both are the perceptual expressions of a presence (the next section will explain this claim in detail). The

15. Cf. Merleau-Ponty's example of our imagining ourselves to be on Sirius. He says that we can only treat the Alps as tiny if we take them as *"molehills"* (440).

painting is the "inside of the outside" (*EM*164) because the icon presents us with the perceptual structure more in its potential than its situational form. In other words, the fictional structure lacks the infinite reference, compossibility, and corrigibility of an actualized situation. Yet we are given the fictional structure in an objective fashion and, hence, we can say that it is the noema of a potential capacity. We perceive the artifact or image as objectively before us and do not possess its correlative potential structure in a strictly noetic fashion, as if it were the object of a reflective act. Therefore, we can speak of the icon as an object-side in isolation or as a noema of a structure, for it is merely the objective expression (with the aid of the flesh of one region) of this structure in its unactualized form. Simultaneously, it is the "outside of the inside" (*EM*164) because it is the objective manifestation of some structures that constitute the body-subject. This vagueness is a result of the essential inseparability of the subject-side and object-side of a situation. If we artificially isolate the subject-side, we can imaginatively describe it from a noematic point of view. Similarly, if we abstract the object-side from the otherness of which it is a part, we can imaginatively describe it noetically (without positing the subject's inherence in the world).

If we digress for a moment on the phenomena of abstract movement and imagination, we shall be able to establish once and for all that our structures can never be given to us in a pure and nonsituational manner or without inhering in the otherness of the world and our bodies. (Thus we shall see that even imagination cannot give us the experience of pure adequacy or apodicticity that is central to phenomenalist epistemologies.) We can understand how acts of imagination presuppose our primordial contact with the world through a discussion of Merleau-Ponty's studies of abstract movement.

Schneider's inability to perform abstract movements (*Zeigen* as opposed to *Greifen*) is a case of his more general incapacity to imaginatively reproduce situations or to create a free space within his present field that can be freely structured. Schneider is capable of *Greifen*, or of producing a sedimented situation, only if it can be supported through its inherence in otherness, or in other words only if otherness specifically demands or triggers it. Hence Schneider can only involve himself expressively or gesturally in standard, inauthentic situations which are always on the near horizon of his present field. He is only open to "centripetal" (111) movements and is thus totally at the mercy of the demands of otherness on the innate and most basic acquired openings to the world. *Zeigen*, which is impossible for him, is an example of an abstract gesture, because when one points one only *displays* or indicates a normal situational bond. One "mentions" it rather than "uses" it, for *Zeigen*, as a creative modification of a grasping, stops itself (the grasping disposition) and only "refers" to its potential involvement in the world. Pointing not only indicates an object, but also "points" to the ways (subject-sides) in which one can concretely deal with this entity.

All acts of imagination must give rise to a free space within the bounds and demands of our natural space because they use (and quasi-actualize) bodily structures which necessarily "project" (111) noemata. However, this free space is a secondary result of such acts, for they are primarily directed at our body.[16] It is only because the structures of our body constitute space that their manipulation must alter and have an effect on this space. Our abstract and imaginary acts are, indeed, not concerned with the world; however, the "material" or structures they use are just our natural openings to this world. Even when I perform an act just to observe it, I disrupt my actual field and cause a space of "nothingness" (111) to penetrate it. The subject does, of course, freely call up such structures, but they are not thereby transparently presented to him. On the contrary, he is once again thrown out into the world and relies on his body's obscure powers to structure this world.

The otherness in which these acts inhere is, therefore, that of the body. However, this is not equivalent to claiming that they are merely embodied, in the sense of having no bearing or dependence on the natural world. We can see that our principle, that the body has the same "materiality" as the world and is only the present actualization of this world, is not refuted by these types of activity by recalling that the body is only present to itself insofar as it is anchored in natural space. Free space presupposes this anchorage and can only come into being through manipulating the present field. Or, correlatively, the subject could not "play" with his potential open-

---

16. "This mimic usage ['this pointing gesture'] of our body is not yet conception, since it does not cut us off from our corporeal situation; on the contrary, it assumes all its meaning" (*Primacy of Perception*, p. 7).

ings upon the world (or open a space for experimentation and imagination) unless he had already organized and attained a grasp of himself (or was already *in* the natural world and space). Thus, free space is grounded in natural space and abstract behavior in concrete behavior. Similarly, we learned that reflective perception modifies our present perceptual field by leveling it to a "fictional plane" (chapter 3.4). It believes that it succeeds in perceiving the world as it is in reality, but it is in fact observing and isolating the structures of the perceptual body and thus necessarily projecting an equally abstract version of the perceptual world.

Let us return now to the study of the icon. Merleau-Ponty says that it is closer than a sign to the actual "since it is the diagram of the real's life in my body, its [the real's] pulp or carnal obverse [*envers*] which for the first time is exposed to the look" (*EM*24F). There is a lived reflexivity in perception which is made obvious by artistic expression. In a painting, the gaze experiences itself as looking at a visible abstract of its own potential structures. It makes the act of seeing into a "visible." The study of painting in "The Eye and the Mind" is a reduction through artistic expression to the same conclusions that are central to *The Visible and the Invisible*. It is a "contribution to the definition of our access to Being" and "any theory of painting is a metaphysics" (*EM*171). This reversibility which makes the invisible into the visible is more thoroughly demonstrated by the fact that painting gives us the "internal analogue" (*EM*165) of the structures of a region other than the visual. "To see is *to have at a distance* [*avoir à distance*]; painting spreads this strange possession to all aspects of Being, which must in some fashion become visible in order to enter into the work of art" (*EM*166). For example, a painter can give us the visual "traces" (*EM*165) of a sound or a tactile quality by transposing the structures of the latter into the visual realm. Yet painting does much more, for, like imagination, it can at least partially present any kind of structure of which the body is capable.

We can grasp the possibility of visually capturing "invisibles" such as emotions, moods, and ideas by recalling, first, Merleau-Ponty's theory of the primacy of perception, secondly, the metastructuring of this primordial contact by all our other regions, and, thirdly, the way in which all of our senses interact in the proximal situation. Since the painting can demand one of our structures with a minimal amount of ambiguity and to an exact degree of specification, the painting is able to reproduce the perceptual world that must face us in any kind of situation. We have learned that we are not overcome by the infinite demands of perceptual contact because we are able to determine the degree to which we will be open. We do so by metastructuring this primordial contact with the interests and concerns of our other regions (practical, interpersonal, and cognitive). The noematic perceptual result of this metastructuring is that our perceptual field's organization reflects our concerns. For example, moods pattern our perceptual awareness in determining both the scope of our present field and the degrees of specification that pertain to our figural entities. For example, we have seen that cognition can level the colors in a field to colored areas and reify its appearances into perspectives. In the same way that the artist can produce an internal lighting by varying the way in which his colors differentiate themselves, he can visually present attitudes and desires by making certain entities in his painting figural and by determining the specificity with which each of these entities is given. He can produce the visual icon of a particular tactile structure by visually creating that mode of appearance which must modify the color and shape of any entity which possesses that tactility. Of course, when he effectively presents us with the genuine color of an object, we must also have its shape, size, tactility, and to a lesser extent its sonority, and taste; for, as we have seen, the color constant of a type of thing is determined by that single proximal compromise in which the maximum articulation of every sense is given. The painter motivates those of our visual structures that are always correlative to such a constant, and hence he communicates the way in which he wishes us to perceive the spectacle.

But the painter can do much more, for he is able to transmit authentic situations. He can give the viewer constants that he has never possessed. He can teach us manners of existing, ways of life, moods or tasks that we have never experienced. More mundanely, he can produce for us a lighting that we have never seen. Yet, like all authentic communication, this cannot be achieved without a creative act on the part of the spectator. When he is confronted with a totally new situation that is as highly delimited as the artistic, his sedimented structures show themselves to be insufficient for mastering its precise requirements. In order to conquer this authentic vision, he must specify and reorganize his sedimented structures in an originating way and acquire the new structure that the artifact demands. The same logic applies to the literary arts or, more commonly, to authentic speech.

Language serves the same role as the artist's icon by giving us an object-side in isolation. Descriptive language triggers cognitive-linguistic structures which either refer to their sublimated prereflective situations or to other cognitive structures. In the first case, speech takes us out into the world through the thematic medium of cognition; "it is but a second version of it [the lived world], a more manageable derivative" (*VI*150). Merleau-Ponty continues by approvingly quoting Proust, who says of the cognitive givenness of a musical experience (by means of its score and abstract notation) that the subject has only "bare values substituted for the mysterious entity he had perceived, for the convenience of his understanding" (*VI*150). Hence language refers us to the world but through the descriptive conventions of the cognitive realm. In the second case, speech refers us to other cognitive-linguistic structures. This is the standard instance of inauthentic speech, "a secondary expression, a speech on speech [*une parole sur des paroles*]" (*F*207,n.). The speaker merely reorganizes and recombines sedimented meanings by using a standard grammatical and logical syntax or perhaps by producing new subject-predicate combinations with the aid of categories of a Kantian type. When we hear or read language, we are given sensible icons which produce an "echo" in our cognitive-linguistic body and which demand a particular transitional synthesis of certain linguistic gestures. Like the artistic icon, we do not perceive the physical marks or sounds for themselves, but we "think in accordance with them." Similarly, in solitary thought, we "speak with ourselves," using our phonetic body to express and hold the meanings with which we are concerned. A listener has the possibility of comprehending authentic speech because he shares sedimented structures with the speaker, who must use the same means to express himself. The incompatibilities and tensions in the given structures will guide the listener toward this new sense but, again, only if he makes a creative effort himself. Until the authentic phrase can be sedimented as a proper cognitive structure and thus become reexpressible in many ways, it remains imprisoned in its original mode of expression. Such is the case with creative literature, and particularly poetry, which uses our linguistic capacities to creatively express other regions rather than cognitively sublimating them or producing a thematic version of them. Like the painting, language

can sustain a sense by virtue of its own arrangement and catch a meaning in its own mesh. . . . As the musical notation is a *facsimile* made after the event, an abstract portrait of the musical entity, language as a system of explicit relations between sign and signified, sounds and meaning, is a result and a product of the operative language in which sense and sound are in the same relationship as the little [musical] phrase and the five notes [notation] found in it afterwards. (*VI*153)

Sublimation is only one side of a process which reverses itself by making the founded structures influence the prereflective situations that ground them. Once our cognitive structures have matured through the extreme articulatory powers of language, "the whole landscape is overrun with words as with an invasion, it is henceforth but a variant of speech before our eyes" (*VI*155). Language not only aids the understanding, but it provides our lived perception with a new structure which will clarify its dealings with the natural world. We noted earlier that not only was the proximal situation attained with the maximum articulation of the different senses, but also it took our other regions, and particularly gross motility, into consideration. We can now begin to see how cognition intertwines with the other constant structures. "The denomination of objects does not follow upon recognition; it is itself recognition. . . . The word bears the meaning, and, by imposing it on the object, I am conscious of reaching that object" (177). Language will provide a handle for the achievement of object situations, which are the main constituents of natural space, by making the differentiations between things and between their properties more precise. It is a major means for retaining sedimented structures and thus for developing increasingly intricate specifications, as well as for using them in imaginative contexts. The presence of cognitive-linguistic structures on the horizon of every percept—"it is on the same footing as its colour or its form" (178)—will give the perceiver the possibility of turning to them in crisis situations that need precise articulation. Hence "naming" in the broadest sense gives us the capacity to take a limited cognitive interest in our field while still being perceptually engaged in it. "Silent vision falls into speech, and in return, speech opens a field of the nameable and sayable . . . , it metamorphoses the structures of the visible world and makes itself a gaze of the mind [*regard de l'esprit*] " (*VI*203F).

3. The Evident and the True

One cannot separate Merleau-Ponty's theory of evidence from his understanding of truth and certainty, and thus these three topics will be interwoven in the following investigation. We shall see that the experience of evidence gives us the foundational experience of certainty. Since it is the experience of our primordial contact with Being, and since "being-in-truth is not distinct from being-in-the-world" (*F*452), it is also our openness to truth. Because it is the "definitive experience of the real" (*VI*40) or generally of the situational unity between subject and object, we shall come to understand it as the key or "privileged experience" (20) on which all of Merleau-Ponty's epistemology and metaphysics is based. We live in and by such experiences because they constitute each present (being given only through the triggering of or merging with otherness), hold the entire spatio-temporal world on their horizons, commit us to a future and a comprehension of our past, and give us the consciousness of our contact with every kind of entity. However, we shall see that these experiences cannot be taken as absolute, apodictic, or incorrigible, and that they are surrounded by, and continuous with, appearance, illusion, and error. Yet we shall also learn that the contingency that characterizes evidence is not due to an imperfection in, or limitation of, consciousness, but is an accurate presentation of the world's and Being's own finitude.

The originality of Merleau-Ponty's theory perhaps lies primarily in his claim that evidence is strictly a characteristic of prereflective experiences. It only occurs with the completion of a lived or operative intention and thus gives us a consciousness of ourselves and the world which is nonreflective and noncognitive. The certainty (equally of our experience and its object) that it yields is a lived certainty as opposed to the certainty of logical necessity or epistemological credibility (i.e., belief "beyond a reasonable doubt").[17] We shall see in the second half of this study (chapter 4.4) that this does not imply that we cannot have evident beliefs. However, when we label a belief as evident (i.e., a cognitive act), this does not result from a reflective appraisal of its credibility (although such an

17. The latter two senses of the word *certainty* present a false alternative that dominates analytic philosophy's studies of the concept of certainty.

appraisal can be implied by it), but rather it refers to the achievement of the propositional truth at which it aims by means of its own form of *operational* intentionality. Thus we shall always have to understand Merleau-Ponty's concept of evidence in contradistinction to the notions of reflective or immanent evidence which have dominated the use of the term. The clearest way to demonstrate this distinction is by returning to the detailed examination of Merleau-Ponty's concepts of the thought of perception and of the lived certainty of the perceptual act. By once again using perception as our main example, we shall be able to thoroughly comprehend what he means by evidence, and then, we shall be in a position to apply this understanding to the much more complex occurrences of evident beliefs and doubts. Similarly, this distinction requires us to keep in mind Merleau-Ponty's two uses of the word *true*. Corresponding to prereflective evidence, he uses it as synonymous with "real," "Being," and more particularly with "things themselves," "facts," or "states-of-affairs" (34, 53, 344, *VI*146, and *VI*150). He also uses it in its more usual sense where it is applied to the beliefs that are expressed in declarative or descriptive language (17, 28, 189, 355, and 388). Both uses are common, but Merleau-Ponty's heavier than usual reliance on the first (which we shall call, following Husserl, "situational truths"[18]), can easily make us forget the prereflective status that he gives to evidence and thus can thoroughly mislead us. In the next section, when we study propositional truth, we shall see that these senses are connected.

Our purpose in these sections is not only to explicate what Merleau-Ponty means by evidence, but more importantly to attempt to disentangle and present his solutions to the many problems and questions that arise from his theory. We shall find that these can be most effectively dealt with by showing how this theory is opposed to others, and thus we shall keep his criticisms of both intellectualist and phenomenalist theories before us throughout.

We can become familiar with the main issues that arise from Merleau-Ponty's theory of evidence by examining how and why he rejects the intellectualist (and, most directly, Husserl's) concept of evidence and its relation to truth. We shall see that he agrees that

18. *Crisis*, p. 132. What Husserl here calls "scientific truths" we shall call "propositional truths."

evidence is intrinsically different from appearance or illusion and that thus it contains a "mark" of truth. His criticism turns on his taking cognition or reflection as a process of sublimation and as immediately and inherently distinguishable from lived perception or prereflective Existence in general. We will have to clarify Merleau-Ponty's own descriptions of the way evidence results from the triggering of otherness, the way it manifests primordial contact, and how it implicates the subject's entire history and all the horizons that constitute its world. These discussions lead ultimately to questioning how illusions, hallucinations, and errors are possible and how they can be described in their relation to evident perceptions. Throughout we shall be able to present Merleau-Ponty's strong criticisms of the phenomenalist's or skeptic's view of evidence. Merleau-Ponty's notions of the teleology of consciousness and the partiality and essential incompleteness of truth will demonstrate that the corrigibility of evidence is essentially related to its certain claim to truth, and that a truth in itself and an absolute falsehood are impossible. These studies will also show us the speciousness of the claim that the act or "thought" of perception gives us a "direct evidence" which is more epistemologically significant than the "indirect evidence" of the perceived object. When we have completed this discussion we shall have a paradigm study of evidence that will allow us to analyze the evidence of the internal states of the subject. The last major portion of our study will analyze the evidence of belief and its relationship to epistemic appraisals and the criteriology of reflection and then turn to Merleau-Ponty's theory of propositional truth.

Merleau-Ponty accepts the claim of the Husserlian type of intellectualism that evidence is the primary epistemological experience because it is an intuition of truth. He, too, maintains that some of our experiences have a mark of truth, and that thus there is an "intrinsic" (296) difference between appearance and reality; accordingly, we are able to identify the true and real and self-consciously separate it from the illusory and apparent. However, within the context of intellectualism the experience of evidence is characterized in ways that are clearly unacceptable to Merleau-Ponty. The intellectualist holds, first, that these experiences are "thoughts," or *cogitationes* and are thus the objects of reflection (which means, in Merleau-Ponty's terms, that they would belong to the region of cognition); secondly, that their recognition as evident stems from the reflective ego; and, thirdly, that the truths that they reveal are third-person (impersonal) and absolute propositional truths. These premises lead to the conclusions that truth is immanent to consciousness, that it is fully available within the privacy of this realm, and that evidence is apodictic, infallible, and incorrigible. For intellectualism, truths cannot help but be a part of our stream of consciousness because evidence is conferred on an experience by a reflective ego whose judgments, or epistemic evaluations, must be perfectly clear to itself. Furthermore, this ego cannot make mistakes or be fooled by illusions or falsehoods, for its experiences have the clarity of ideas and can, thus, be exhaustively thematized and grasped by means of cognitive categories. Merleau-Ponty frequently criticizes this theory both because it makes illusion and error impossible, and thus equates appearance and reality (294), and because there is nothing in our experience that corresponds to such immanent, apodictic, or "absolute evidence" (295).

Merleau-Ponty escapes these conclusions by denying all the above premises. He denies that evidence is the result of a reflective epistemological appraisal and that these experiences are part of an immanent cognitive realm. On the contrary, for Merleau-Ponty evident phenomena are lived or prereflective experiences which open us to a truth that is not absolute and in-itself, but temporal and closely tied to subjectivity. Since an evident experience is defined as what presents us with the real and true, since we have learned that perceptual experience is situational or is a being-in-contact-with the world, and since the cognitive version, translation, or sublimation of perception leaves behind this opaque bond with reality and truth, the evident must be understood in terms of our lived contact with Being. Furthermore, far from constituting the evident and having it as its object, reflection in fact negates and abolishes the evident certainty of our lived experiences. Merleau-Ponty can thus maintain that evidence is a mark of the real and is intrinsically different from the illusory and fictitious, without maintaining that evidence can be a reflective or analytic test, criterion, or definition (such as a "pragmatic definition," which would claim to be able to give the necessary and sufficient conditions of our experience of the real). The evident is to be found in those very aspects of our lived experience that cannot be sublimated by cognitive reflection. The "relationship" (*VI*35) that cannot be thematized is characterized by Merleau-Ponty as our "initiation to" (*VI*35), "openness upon" (*VI*35), "blending with" (*VI*38), and "mute contact" (*VI*38) with the world. This relationship is cut by the "hypothesis of inexistence" (*VI*36 and *VI*38), while evidence is just the experience of existence.

Merleau-Ponty's argument is strong, for it appears to be a correct analysis of the meaning of the word *evident*. Austin supports Merleau-Ponty, for both argue that "evident" talk cannot be reduced to, or is categorically different from, "justification" talk, which corresponds to reflection. In other words, as Austin states, we only speak of inductive evidence, reasons, credibility, and principles and criteria of justification when our subject-matter is beliefs or opinions; and this practice is categorically opposed to the ordinary use of *evident*, whose subject matter is truths, facts, things, and in general the objects of knowledge.[19] Merleau-Ponty, of course, would unhesitantly broaden "knowledge" to include that of the noncognitive body-subject, but he similarly maintains that belief-claims hedge knowledge-claims when he speaks of reflection reducing our "assurance" (*VI*12 and *F*438) and "confidence" (*F*343) of being-in-the-world. Therefore, *evident* is not normally or properly applied to reflective beliefs or thoughts (for example, to statements of the form "*S* believes that *S* perceives *p*" [*S* thinks that . . . ; It seems to *S* that . . . , etc.]), but only to existential or lived acts of knowledge and their objects.[20]

However, Merleau-Ponty maintains, as against Austin, that evidence is a mark or a type of experience that gives us a knowledge of the world and truth. What he must show, then, is how evidence can be experienced and recognized as such (and how we, thereby, actively distinguish appearance from reality) without our being reflectively conscious of it. Merleau-Ponty states that "I can experience more things than I represent to myself, and my being is not reducible to what expressly appears to me concerning myself" (296). Nevertheless, there is no pure "unconscious" (296), for consciousness or any form of Existence is "not concealed from itself" (296). In order to understand the consciousness of self that accompanies all nonreflective acts of Existence, we need only recall the logic of

19. E.g., *Sense and Sensibilia*, p. 115.

20. Later we shall see that when we characterize a belief as evident, we might be stating that it is true or that its physical expression is evidently perceived, but not that it has been reflectively appraised as reasonable or well supported.

operational or motor intentionality that we explicated through the notion of perceptual proximity. We saw there that "perception is inseparable from the consciousness which it has, or rather is, of reaching the thing itself" (374). Perceptual subjectivity knows and meets itself when it belongs to or actively inheres in an evident object. Its self-consciousness is a result of gathering itself together in "the term of an approach" (*VI*40) by achieving a maximum grasp of its lived intention. An evident perception, like temporality, grasps itself when it "gathers together [*recueillir*]" (*F*269) all the motives, occasions, and unfulfilled appearances which it seeks to articulate. This "present" of perception coheres with its whole sedimented past, and its present horizons, and it lays out a future on which it pins its faith and which it approaches with confidence. Perception only knows itself as such when its appearing or blurred structures resolve themselves by, and culminate in, an evident perception. It is a process of reaching truth through encountering otherness (that is, through uncertainty, illusion, error, or "untruth"), and thus it must essentially be able to distinguish the real from the fictitious and deceptive. However, it is understandable that "I am capable of omitting this distinction, I am capable of illusion" (*F*343), and that appearance and reality are not separable in the manner of "adequate and inadequate thought" (*F*343).

This action and operation of lived perceptual intentionality makes the experience of evidence possible and, since it is just what distinguishes the prereflective from the reflective, its mark or "sign" cannot be thematized (and thus cannot serve as a reflective test or criterion of the evident). Merleau-Ponty has not only shown us that there is an intrinsic difference between appearance and reality, but also that there is an intrinsic difference between reflective and prereflective consciousness. When we recall that the prereflective is a being-outside-itself and in-the-world, we can see that Merleau-Ponty has shown that "there is no sphere of immanence" (376) or "private" (377) realm of consciousness that might be correlative to the world. One can indeed hold that there is a stream of experience, but the phenomena that constitute this stream essentially differ according to their own regions, as does the form of subjectivity or *cogito* that lives in them. All regions have a distinctive mode of making present such that their intrinsic difference from one another is available to us "immediately" (*VI*39). This stream consists only partially of *cogitationes* (in the sense of objects of reflective thought) and thus is only partially open to the *logos* and categories of the reflective ego. These experiences constitute our life with all its obscurity and inaccessibility to thetic and thematic reflection, and they are thus not the leveled and homogeneous experiences that constitute Husserl's or James's immanent realm of consciousness. There is a substantive and not merely a temporal distinction between these phenomena such that they transcend the reflective ego in the same way that the thing transcends perception. However, one must not conclude that Merleau-Ponty equivocates between two types of intrinsic difference (between appearance and reality, on the one hand, and perception and reflection, on the other): the evident perception is the epitome of perceptual experience (it is where perception knows itself), and its mark as an evident experience is one and the same as its mark as a perceptual experience. The experience of evidence will not, therefore, be of a propositional truth but of a situational truth, and it will be "ambivalent" (296) and ambiguous to the thetic powers of reflection.

The evident certainty of an act of perception (as opposed to a "thought of perception") must include the certainty of its object being an actual entity within the world. The experience of evidence does not refer either to an act or an object in isolation from the other but to their unity within the perceptual situation. It is inconceivable for Merleau-Ponty that one could "possibly dissociate the certainty [or uncertainty] of our perceptual existence from that of its external counterpart" (375). This follows because evidence is the "adequation of my visual intentions and the visible which is vision in act" (*F*430), because the quality or thing "is the suggestion of a certain way of existing put to us, and responded to by us, insofar as we have sensory fields" (*F*429), and because "there is no transcendent interpretation . . . which does not spring from the very configuration of the phenomena" (*F*430). Merleau-Ponty is reminding us of his theory of productive specification, or contact. We perceive when our sedimented perceptual structures are motivated, demanded, or triggered by otherness. When we are open to the perceptual world (and we must be to some general degree as our senses are a thrown and primordial openness to Being), the entities within the field "articulate" (*F*430) and constitute themselves through a specifying selection of the most adequate or appropriate perceptual structures. If one is certain of a particular perceptual act or structure, then one must be certain of the existence of the entity that actualizes or demands it. As we have learned, there is an intertwining between subject and object and both belong to one "element" (*VI*140) or dimension of Being. Merleau-Ponty can speak of the thing or quality, in the same way as he does perceptual consciousness, as "existing in act" or as a "way of existing" (*F*429), for evidence is an experience of a mode of Being which includes both subject and object as abstract poles. Therefore, "perception and the percept necessarily have the same existential modality" (*F*429) and evidence is an "ontological function" (*VI*40). The certainty or uncertainty of both depends on the grasp or "hold" (294) we have on the world (and that it has on us), but this is not merely an epistemic appraisal; it is instead a foundational metaphysical relation. Since this ontological correlativity is a defining feature of evidence, we can conclude that the "thought of perception" (taken in the most favorable sense as the "consciousness of perceiving") cannot be held to be directly evident, and thus it cannot have a type of certainty that is more epistemologically significant than the indirectly evident or the certainty of the thing itself.[21]

Let us continue to describe the essential features of an evident perception, for we shall have to see whether the same holds for the less obvious case of an evident belief or doubt. Since the experience of evidence is identical to the perceptual experience of proximity, evidence will have all the characteristics of the real or the thing itself. We saw that the thing was defined as the accent of a multiplicity of properties and predicates and of an infinity of appearances and specifications. Similarly, we saw as early as in chapter 1 that "the presence of the whole world" (*VI*40) is to be found in each evident or veridical perception. Thus, we were able to show that the otherness that actualized our structures could be described as infinite structurability, which meant that each perception held the entire spatio-temporal world on its horizon and indicated an inexhaustible future. However, this world is individual not only in the sense that all our experiences "manifest ... and are *possibilities of the same world*" (*VI*41), and are thus inherently interdependent, compossible,

21. Later we shall discuss in detail this distinction between indirect and direct evidence, which Chisholm uses following Brentano. Cf. Brentano's *The True and the Evident*, p. 130.

coherent, and "concordant" (*VI*38); it is also open (cf. chapter 2.1) in the sense that it is essentially incompletable, corrigible, and contingent. Every evident perception contains this inexhaustible complex of present levels, past fields, and future protensions, and thus one can never "thematize all its motives, that is to say we [can never] cease being situated" (*F*453) nor list the "reasons" (*VI*42) for taking it as evident.

The assurance that evidence gives us of having reached the real and true is the present focus and mundane "actualization" (43) of the primordial certainty of being in contact with Being itself. We have seen that this primordial contact is beyond question, and its primitive certainty that which is most genuinely given when subjectivity, temporality, and Being merge at that privileged existentialist moment (chapters 2.1 and 2.4). Each evident experience is a specification of this tacit *cogito* or "the profound movement of transcendence which is my being itself" (377), and we can experience this general thrownness only through such particular phenomena. The tacit *cogito* "is only a global and inarticulate grasp on the world . . . and if it is true that all particular knowledge is founded on this first view, then it is also true that it waits to be reconquered, fixed and explicated by perceptual experience and by speech" (463).

It is most important that we comprehend this connection between primordial faith and evidence, for otherwise we should be tempted to give primordial contact a certainty that was in some sense greater than that of evidence. It makes no sense to say that there is a higher degree of certainty than evidence, although it appears possible that there might be a different kind of certainty than the evident that we have described—that is, apodictic or direct evidence. However, we shall continue to see that it is essential to Merleau-Ponty's metaphysics and epistemology that he reject the idea that there are two such types of evidence. Merleau-Ponty confirms that a particular evident and Being in general have the same sort of certainty when he describes each separately as "being beyond contestation" (*VI*64*F*). However, he also states: "There is an absolute certitude of the world in general, but not of anything in particular" (*F*344). This absolute certainty cannot be apodictic, for Merleau-Ponty's notion of Being does not permit us to conceive of it as *a* truth or as having a necessary content or final description.[22] Similarly, it cannot be

22. Merleau-Ponty criticizes Spinoza for taking primordial faith as "absolute evidence"

direct, for this would be to affirm a Cartesian *cogito* and to contradict Merleau-Ponty's extensive arguments against a direct evidence. He can call our general experience of the world and Being absolute because in contrast to any particular evident it cannot break down or deceive us. Yet what this experience gives us is a glimpse of the "openness" (*VI*40) or finitude—or "nothingness" (*F*455 and *VI*88)—of Being and the world, or an indication that Being is a process of *écart, ekstase*, making-visible, or inexhaustible specification and articulation. This experience is thus the general certainty that we are *actively* engaged in "being in truth" (*VI*12), or that any particular perception of reality can only be shown to be untrue by yielding its claim to truth to another perception which serves the same "ontological function" (*VI*40). In other words, the experience is one of a "teleology of consciousness" (*F*453) and truth which is, in fact, an essential aspect of every experience of evidence. Therefore, our faith in particular evidences and our faith in Being in general are essentially the same; for the former can disintegrate and be proven illusory, but only in the name of the latter, and the latter is only given in the oscillations and corrigibility of the former. It is clear that in order to understand evidence we must turn to an examination of illusion and the teleology of truth.

The fact of perceptual illusion is a cornerstone of the skeptical and the phenomenalist positions and their attack on realism. However, Merleau-Ponty turns the argument from illusion against the phenomenalist by showing that, if we actually describe the experience of illusion, we shall see that it presupposes the same openness to the real and true as do our veridical experiences. Merleau-Ponty holds that the conclusion of the argument from illusion—that all perceptual experience must be as untrustworthy and deceptive as illusory experience—places perception on an equal footing with imagination (295 and 379). Therefore skepticism, like intellectualism, levels and "neutralizes" (*VI*38) all our experiences to *cogitationes* that belong to a homogeneous and atomistic stream of reflective consciousness, such that an image is distinguishable from a perception, if at all, only by means of reflective or analytic operations. Merleau-Ponty agrees with Austin that such a theory equates illusions with hallucinations,

---

(*F*455), as Spinoza does, for example, when he makes a necessary Being, which is perfectly adequate to itself and is a pure positivity, the starting point of his ontological argument.

for the hallucination does approximate the noema of an act of imagination since it lacks contact with the natural perceptual world.[23] On the other hand, illusions "belong" (VI41) to the perceptual world and region, and, as we have learned, there is an immediate intrinsic difference between perception and other conscious acts. We shall show that illusions are part of the perceptual realm for, although they are mistaken evidents, they are solicited or triggered giving us, at least, a partial truth and are stages to a genuine experience of truth.

Merleau-Ponty also uses the standard contemporary argument against skepticism which points out that the concepts of illusion and error presuppose an understanding of truth or veridical perceptual experience (F341). However, he goes beyond the usual formulation of this argument (as given by for example, Austin and Strawson) by understanding it in the way that Hegel originally presented it.[24] Thus he does not merely maintain that these terms would be vacuous without the contrasting experience of truth (which, as Ayer shows, is a relatively weak argument), nor does he wish to imply, as Strawson does in presenting this argument, that we must somehow have a knowledge of "pure" truth in itself.[25] On the contrary, what his descriptions of illusion show is that, paradoxically, the experience of truth is itself an experience of fallibility and, conversely, that an illusory experience actually testifies to our hold on truth. Merleau-Ponty thus confirms Heidegger's position that truth and untruth are interdependent notions.

He states that the key to understanding illusions is to recognize that they are only experienced as such retrospectively; that is, we only know that we have been deceived when we are disillusioned. Now "disillusion" implies that we have already experienced the true perception that corrects or is latent in the illusory perception. Phenomenalism "ill-describes ... the experience of dis-illusion" (VI40), because the corrigibility of our evidences or the experience of perceptual error does not make us skeptical but actually affirms our faith in our ability to experience truth. Unless we affirm that our present perception is veridical, we cannot condemn the previous as deceptive or even authentically doubt it.

23. *Sense and Sensibilia*, pp. 22 ff.
24. *The Phenomenology of Mind*, pp. 248-50.
25. See A. J. Ayer, in K. T. Fann, ed., *Symposium on J. L. Austin*, p. 294 (and L. W. Forguson's reply, pp. 324-26); Strawson, *Individuals*, p. 35.

When an illusion dissipates, when an appearance suddenly breaks up [éclate], it is always to the profit of a new appearance which takes up again for itself the ontological function of the first. . . . The dis-illusion is the loss of one evidence only because it is the acquisition of *another evidence*.(*VI*63F)

There is a necessary connection between the evident that deceives and the evident that corrects this first. Our contact with the world is not cut when we discover our illusions, for the evident that makes the first appear illusory takes over its ontological function (being-in-the-world) so completely that the first is no longer considered a case of *"really"* perceiving (374 and 375). However, in strict accordance with the Hegelian dialectic, the veridical perception presupposes, preserves, and transforms the "truth of" (380) the first at the same time that it negates it. The relation between these two experiences is the same that we found in temporality's movement of lapse or autoposition. In other words, the breaking up (*éclate*) of a case of evidence or a present is an experience of the otherness that it has not captured (its corrigibility), which is already the positing of a new evident or present grasp on the ground of this past. Thus Merleau-Ponty also describes the single thrust or movement of temporality as *éclatement* (*F*482). This teleology of evidences is grounded in the form of temporality, which is, of course, the form of all operative intentions and transitional syntheses. These two evidences "are not successive hypotheses about an unknowable Being, but perspectives upon the same familiar Being, which we know cannot exclude one without including the other" (*VI*41). This phenomenological fact that two contrary evidences cannot be contemporaneous shows conclusively that the accounts of illusion given by analytic philosophers are false. If it is empirically impossible that two contrary perceptions could present themselves as equally evident, one cannot possibly hold that an evident or veridical experience is a "judgment" or "claim" about reality. One does not experience "repeated failures in the determination of the world, but . . . progressive approaches" (*VI*64F). Since there is an inescapable optimism and positivity that accompanies the recognition of the corrigibility of our evident perceptions, *corrigibility* has entirely different connotations for Merleau-Ponty than it does for the analytic philosopher. For the latter, it is entirely negative, for it only casts the present evident into doubt and raises the specter of skepticism; for Merleau-Ponty, on the contrary, it is an experience of truth itself. *Corrigibility* is synonymous with *evidence* understood as our perpetual faith and lived affirmation that we are in truth, that "there is a true vision" (*VI*146), and that we have a "hold on truth" (*F*453).

Neither illusions nor veridical perceptions are discrete and independent present phenomena (295). It is not by mere chance that an illusion is corrected by another experience nor are the two externally related; it is instead the case that illusions carry the germ of, and protend, the experiences that will reveal them to be what they are. "In the very moment of illusion, the possibility of correction was presented to me" (297). Because illusions are not merely errors of judgment but are "definitely lived" (*F*436), like the evident they center my entire field, gather together and reconfirm my past, and protend a variety of future possibilities that must be fulfilled (in both the inner and the outer horizons). To be perceptually deceived is to live as if the percept were veridical, such that "my whole perceptual and motor field" (*F*343) is committed to certain systems and patterns of future experience. As we have learned, our experiences and their noemata temporalize themselves or spread from the past through the present and into the future. If the experience did not ready me for a future that could confirm or disconfirm it, if the perception was merely a *cogitatio* or instantaneous experience, and if there was not the thrown faith in the unity, interweaving, and compossibility of our experiences and our world, we could never be sure of our errors nor experience disillusion. Therefore, Merleau-Ponty makes Husserl's notion of the crossing-out of errors or deceptions central to his understanding of evidence and truth, but he ties it directly to our *"openness upon being* which is perceptual faith" and to a teleology of consciousness (or the replacing of one truth by another).[26]

It is, of course, indisputable that illusions occur and that evidence is always "conditional" (*F*454), but it is not immediately apparent how illusions are possible at the prereflective level. If we examine some of the ways they can occur, then we shall begin to understand how they must also be partially true. Descartes's dictum that errors are due to judgments that go beyond the given is correct to some extent. When we focus on an entity that is nonproximal or in an epistemologically unfavorable position and for some reason make it

26. The importance of the relationship between these notions for Merleau-Ponty is shown by his stating it in almost identical language on three separate occasions (297, *VI*88, and *VI*128).

the center of our field, we must give it that level of specificity which permits us to anchor our global body and all of the field's levels within it. Rather than the entity constituting itself (triggering its appropriate structures), we go beyond the degree of specification that is given, overspecify it, and open ourselves to the error of a transcendent judgment (but a prereflective one). However, this overspecification is grounded in the more general structures that are warranted by our epistemic situation and these would have given us a true, if very indeterminate and general, perception of the entity. Thus this type of illusion is not totally false (or is partially true), for the correct perception, when it is achieved, is based on or compatible with the same general modes of presentation that founded the false perception. It is easy to see why such illusions are common, for they are due to our interests and concerns "being ahead of" our perceptual being-in-the-world. Because our metastructures intertwine with, delineate, and make use of the openness of the perceptual region, their purposes can often displace those of normal perception. For example, when moving, say, walking or driving, I place myself well beyond my proximal field, for my interests demand that I be overcautious and err on the side of overdetermination. When I drive, I constantly meet with illusions, because I prefer to ready myself for possible dangerous and threatening entities at the least suggestion. Thus my "biological" concerns for self-preservation overrule my perceptual concerns for a maximum and accurate grasp of my field.

However, perception is constantly open to other sources of error besides the interference of our metastructural concerns. We have learned that the real and the evident are such because they actualize the entire world on their horizon and center all our sedimented structures. "The close, the far-off, the horizon in their indescribable contrast form a system, and it is their relationship within the total field that is their perceptual truth" (*VI*22). Since the thing is a precarious balance of all the field's levels and implies the other entities within the field (and even other fields), an illusion can be symptomatic of a weakness in one or more levels or in their combination. This also implies that we might be mistaken about our figural entity because we have mistaken other entities on its horizon (this contextual source of error is inexplicable for phenomenalists). No such field or global system can be totally delusive, and thus no illusion can ever be absolutely false. When the perception becomes veridical, we can see why it will retain what was true of the illusion's field. "Illusions are not mere constructions, the significance [*sens*] of the perceived was motivated" (*F*529, topic of *F*303ff.).

Because for Merleau-Ponty there are only "degrees of reality" (378) and one can speak strictly only of the "more true" (*VI*128) and of "partial truth," evidence is equated with truth.[27] There can be, therefore, no absolute, third-person, or impersonal truth or Being behind and beyond that which is given to the subject within his experience of evidence. Just as Merleau-Ponty's philosophy has consistently denied that there are things-in-themselves, that Being is absolute plenitude and positivity, or that there is an exhaustively determinate world, he must also deny that there can be truths in themselves.[28] Merleau-Ponty cannot possibly allow a truth that fully transcends the finite and partial truth given in the experience of evidence because he makes this experience both epistemologically and metaphysically primary. He thus shows that one can treat this experience as lacking the full positivity of Being and truth only if one posits an absolute, as for example, Spinoza and other rationalists do (397). Similarly, the skeptic or phenomenalist can derogatorily equate evidence with a "psychic fact" (377) or mere appearance only because his philosophy is grounded in the tacit belief that there is truth in itself and in the hypothesis that there is an absolute knowledge that is correlative to such truth. However, there is no such knowledge or truth to contrast with evidence in this way, for, as we have seen, for Merleau-Ponty there is no "other being beyond apparent being" (*F*455); Being is situational and constitutes itself in the necessarily corrigible and temporal relating of "subject" and "object." Being itself is finite, because it has no more to offer than what it gives to our experience. We have attempted to demonstrate throughout this study that the logic and positivity of Being and evidence are one and the same. The teleology of evidence has shown us that the false and the deceptive can be understood only retrospectively, and that the true and the real, with which they are contrasted, are themselves given in experiences that are ontologically relative to them (the false and the deceptive). Merleau-Ponty's

27. Merleau-Ponty uses the expression "partial truth" in *The Primacy of Perception*, p. 20; for the equation of evidence with truth, see, for example, *The Primacy of Perception*, pp. 6 and 20-21.

28. Although we are now more concerned with situational truths, we shall see that these considerations apply equally to propositional truths.

characterization of freedom, Existence, and transcendence as the ability to "fly from being only into being" (360) is, therefore, equally applicable to our involvement with truth. At most, one can say that the true temporally "transcends" or distinguishes itself from the false. Merleau-Ponty's point is that all truth is experienceable and that the experience of evidence is a "value-fact" (*F456*) that conditions and makes any other fact possible (or, in Heidegger's terms, that it is "facticity" which makes "factuality" possible).

Similarly, there can be no absolute falsehoods, for only if there were a truth in itself beyond our evident experiences could our beliefs or perceptions be totally and irredeemably false. If we have established that every evident experience must be true to some degree, then the phenomenalist is already defeated. He cannot logically maintain that every experience can or should be treated as false, for his notion of falsehood is as inconsistent and unrealizable as his presupposition of the absoluteness of truth. Our errors can "never revert to nothingness or to subjectivity as if they had never appeared" (*VI*40) nor can an illusion be "nullified" to the extent of leaving "a gap in its place" (*VI*140); for "the principle of visibility, as though through a sort of abhorrence of a vacuum, already invokes the true vision" (*VI*140). Even in error one cannot totally "detach" (*VI*146) oneself from Being, for every activity is an expression of the visibility that defines both subjectivity and Being. "What I can conclude from these disillusions or deceptions, therefore, is that perhaps 'reality' does not belong definitively to any particular perception, that in this sense it is *always further on*" (*VI*40-41). Thus, from the fact of illusion, one can draw conclusions about the beyondness and otherness of Being itself and not only about the corrigibility of evidence. What is important to recognize is that the corrigibility of an evident experience is a direct reflection of the finitude of Being (its being-outside-itself), just as its certainty is derivative from the basic certainty that arises in the experience of primordial contact when subjectivity merges with Being's *écart*. Illusion, "far from authorizing us to efface the indices of 'reality' " from all experiences, forces us to consider them "as 'all true' " (*VI*65F).

One wonders, then, about hallucinations, which appear to be totally delusive and thus absolutely false. Merleau-Ponty has produced a strong and detailed theory of hallucinations and their related phenomena, such as dreams and the phenomena of primitive (mythical) and childlike anthropomorphic worlds (283 ff. and 334 ff.). Such a theory is vital if he is to preserve his first principle that there are no situations that are not somehow dependent on otherness and expressive of Being. To explore this theory fully would, however, require much more space than the present context warrants, and thus we shall give only the briefest outline of it.

Merleau-Ponty's main insight into the status of phenomena of this sort is that they express in perceptual terms a *presence* which properly belongs to another region of Existence and Being, especially the sexual-affective region (341). Thus, for example, problems, needs, and fixations in the biological, motor, sexual, or interpersonal spheres are the overriding preoccupations of the schizophrenic (and the sole concern of the dreamer). They "forget or repress" (344) the primacy of the natural world in order to put all of their articulatory capacities into the service of their obsessions. They use perceptual structures and often linguistic ones, preserving only their normal affective or emotive sense (340), to articulate this inescapable presence because these regions contain our richest and most highly varied structures. It is possible for them to successfully articulate these normally vague and highly indeterminate and unstructured regions by these means because, as we have seen, all of our regions are to some extent constituent of natural objects and natural spatiality.

What is most important to us here is that even though they express a nonperceptual presence (or otherness) in perceptual terms, they rarely mistake or confuse the reality with which they are struggling (and which is the one that counts for them) with the natural perceptual world (342). Hallucinations overlie this world, but they do not replace it and, therefore, they are not strictly errors and do not strictly fool the subject. Since the ambiguity of prereflective life does not allow this distinction to be clear and unmistakable, when hallucinations do deceive us they fall under the logic of illusions (mistaking one region for another and only teleologically discovering the confusion). They are "true" in the broad sense when they are understood as accurate and fitting expressions of an obsessive bodily presence (rather than, for example, as merely the signs or symbols of unconscious thoughts). This presence, although resulting in a bizarre world and a complete imbalance in the subject's maximum grasp of

Being, is still not nothing; and this world is triggered and motivated by one of the dimensions of Being. Hallucinations, then, are also manifestations of our primordial faith or contact with Being itself (343). They are indeed projected into the world, but not in the intellectualist sense. It is because the perceptual grounds all meta-structural regions—all bodily disturbances modify the natural world (339-40)—that hallucinations use perceptual structures, which must be at least noematically presented on a "fictional plane," as are reflective or analytic perceptions (cf. chapter 3.4). Like even the simplest act of imagination, they hollow out a free space within natural space (and, as we have seen, the former space presupposes and is made possible by rooting itself in the latter). Thus hallucinations are not part of our perceptual life nor do they have the mark which distinguishes perception within our stream of experience. (Merleau-Ponty shows in detail how hallucinations lack, for the subject, that coherence and interconnection with the rest of his field and with his past and future horizons which characterizes perceptual reality [338-39].) They are thus not part of the truth and teleology of evidence which are proper to normal perception. They are indeed closest to imagination, for they are the translating of a nonperceptual presence into the *logos* of the perceptual realm, and this process of creative expression and translation is just the definition of imagination.[29]

4. Cognitive Evidence and Truth

This section will continue the discussion of the issues raised in the previous one, for it will concentrate on the concepts of evidence and truth as they are applied to the cognitive region. In order to make these notions clear, we shall investigate in depth Merleau-Ponty's phenomenologies of belief, doubt, and reflection and their relationship to noncognitive situations. Therefore, this study will also complete our analysis of cognition. We shall see that the sense of the term *evidence* does not change when it is applied to beliefs and that propositional truths have the same general characteristics and the

29. For this reason, Merleau-Ponty's frequent equation of the imaginary with appearance and illusion is quite misleading (e.g., 231, 379, and *VI*40).

same inherent connection to the experience of evidence that we found in our study of situational truths.

By beginning with a critical discussion of Chisholm's theory of evidence as presented in *The Theory of Knowledge*, we shall be able to summarize what we have thus far learned and introduce the issues that will occupy us throughout this section. Chisholm's epistemology, to which we shall frequently allude, is of interest to us because it incorporates a Husserlian notion of evidence into the context of contemporary Anglo-American epistemology. This will allow us to carry on Merleau-Ponty's dialogue with Husserl from a different and more contemporary perspective, as well as to maintain the dialectic between intellectualism and empiricism that occupies Merleau-Ponty throughout his investigations. We shall then immediately turn to the question of propositional truths in order to comprehend how they are constituted by evident beliefs and, like situational truths, are always present on the horizon of every evident belief. We shall proceed to a discussion of how Merleau-Ponty can understand truth as correspondence, which will be interrupted by a detailed analysis of belief and reflection and their relationship to one another. Once the structures of belief and reflection are clarified, we can return to the consideration of truth as correspondence.

Chisholm's theory is philosophically interesting because he proposes a definition of evidence which clearly relates it to the reasonableness of a belief. He makes evidence one of a family of epistemic terms and shows that they all belong to the same category by defining them in terms of one another.[30] He is thus able to place these terms on a single comparative scale of evaluative epistemic attitudes. He defines an evident proposition as one which has the highest degree of reasonableness, or as one whose reasonableness is as high as that of any other proposition the subject may hold. An evident belief, therefore, gives us that privileged type of certainty which fully satisfies the justification condition of "knowledge," which is now itself partially defined in terms of evidence. One cannot actually quantify an evaluative scale, but rough numerical values can be assigned to each member. Thus it can be said that "gratuitous" propositions have 0.5 degrees of credibility, "unacceptable" have less than 0.5, "acceptable" have 0.5 and over, and "reasonable" have

30. Cf. *Theory of Knowledge*, pp. 21-23.

more than 0.5. Since our most evident, certain, or justified beliefs do not unexceptionally guarantee their truth (and only such infallibility could hold the position of 1.0 degrees of credibility), evidence must fall somewhere between 1.0 and 0.5. Chisholm would give it a value of something like 0.8, for this would allow, first, that its degree could increase over time, as do the most credible of a subject's beliefs, and, secondly, that one could compare a number of propositions by assigning different degrees of reasonableness to them (between 0.51 and 0.79).

Merleau-Ponty would hold that such an understanding of evidence would "reduce the true to the credible, the real to the probable" (*VI*39), or "reduce the real to appearance" (*F*455) or to the "imaginary" (*VI*40), or, finally, make the "real . . . only the less improbable or the more probable" (*VI*40). We have seen that these criticisms hold because evidence is the experience of the true and the real and because talk of "credibility," "probability," or "reasonableness" belongs strictly to the realm of reflective appraisal (which is intrinsically different from the prereflective experience of evidence). Chisholm's scale is attractive at first glance because it seems to take into account Merleau-Ponty's notions of the teleology of evidence or degrees of reality and truth, but we shall see that this is not the case. Chisholm indeed wishes to keep the connection between evidence and truth, and he thus places them on the same scale (by somehow making a "pure experience of truth" count as the upper limit of the scale, 1.0). However, by tying evidence to reasonableness he reintroduces an unbridgeable gap between evidence and truth and thus loses the sense of "evidence" (something like the Husserlian sense) that he set out to preserve. This accounts for his vacillations throughout *The Theory of Knowledge* about the relationship between evidence and truth (see pp. 20, 48-49, and 111-13). Let us look at some of the inconsistencies that arise from this tension.

Chisholm cannot help but take back the connection that he initially establishes between evidence and truth, for by making evidence a type of reasonableness he simply makes it into a predicate of the kind that results from any other epistemic judgment.[31]

---

31. One can accept his account of reflective epistemic judgments or appraisals while omitting his use of *evident* for the most certain degree, and we shall do so throughout the remainder of this section.

Chisholm's epistemic principles, like even the logical positivist's theories or rules of inference, are meant to sort out true from false beliefs (and, correlatively, real from unreal noemata of these beliefs), and thus "true" and "real" become predicates of the same type as "probable" (in its epistemic sense) or "credible."[32] The only way left to overcome this distance between appearance and reality is to somehow be able to infer or judge a proposition's truth. If one is satisfied with the skeptical position, one can hold that "is true," "is real," and "is evident" are merely reflective predications of propositions, states-of-affairs, and experiences, predications that do not get us any closer to reality than other epistemic appraisals do. But if one refuses to take a skeptical position, then, like Chisholm, one must attempt to separate this type of reflective judgment from the others by giving it some kind of substantive sense, which means that these predicates cannot be understood in a nominalist fashion. It is because of this that Chisholm's scale attempts to keep evidence tied to truth and knowledge. But how then can he or any antiskeptical phenomenalist escape the fact that he has made "existence" into a predicate of the belief's *cogitatum* or object (and "is true" into a substantive predicate of a belief)?

Because Chisholm refuses to allow the "difference of nature" (*VI*40) between evidence and credibility, his scale is bound to be inconsistent. For example, let us examine the implications that disillusion or the replacing of one evident by another has for this scale (Chisholm would agree that there cannot be two contrary beliefs that are simultaneously held to be evident). Chisholm would have to hold that there was a difference in degree of credibility between these two evidents and not that one took over the ontological function of the other. Whenever one evident replaces another, Chisholm has to maintain either of two unacceptable positions. Since no evident can ever reach 1.0 on the scale (since it is known to be corrigible) and since the discovery of illusion is very frequent, there must be a progressive, but infinite, approach to this final degree. Even if this is conceivable, it is hardly convincing. The second alternative is to maintain that the new evident replaces the old at the same level on the scale (0.8), with the old now being merely "reasonable." However, this implies that an evident experi-

32. *Theory of Knowledge,* pp. 44 ff.

ence is corrigible not only because it might be false (the difference between 0.8 and 1.0) but because it might not be evident (or at 0.8). The absurdity of this alternative is just the reverse of the first, for now every new evident will push the previous ones further down the scale until some are no longer even reasonable or acceptable. The only way to escape this dilemma is to affirm that there is a qualitative difference between the evident and the highest degree of credibility. Thus Chisholm's scale does not express Merleau-Ponty's teleology of evidence, for the latter is not a "blind progress of probability founded on a number of signs and concordances" (*VI*42). As we have seen, there is no break between evidence and truth, for the corrigibility of evidence reflects the finitude of truth itself, and, if evidence has degrees, these are degrees of truth and reality and not of reasonableness.

We have seen that "the real is coherent and probable because it is real, and not real because it is coherent" (*VI*40), since the experience of the real is the experience of the concordance and intertwining of all our horizons and structures in the present evident. This main characterization of evidence explains what Chisholm is seeking with his epistemic principles of indirect evidence and why he must fail. His last principles depend on the notion of concurrence, which attempts to duplicate, in reflective and thetic terms, the gestalt of the world that is given in an evident perception. Thus, in order for a claim about the perceptual world to be evident or justified, it must be concurrent with every other reasonable perceptual claim.[33] This notion of concurrence appears artificial and abstract because, as Merleau-Ponty has shown, all the motives for an evident experience cannot be thematized (as this would in fact amount to a total description of the world). Even if we could exhaustively thematize or put into propositional form an evident's total horizon—which is an "infinite task" (*F*455)—, it is incomprehensible how the subject could be aware of this seemingly unlimited number of propositions. Similarly, Blanchard's claim that coherence is a test of truth makes the same mistake, for in order for it to be a successful reflective test

---

33. "Any set of propositions that are mutually consistent and logically independent of each other . . . is *concurrent* provided that each member of the set is confirmed by the conjunction of all the other members of the set" *Theory of Knowledge*, p. 53.

or definition of truth, all the cohering members and their interrelations would have to be thematizable.[34]

This might seem unfair to Chisholm, for he is not concerned with prereflective experiences of evidence but with establishing that our perceptual knowledge-claims are indirectly evident. Furthermore, he bases such evidence on the apodictic evidence of the "thought of perception" or of "self-presenting states."[35] We have shown that the "thought of perception," if certain, is only as certain as the perceptual act which, in turn, implies the same degree or type of certainty in its object. However, we shall make Merleau-Ponty's arguments against the dichotomy of the direct and indirect clearer and more convincing by examining how he demonstrates that even cognitive acts, such as belief or doubt, are not self-presenting, nor their evidence direct. We shall then see that cognition's type of evidence fully confirms our criticism of Chisholm.

We shall turn now to the study of the evidence of belief in order to show that it has the same essential characteristics as the evidence of perception. We shall find that the evidence of belief is the experience of our openness to propositional truth; that it is triggered by, or in contact with, our noncognitive existence; that it gathers together the entire cognitive horizon in a present act which is nonthematizable; and that it protends a future, has a teleology, and is susceptible to illusion because it can never be exhaustively determined or accomplished. In other words, we shall have to understand how a cognitive act like belief can be prereflective and lived or how it can have a situational form. Thus one of our main tasks will be to distinguish reflection, as the second-order cognitive act, from all first-order cognitive acts.

Every form of Existence, including belief, doubt, will, and emotion,

is action or doing, and because action, by definition, is the violent passage from what I have to what I aim at, from what I am to what I intend to be, I am able to affect the *cogito* and have the assurance of willing, loving, or believing on the condition that I first actually wish, love, or believe, and that I accomplish my own existence. (*F*438)

---

34. Brand Blanshard, in Nagel and Brandt eds., *Meaning and Knowledge*, p. 139. Confirmation theory suffers from the same weakness, for it states that the highest degree of inductive evidence that a statement can possess is determined by *all* the knowledge that one possesses. See, for example, Brian Skyrms, *Choice and Chance*, pp. 15-18.

35. Chisholm, *Theory of Knowledge*, pp. 111, 44.

It can be evident to me that I believe only within the actual performance of the belief. Thus, for example, the only way that I can silence all my doubts about my doubting is to actually "doubt something" (F438). Cognitive action, like all forms of operational intentionality, is only present to itself in its objective and in the process of its accomplishment. There is, therefore, a lived form of self-consciousness that accompanies our cognitive acts, which, as we shall see, must not be confused with the clear self-consciousness of the reflective ego. We have learned that the essential activity of believing (or cognitive "knowing") is the sublimation (translation or expression) of our noncognitive situations into the thematic and linguistic structures of our cognitive region. Therefore, what belief seeks is the adequate expression of the facts that are given, for example, in perceptual experience, and what it accomplishes are the propositional truths that *correspond* to these situational truths. The operation of belief is to hold a certain proposition as true, and it grasps its own "life" only to the degree that it achieves this aim. Like perceptual evidence, the evidence of belief is equally and correlatively certain of itself (the act of belief) and of its object (the propositional truth or "idea"), for these are the two sides of a unified cognitive situation. Merleau-Ponty therefore insists on understanding belief as he did attention (chapter 2.2), that is, not as a *fait accompli*, in the way it gives itself after it has already been constituted, but in the way it grasps itself when it authentically articulates or creates a propositional truth or cognitive meaning.

Although we shall return to Merleau-Ponty's theory of declarative truth in the last part of this section, it will help our understanding of cognitive evidence if we gain some familiarity with it at this point. Since an evident belief refers to a lived situation and describes it in cognitive terms, Merleau-Ponty would agree that correspondence is an essential feature of truth. A truth comes into being when the "descriptive conventions" of formulating a belief are satisfied, because believing is an operation that uses the subject's entire system of cognitive-linguistic capacities in order to express or constitute a meaning. Furthermore, an evident belief must satisfy "demonstrative conventions," because the meaning it intends is a noncognitive perceptual situation before it is acquired as a cognitive meaning. "Thought . . . envelops the affirmation of the thing . . . [and] presupposes that I assume at the same time the existences at which it aims" (F430). These Austinian categories are helpful because they allow us to show that an evident expression is at the same time a reference to a noncognitive significance and that the cognitive grasp can only be successful if it makes proper use of its own cognitive structures. Therefore, this is not a third-person theory of truth and correspondence is not an external relation, for correspondence is precisely what is *experienced* when we take our belief as evident. Similarly, the adequation of our belief to the phenomenon that it is attempting to sublimate is a relation internal to the subject because what is expressed (e.g., a perceptual situation) is always as much a part of the subject as is the act of expression.

Like all structures, those of cognition are interconnected through a kind of hierarchical system of thrown and sedimented structures. Thus, as Merleau-Ponty frequently shows, any authentic use of a structure modifies its sense, and thus, because these structures form a gestalt, indirectly modifies the sense of every other cognitive-linguistic structure. Furthermore, every authentic belief is sedimented within this system of structures and is therefore related to every other previously acquired or sedimented belief. Because these sedimented truths retain and preserve, in cognitive terms, the natural phenomena they have sublimated, they become part of our "semi-permanent" world (cf. chapter 5.1) or are held within and permeate the constant natural world which we reaffirm in every present (*VI*189). This system of cognitive truths, which helps constitute our world, can be taken as the sediments (*VI*189) or institutions (*VI*14) of which the cognitive region consists. The universe or world of propositional truths is, then, an abstraction of the cognitive layer from the one unified world which contains the articulations of every region (and of which it is one of the metadimensions). It is thus hardly the complete and fully determinate world of most philosophies. Every belief which formulates a new truth therefore brings this entire horizon of cognitive structures and truths to bear on the phenomenon it seeks to express. In other words, for our descriptive conventions to be satisfied, not only must the act of expression use available cognitive-linguistic structures and be consistent with their logic, but it must also be compatible and compossible with every other truth that constitutes the cognitive region or is part of our sedimented world. (Hence, once again, the demonstrative conventions must be satisfied simultaneously in the same act.)

We saw that an experience of evidence had to be motivated, occasioned, or triggered by otherness, for evidence must be understood as presence or as our bond to otherness. Cognitive evidence has this same characteristic of contact, but it is not as plain since cognition metastructures other regions. Beliefs or "ideas . . . always express our contact with being and culture."[36] The otherness upon which cognition opens consists primarily of the lived situations of our perceptual region. These obviously "guide" (36) the entire process or transitional synthesis that results in an evident belief, for it is these situations that our cognitive acts labor to express. We need not, of course, formulate beliefs about our perceptual life, but if we are interested in doing so cognition opens itself to the demands and presence of these experiences. It is essential to the understanding of Merleau-Ponty's theory that we realize that the meaning that cognition desires to achieve and express does not exist as a "thought" or "proposition" prior to its expression. On the contrary, the meaning that it initially sets out to capture is, for example, the significance contained in a perceptual situation and the proposition at which it arrives is constituted by the actual process of expression.[37] In this way there is a kind of meaning or thought before language, if we understand meaning or thought as the initial opening our cognitive region has on those lived significances it is interested in articulating.

It becomes impossible to maintain that Merleau-Ponty changes his sense of *evident* when applying it to beliefs if we note that an evident belief has an inexhaustible and nonthematizable horizon like the one that essentially characterizes an evident perception. Therefore, an evident belief must also be corrigible and imply a teleology of consciousness. These characteristics hold because, as we have just seen, every evident belief gathers together its entire system of sedimented knowledge or becomes the present "focus" (F54) which concretizes the world of cognitive truth. Besides implicating cognition's whole past, each evident belief also protends a future that will confirm it or reveal it as illusory. As in evident perception, "I collect myself together [*rassemble*] in order to transcend myself" (F439).

36. *Primacy of Perception*, p. 21.
37. Thus, for example, Strawson is *technically* correct to prefer the use of *statement* to *proposition* and to deny that there are propositions independent of their linguistic expression.

Evident belief can only be certain of itself while in act because the horizon and the past which it assumes can never be verified or made totally clear.

> It is no accident that evidence itself can be called into question, because *certainty is doubt*, being the taking up of a tradition of thought which is only able to be condensed into an evident "truth" if I renounce all attempts to make it explicit. (*F*454)

As soon as I step back from my present affirmation and reflect on it, the infinite complexity of its horizons becomes conspicuous and cannot help but throw my present belief into doubt. Since these horizons can never be exhaustively thematized (and, thus, all the motives for my affirmation cannot be made clear), no belief can remain evident for such reflection. It thus becomes a defining characteristic of reflection that its object can never be predicated or evaluated reflectively as "evident." For the same reason, no evident belief is incorrigible. Since one never has a grasp on all of its implications and can never guarantee the other truths on which it is grounded, the present evident proposition may be revealed to be false. However, it can only be shown to be illusory by means of another future evident belief which itself suffers from the same incompleteness.

> The actual possession of a true idea . . . only founds a "teleology" of consciousness [reference to Husserl] which, from this first instrument, will forge more perfect ones, and with these even more perfect ones, and so on, without end. (*F*453)

Therefore, cognitive evidence has the same logic as perceptual evidence, and propositional truths are nonabsolute, relative, and partial like perceptual truths. Because every evident belief focuses and gathers together every other belief, all beliefs are interdependent and share a single primordial faith; and "in one sense, there are no more acts of consciousness or distinct *Erlebnisse* in a life than there are separate things in the world" (407).

Although Merleau-Ponty holds that every evident belief maintains our whole system of beliefs on its horizon, he is not susceptible to the criticisms made of Chisholm, Blanshard, and Skyrms when we discussed "concurrence" at the beginning of this section. His main point is that in order to posit a belief it is not necessary that the subject have a clear grasp of every piece of knowledge he possesses.

On the contrary, this type of reflective awareness of a belief's horizons prevents the affirmation from being evident. As we have seen, a horizon is not a sum of particular entities but a system that contains these particular truths within more general truths, and these within general "fields" or regional principles, and so on. For example, Merleau-Ponty says that the principles of Euclidean geometry or those of Marxist sociology are "orders of thought" (*F*454). Once these are assumed, within their contexts we can discover evident truths; but if we consider these regions themselves, they are not "without appeal" (454). In other words, our particular certainties presuppose our taking whole areas of belief as true and "unquestionable" (*F*451).

Toulmin's philosophy of science supports Merleau-Ponty's theory, for it is built on the view that there are regional beliefs which make possible our particular beliefs.[38] He shows that scientific theories give us highly general principles which lay out a region for the production of scientific truths and that these principles are by themselves always questionable. He even refuses to apply *true* or *false* to these principles (and, thus, to the scientific judgments that are grounded in them) because, even when they break down or are replaced by other principles, they do not become absolutely false. Since they will continue to be useful in certain contexts and to delimit an area of scientific concern, they will always have at least a partial truth. Using the truths of Euclidean geometry as an example of all mathematical and scientific truths, Merleau-Ponty says that they have "a coefficient of facticity" and a "pretended transparence" which "reveals itself one day as a transparence for a certain historical period of the human spirit" (*F*451). He would, of course, maintain that this is the case with all truths and that there is no more justification for withholding *true* or *false* from scientific and analytic statements than from any other evident beliefs. There are no absolute truths or falsehoods to be found anywhere and we have nowhere else to put our faith than in the experience of evidence and its teleology.

Merleau-Ponty's entire theory of cognitive evidence hangs on the distinction he makes between first-order cognitive acts and re-flection. Therefore, we must now turn to an exhaustive description

38. Stephen Toulmin, *The Philosophy of Science: An Introduction.*

of the characteristics and modes of interrelation of first-order and second-order cognitive acts. By doing so, we shall prove once and for all that cognitive evidence is categorically different from and not on the same scale as "credibility." We shall explain how reflection's function is to reduce, neutralize, or level the lived evidence of our cognitive experiences, just as it does that of our perceptual experiences. This will show that any "thought of" statement (e.g., "I believe that p" or "It seems that p") is a hedge of a first-order belief and essentially a reflective statement. It is only in such cases that crisis techniques (cf. section 1) and criteriology become appropriate, and thus none of these types of statements can be said to be evident. Thus we shall see that all first-order acts of the *cogito* are as "indirect" or open to doubt as our perceptual acts, and that reflection in fact must doubt them to the extent that their evidence is necessarily inaccessible to it.

Although the logic of evident belief is our central concern, we shall begin by examining first-order doubt and then apply what we learn to belief. This procedure is useful because reflection usually has the form of a belief (but a second-order belief), and thus is very easily confused with first-order belief. We must begin by investigating Merleau-Ponty's claim that doubt can be lived and is inherently distinct from reflective doubt, affirmation, or appraisal.

> One can call into question thought which is loaded with historical sediments . . . , one is able to doubt doubt itself, considered either as a definite mode of thought or as consciousness of a doubtful object. (*F*457)

There are two sources of error about cognitive acts. First, one can always be mistaken about the fact that one is, for example, doubting rather than willing or believing. Secondly, there is room for uncertainty about the precise object one is in fact doubting. However, these questions about our actual evident cognitive acts, like those about our lived acts, can only be raised when we distance ourselves from them by reflecting on them. Merleau-Ponty's entire position is contained in the tension between the statement quoted above and the neighboring statement: "He who doubts cannot while doubting, doubt that he doubts" (*F*457). Cognitive acts are not any more self-presenting or direct than perceptual acts, for there is no way of silencing one's reflective doubts about them. "What has been said of external can equally be said of internal perception: that it involves infinity" (*F*439), and "all inner perception is inadequate . . . because I make my reality and find myself only in act" (*F*438). However this does not mean that we are thrown into an endless doubt about our doubts or beliefs, for at the level where these doubts can be lived they are given with evidence. When one doubts a proposition or an object, one can be sure of one's act and the entity at which it is directed. Like any evident experience, this certainty is the result of bringing one's whole cognitive system of beliefs and structures to bear on the object at hand. One therefore pins one's cognitive life (or faith), and centers one's whole Existence (*VI*37), on taking the object in this way, thus excluding the possibility of performing a second act of reflection at this moment.

When I reflect on a first-order act of doubting, it becomes the "mere thought" (382) of my lived doubt. Thus if "I doubt that *Fa*" (or "That *Fa* is dubitable") expresses my present act of doubting, then "I believe that I doubt that *Fa*" ("I think that . . . " or "It seems that . . . ") expresses my reflecion on this doubt. One can equally describe the first-order act as "It is evident that *Fa* is dubitable" or "I doubt that *Fa* with evidence" (although we rarely say this because it is redundant). But we do not say that we doubt "*with* reasonableness" or "*with* acceptability," as we can say that we doubt "*with* evidence." That is because the latter expression refers to the "assurance" (377 and *VI*12) or confidence we have in our present act, while the former expressions refer to its credibility.[39] In other words, to characterize a doubt as reasonable is to make a statement about the degree to which is should be believed. It is a statement about a statement, for it *refers* to the actual act of doubting and predicates such epistemic values of it. It is of the nature of talk about justification, the giving of reasons (the supplying of inductive evidence), or the appraising of credibility that it be a second-order description and thus belong to the order of reflection. If it was possible that all the motives that constitute our evidence could be exhaustively thematized, these second-order descriptions would be mere explications of our first-order descriptions. But the fact that this is not possible confirms and is confirmed by the fact that there is a category difference or logical leap between these two

39. Chisholm's main principle, pattern your confidence in a proposition to its degree of credibility, shows some recognition of the split between reflection and first-order acts. However, he fails to see that "confidence" describes the way we live in an act (or its evidence), while "credibility," on the contrary, is a reflective category.

orders.[40] Therefore, locutions of the form "It is reasonable (un-reasonable) that I doubt that *Fa*" or "My doubting that *Fa* is reasonable (unreasonable)" are metalevel statements that reflectively predicate "is reasonable" to my first-order act or statement of doubting. In such circumstances, we more commonly speak in the third-person and say, for example, "It is unreasonable to doubt that *Fa*." However, this should not mislead us into asserting that there is no first-order statement that is being appraised in this case; for this statement is elliptical for roughly "Reflection would show that it is unreasonable to doubt that *Fa* if anyone should hold such a doubt."

The reflective act of appraisal can itself be evident like any other cognitive act. However, what will be evident is not my first-order act but my appraisal, or the predicating of reasonableness or unreasonableness to this act. Thus it makes perfect sense to say "My doubting that *Fa* is reasonable (unreasonable) is evident" or "It is evident that doubting that *Fa* is reasonable (unreasonable)." These phrases state that my first-order act of doubting, which is evident to me, is reasonable, and that this appraisal is evident to me in the reflective act of appraising. (It is evident to me that I am appraising the first-order act as reasonable and that it is reasonable.) According to Chisholm's scale these statements would be nonsense or contra-dictory because he has leveled the intrinsic difference between evidence and credibility. One can significantly add "is credible" and "is evident" to a first-order statement indefinitely, not because (as most hold) one is merely reproducing thought about thought *ad infinitum*, but because a definite change in standpoint is implied by these terms. Thus Chisholm must be wrong, for according to his scheme it would be a contradiction to state "It is evident that my doubting that *Fa* with evidence is unreasonable." Furthermore, for him it makes sense to say "It is evident that my doubting that *Fa* is evident," with *evident* having the same sense in both places. Yet for this to be sensible *evident* in one of its occurrences must mean "beyond a reasonable doubt" (or "with the highest inductive evidence") and in the other occurrence must mean "lived evidence." That there is an equivocation here shows that Chisholm's whole enterprise has failed.

40. The fact that one can hold a doubt or belief as evident and then, on rationally appraising it, hold that it is unreasonable to do so, demonstrates this distinction.

The above distinctions apply equally to belief. However, the first-order knowledge claims which are parallel to "I doubt that Fa" are not expressed as "I believe that Fa," but merely as "Fa."[41] There is good reason for this, for we reserve "I believe that Fa" for a second-order reflective statement about our belief in order to keep its form parallel to all other "thought of" statements, such as "I believe that I doubt that Fa," "I think that I see that Fa," "It seems that I am angry," and so on. Therefore, as soon as we make epistemic appraisals of our own beliefs (knowledge claims) we can move into this form of locution. We say "My *taking* the a to be an F with evidence is reasonable (unreasonable)" or "My *belief* that Fa is reasonable (unreasonable)."[42] Once again, we more often adopt a third-person form of discourse, such as "It is unreasonable that Fa," but such statements are equivalent to "It is unreasonable to *believe* (affirm, think, etc.) that Fa," or "To *affirm* that Fa is unreasonable." These, again, are elliptical for a statement like "It is unreasonable for anyone to *believe* (with evidence) that Fa." Now I can refer to the certainty I have of my reflective appraisal, if I wish, merely by prefixing all these statements with "It is evident that. . . ."

Ryle and Austin are correct that statements of the form "I believe that Fa" are hedges. However, what is interesting to us about such statements is that we make them only when we have taken up a reflective point of view on our beliefs but when, also, our first-order belief is not evident (that is, not successful or not intentionally achieved).[43] In other words, I treat all my nonevident beliefs from a reflective point of view, for I cannot live or "put my faith" in them. We never say "Fa" unless it is evident, and, if it is not, we always say something of the form "I believe that Fa" or "That Fa is reasonable (unreasonable, acceptable, etc.)." In the case of all nonevident statements, I take up a "crisis attitude" which is equivalent to the

41. It should be obvious that I agree with Austin that statements of belief are different from statements of knowledge, but it is more in keeping with Merleau-Ponty's usual usage and philosophical tradition to continue to use "belief" to refer to claims of knowledge, affirmations, or assertions.

42. Of course, while I believe that Fa, I cannot affirm that it is unreasonable to do so. This is precisely Merleau-Ponty's point, but it only becomes clear when we see that, equally, we cannot affirm that it is reasonable.

43. It is equally important to note that a statement such as "It is unreasonable that Fa" is also a hedge, and that the statement "It is reasonable that Fa" is *less* of one.

reflective attitude, for its methods of rational assessment can give me some direction about what I should believe. These hedges pose questions to myself or others when their resolution is of importance to us; and determining a statement's credibility supplies me with an answer that most often will not mislead me and will be worth accepting if I must act on the statement.

One of Merleau-Ponty's main claims was that the "thought of perception" reduces "the true to the credible" (*VI*39) or, more broadly, that cognitive statements reduce the evidence of perception. However, he has also stated that cognitive acts can be evident. We can now understand how these two assertions can be consistent and how the ambiguities in the concept of thought of perception make the phenomenalist's argument appear sound. If by the "thought of perception" the phenomenalist means statements of the form "I believe that I perceive that *Fa*" (or "I believe that I sense *F*"), then he has taken up a second-order reflective standpoint whose own evidence does not bear on the evidence of a first-order belief or on an act of perception. Thus Merleau-Ponty says of such a "thought" that we consider it "unshakable only because it presumes nothing about what effectively is, only because it entrenches itself in the apparition to the thought of what is thought" (*VI*36). However, this "type of certitude" is "onerous" (*VI*36) because it is merely that of performing a reflective act (a second-order belief or appraisal) and thus loses whatever substantive content it had intended. If the phenomenalist means a statement of the form "I perceive that *Fa*" (or "I sense *F*"), then this statement may also be evident, but its evidence is that of a belief which is a successful sublimation and expression of an evident act of perception. In both cases the evidence of the perceptual act is taken out of action (and to this extent the first-order belief is also a "reflection" on the first-order perceptual act). However, in the latter there is at least a reference, in some sense, to the original perceptual evidence, while the former is twice removed from this perceptual act. (An evident belief that is directly verifiable by a perceptual act can be formulated only if it sublimates an *evident* perception.) It is likely by confusing or playing upon these three different senses of a "thought of perception"—(1) the actual perceptual act; (2) the cognitive claim corresponding to it; and (3) the reflective claim about the first-order cognitive claim—that the phenomenalist can maintain that it presents us with a foundational certainty. Chisholm, for example, confounds the lived evidence of a first-order belief with the reflective evaluations that can be made of this belief.[44] Furthermore, early phenomenalists frequently took these reflective statements to be equivalent to actual perceptual experience and thus confused their logic.

We shall complete this chapter with an examination of the way in which Merleau-Ponty would understand the standard character-ization of truth as correspondence. Although we have discussed his theory of truth throughout our analysis of evidence, the present discussion will summarize and put into perspective his understanding of propositional truth.

We have seen that Merleau-Ponty would be sympathetic to the description of synthetic propositional truths as correspondence. However, he would not agree that correspondence thematically defines truth and his understanding of this relation would, at most, attempt to explain the motive and ground behind such definitions. It cannot be treated as a test of truth because it is not a relation that can be made thematically clear to cognition or reflection, nor can this relation's terms be clearly separated. We have seen that it is a useful characterization because Merleau-Ponty sees cognitive truth as resulting from the process of sublimating lived situations into the *logos* of cognition or, equivalently, from the capacity of language to creatively express by means of its structures every form of Existence. A propositional truth can be defined, therefore, as an evident cognitive sublimation, or an evident linguistic expression, of a lived situation. If we now turn to an examination of this relationship and its two terms and then to the possible objections to Merleau-Ponty's analysis of truth, these points will become clearer.

The facts or states-of-affairs that are spoken of as corresponding to a true proposition *are* the lived situations of any existential region. Thus Merleau-Ponty has solved a number of the problems that have frequently been raised about this term of the relationship. If we can

44. Chisholm is, no doubt, correct that "appear" statements are sometimes used to give descriptions of perceptual experience (*Theory of Knowledge*, pp. 31-32). However, since this puts them into the category of first-order belief statements about sensing, their evidence cannot be a mirror image of the categorically different evidence of the act of perceiving itself. In any case, as we have seen, the evidence of a perceptual experience includes or is one and the same with the evidence of its objects, such that they cannot be significantly distinguished as direct and indirect.

accept that these facts are situations, then he has shown that they do indeed exist and his whole philosophy is a study of their logic. Furthermore, because situations can be presented to us in a noncognitive way, they are available to us independently of their cognitive statement and are obviously more than just a projection or reproduction of the form of such statements. They are, thus, conceivable and experienceable apart from cognition's propositional version of them.

However, such an interpretation of this particular use of "fact" does not give the correspondence theorist what he requires, for a situational truth or evident prereflective experience is not available as such to the analytic or reflective ego. Cognition cannot compare, from a distance, the fact with the statement of the fact. The correspondence relationship is not a reflective structure, not a cognitive-linguistic meaning that could bind two other cognitive meanings or objects of reflection. We have seen that this comparison is just the process of sublimation or creative expression—an operational and transitional synthesis that cannot be reflectively articulated. Cognition indeed, experiences this correspondence, but in a prereflective manner, for it is its attempt to formulate a lived or evident belief. The experience of evidence is the cognitive experience of the adequacy of this relationship. It is indeed the case that from the beginning cognition has a grasp of this lived significance, but it is a vague and highly indeterminate one. (The lived meaning is held only within our most general meaning-giving capacities, that is, within broad areas or fields of our cognitive-linguistic system.) If this grasp is not fulfilled by specifying it to the degree that our interests demand, cognition quickly loses its grasp of it. However, once it is articulated, cognition only possesses it in the form of a statement and not as a fact or lived situation. Therefore, although Merleau-Ponty shows that this "operative" correspondence must remain fundamentally obscure (thus leaving much room for illusion), he establishes that this relationship is metaphysically grounded in the intertranslatability of the body-subject's regions and is epistemologically experienceable as the evidence of belief.

Finally, the statement or the belief, as a term of the relationship, is neither independent of the other term nor of the relationship itself. If it is indeed a propositional truth of our world, then noetically it retains its grasp on the experience that it meant to express, and noematically it becomes a layer of cognitive significance which from its inception constitutes this particular fact of the natural world. Propositional truth is only possible because it is grounded in the concrete structures which give us our primordial contact with Being and because these natural structures are inherently intersubjective (*VI*13-14). "It is necessary that it [true thought] remain true not only as a past actually lived, but also as a perpetual present always retaken [*repris*] in the passage of time" (*F*451). Once they are acquired, these truths remain on the horizon of every present in such a way that they become part of the world with which each present must be concordant and consistent. Although our sedimented truths appear to be independently available to us, Merleau-Ponty repeatedly stresses (chapter 4.2) that this is an illusion of secondary or inauthentic language and that the obscurity of their originating experiences will always be discoverable in them on inspection.[45]

The definition of truth as "evident cognitive creative expression" seems to be too narrow, for it appears to exclude the bulk of our knowledge and most of what we consider to be true, that is, the sedimented and institutional truths that comprise our culture and cognitive life. Merleau-Ponty does recognize the status of such knowledge, but he insists that "secondary" or "inauthentic" descriptive language be considered to have truth only insofar as it remains in touch with its originating experience. Its truth stems from its lived interrelationship with a situational truth. Thus, for example, if a proposition becomes merely a cliché of our society through overuse (or is forgotten by or irrelevant to our time), it loses this attachment to its foundation and must be reexperienced (verified) in order to again become part of the cognitive dimension of our lived world (390-91).

From another point of view this definition appears too broad, for it seems to include every type of creative linguistic expression. Our linguistic capacities can, indeed, be used to express (in the sense of concretely manifest) any type of activity in which the subject is involved (for example, pain is manifested by "ouch").[46] However,

45. Therefore, Merleau-Ponty says that the meaning of a descriptive term (for example, a noun) is constituted by the way we "experience" what it describes, its "generality" is that of "the world as typical," and its future authentic uses, which will also express lived situations, will compound this sense (403).

46. Max Black also understands this type of expression as an important function of language. Cf. *Labyrinth of Language*, p. 139.

the expression to which the definition refers is a species of this broader expressive power that belongs to any bodily region and it denotes the process of sublimation or the creation of "intellectual significance (*Bedeutung*)" (*F272*). Yet, Merleau-Ponty would hold that in every case where a lived situation is expressed by means of cognitive-linguistic structures some cognitive truth is involved as there is at least an implicit descriptive content to the utterance. Thus, for example, poetry and emotive utterances that successfully communicate an emotion, mood, way of life, and so forth, can be experienced as cognitively evident and thus can be constitutive of truth to some degree.[47]

With this analysis of cognitive evidence and truth, and of belief, doubt, and reflection, we come to the end of our examination of Merleau-Ponty's philosophy of cognition. Through a comprehensive review of his descriptions of the region, we have come to an understanding of its unique capacities and limitations. The discussions of his phenomenologies of language, essence, propositional truth, and imaginative expression have finally shown us that all types of *cogitationes* are grounded in the body-subject and in our primordial contact with the world, and therefore that there can be no privileged realm of immanent and apodictic states of mind. Similarly, because the cognitive region has its own form of operative intentionality and displays a situational logic, we have seen how Merleau-Ponty can account for reflection, or cognitive abstraction, within a philosophy of the body-subject and the lived world. Furthermore, we have shown that he has an adequate theory of propositional truth and evidence that is intrinsically related to his comprehension of noncognitive truth and evidence. His philosophy cannot be said to suffer from a "problem of truth."

Our study of cognition as a metastructure in its relation to perception presented a detailed examination of how these regions intertwine. Taking into account our previous analysis of the relationship between perception and motility, we are well on the way to attaining a full and concrete grasp of the reversibility and intertwining through which Merleau-Ponty ultimately defines Existence. This will be completed with our study of sociality and its

---

47. Merleau-Ponty therefore favors a form of "multifunctionalism" of ethical or emotive language. This term is Brandt's (cf. *Ethical Theory*, pp. 231-39), although P.H. Nowell-Smith is the most famous proponent of this theory of language (see his *Ethics*).

blending with nature in the next chapter. Similarly, it has now become clear how cognition necessarily structures and gives sense to our experience of any entity within the world (this becomes important in chapter 5 for understanding the permanency and depth of both the natural and socio-cultural worlds). We have also learned that cognitive structures are as much a part of our facticity as are the structures of the other regions of the body-subject. This chapter has also completed the discussion of a number of major themes that have occupied us throughout. It has further extended our understanding of Merleau-Ponty's philosophy of perception by examining perceptual truth and evidence and by clearly establishing the possibility of analytic, or reflective, perception. It brings to completion our studies of the experience of evidence, which, we learned, was the key epistemic experience for describing primordial contact (chapter 2.1); the relationship between subjectivity, temporality, and Being (chapter 2.4); and the relationship between appearances and the thing itself (chapters 3.1 and 3.2). Finally, it has demonstrated the efficacy of Merleau-Ponty's notion of situation, for it has shown us how he can productively apply the logic of situation to the region which at first glance appeared least amenable to it.

Most important is the fact that by means of this study of cognition and the previous study of perception, we have achieved a thorough grasp of Merleau-Ponty's treatment of standard phenomenological and epistemological issues. Through the examination of how existential, or situational, analysis deals with these types of philosophical problems, we have revealed original (and rarely explicated) features of Merleau-Ponty's phenomenological studies. Finally, these studies have justified our earlier interpretations of the central phenomenological descriptions that Merleau-Ponty uses as the starting point for his metaphysics. We have now observed concretely how, on the one hand, Merleau-Ponty's phenomenology constantly directs us to metaphysical questions for its completion, and, on the other hand, how his ontology and deepest metaphysics presuppose an initial inquiry into phenomenological questions.

5 Being and Man

The purpose of this chapter is to give an exhaustive analysis of Merleau-Ponty's views on the constitution of Being, and thus to deepen our understanding of Being's regions and essential character-istics. Besides justifying many of our previous statements about Being (especially those in chapters 1.4, 2.1, and 2.4) and drawing the conclusions from them, we shall take up a number of new topics, the most important of which will be connected with Merleau-Ponty's theories about the relationships between people. The main theme of the chapter is the metaphysical relationship of Being to man and our main task is to systematize Merleau-Ponty's extensive and diverse thoughts on this subject. We shall be a long way toward achieving this goal if we first comprehend the subject as a "clearing," opening, or making-visible of Being by itself, and, on this basis, comprehend the social world and the whole of history as the concrete ontic manifestation of a Being that is no more than the synthesis and interweaving of such clearings. All of these aims will be satisfied by structuring our investigation around the problem of others and the way in which a multiplicity of subjects can interrelate within Being. In the course of this study of Merleau-Ponty's deepest metaphysics we shall frequently appeal to his last works and hence become better acquainted with them. Yet we shall also make extensive use of his earlier work, for as we have tried to demonstrate throughout he was already committed to metaphysics in the *Phenomenology of Perception* and his solutions to its main problems did not change. This is not to deny that his metaphysical perspective was obscured in his main work by the richness, extensiveness, and complexity of its phenomenological studies.[1] Indeed, many commentators were unaware of the centrality of metaphysics to his thought until the publication of the later works.[2]

We can best introduce the discussion in this section by examining the types of questions that arise within Merleau-Ponty's theory of sociality. It appears prima facie that Merleau-Ponty, like most phenomenologists, has a problem with "other minds." His problem is, however, as much metaphysical as phenomenological. Not only must it be explained how the experience of others is possible, but also how it is conceivable that there can be other subjects, given the relationship of the subject to Being that we have so far discussed. If we briefly review the subject's central place in Being, the problem will become clearer.

Our previous analyses have shown that the body-subject and the senses in particular are in primordial contact with Being. This means that the body and the world are ontologically one and the same: the Being of the world is the "corporeity" (*F*294) and the "flesh" (*VI*138) of these senses (and of the other primitive regions). We analyzed this central thesis of Merleau-Ponty's in terms of the "generality" and "anonymity innate" (*VI*139) to the senses, that is to say, in terms of the *on*. We concluded that the body is present to the whole of Being. Our study of temporality showed that sub-jectivity has even greater metaphysical importance; it was shown to be the unifying thrust and coherence of temporality, and thus the manifestation of Being's own drive to determine itself and make itself explicit. A subject, therefore, is a point where Being clears itself; that is to say, it is "a field of Being" (*VI*240), "the pivot of being" (*VI*99), the "location" (*VI*140) and "Being-there" (*VI*258) of Being, its "measurant" (*VI*103 and *VI*206), its "natural light" (*VI*118), and its "Opening" ("*Eröffnung*" [*VI*206], "*Offenheit*" [*VI*185, *VI*196, *VI*213, etc.]).

This understanding of Being leaves us with many questions. We

---

1. Merleau-Ponty chides himself in his last notes for not unambiguously bringing the conclusions of the *Phenomenology* "to ontological explicitation" (*VI*183) and makes this a main goal of his projected work.

2. For example, see Kwant's introduction to *From Phenomenology to Metaphysics*, pp. 11 ff. (although Kwant puts too great a distance between Merleau-Ponty's earlier and later works).

must explain how a number of "constitutors" or "articulators" of Being can coexist within one Being, witness and communicate with one another, and at the same time be individual or contingently different from one another. We must ask why there should be more than one subject since each subject actualizes and contains every dimension of Being through his own thrown structures. We must demonstrate the necessity of Being giving rise to a multiplicity of individuals, rather than to one lone and absolute subject. We must clarify how sociality can be an irremovable dimension of Being,[3] how it is even conceivable that the subject have a singular and thrown capacity to experience other subjects, and how such a dimension can be possessed (as each *on* is) by an individual.

The solution to these problems lies in making Merleau-Ponty's metaphysical descriptions of the subject fully explicit. This will involve an ontological understanding of the ontic subject as a spatio-temporal field or as *Being clearing itself perspectivally*. That it is epistemologically possible for there to be other subjects will be shown by establishing how these perspectives and presents (with their general horizons) can contribute to and permeate one another without denying the subjectivity of one another. The problem of how others can be given phenomenologically is solved by Merleau-Ponty's theory of the necessary visibility of intentions, gestures, and conducts.

By taking into account this view of the subject and the main principle of Being that we have discussed—that Being seeks to maximize its self-comprehension and determination by its constant drive into multiplicity—we shall be able to explain how a multiplicity of individuals is a *necessary* feature of Being. As a result, we shall show that Merleau-Ponty's understanding of Being makes it inconceivable or contradictory not to allow for a plurality of subjects to maximize Being's articulation of itself. This will be explained by showing, first, how one individual's present field is further clarified and determined by the presence of others, and, secondly, how it is greatly expanded. This will lead to an account of how a highly determinate and permanent world is conceivable for Merleau-Ponty.

---

3. Sartre, to his credit, shows a clear awareness of this set of problems and of their importance to an existential phenomenology, for, although he does not undertake their solution, he outlines them thoroughly in *Being and Nothingness* (pp. 297-302).

Furthermore, we shall see that many subjects make possible a socio-cultural world whose resulting language, institutions, and cultural products greatly increase Being's self-expression. But equally we shall comprehend how Being itself is historical, for the societies and civilizations which are founded by a multiplicity of individuals allow Being to develop itself well beyond the evolutionary capacities or the historicity of any one individual or society.

Prior to establishing the epistemological possibility and metaphysical necessity of others, we shall attempt to exhaustively analyze the subject as a spatio-temporal field or clearing; this means that we shall understand subjectivity from "the point of view of Being" (i.e., within a strictly metaphysical context). Not only will this be helpful for the following discussion, but it may clarify Merleau-Ponty's metaphysical perspective and thus set right a number of serious misinterpretations of his philosophy. Certainly, part of the advantage of such strictly metaphysical descriptions of the subject and the world (which Heidegger would call "existential" and "formal" as opposed to "existentiell") is that they confront to a much greater degree our Cartesian prejudices concerning individuality. It is harder to slip into a dualist ontology if the subject is understood to be a field of Being, or a contingent manifestation of Being's own perspectival illumination of itself. However, this is not to say that Merleau-Ponty ceases to be a genuine phenomenologist when he turns to deep metaphysical issues.[4]

It is, of course, axiomatic that phenomenology cannot take up a point of view external to the subject and that any entity must be described as it is *for a subject*, or as it is given *to me*. But as both Merleau-Ponty and Heidegger have demonstrated, this *mineness* (*Jemeinigkeit*), or phenomenological limitation and principle, also gives us a direct access to Being.[5] Indeed, we have argued this point throughout and we have shown, for example, that our self-givenness and general self can be experienced as a reflection of Being on itself and that a description of subjectivity can lead to a description of

4. For example, Zaner, in failing or refusing to see how the phenomenological perspective can become metaphysical, implicitly assumes that the world (and Being) can only be described as it *appears* to be by means of a subject who is correlatively posited as an external and purely transcendental source of this world (cf. *The Problem of Embodiment*, particularly pp. 233-38).

5. Cf. *Being and Time*, pp. 68ff.

temporality and Being. Merleau-Ponty's argument that the subject is in primordial contact with Being provides a strong justification for his form of "descriptive metaphysics," which uses phenomenological description as the basis for more general conclusions about Being itself. Furthermore, like Heidegger he is directly in the existential phenomenological tradition, for he believes that limiting experiences (such as anxiety, love, shame, depression, and boredom) make possible an authentic state of mind which produces a privileged intuition of the situation. This deepest vision and experience of the reality of man, the world, and Being can profitably be viewed as the existentialist equivalent to Husserl's final reductions.[6]

Let us outline the form of our argument, its methodology, and the conclusions it will attempt to establish. All of our arguments will presuppose the essential characteristics of Being that we have established, and that Being must give rise to a subject understood as a spatio-temporal clearing. After explicating the notion of clearing, we shall be able to show that, on the basis of the understanding of Being that we have achieved thus far, it is logically possible for Being to have a plurality of such clearings. Given the contingent fact that there are *many* subjects that interrelate in a common natural world (one that Merleau-Ponty has phenomenologically analyzed), we shall then be able to conclude that Being must necessarily be constituted by a multiplicity of interrelated clearings. Using the above conclusions in section 2, we shall demonstrate that it is logically possible for Being to contain sociality as a distinctive dimension (flesh, element, or stuff) which will bind these natural clearings in a new and categorically different manner—interpersonally, socio-culturally, and historically. Once again, when we take into account the contingent fact that there is a socio-cultural world, we can show that it is necessary that Being have sociality as one of its essential dimensions. We shall then be able to conclude that Being necessarily manifests itself concretely by means of contingently different societies and interpersonal relationships.

The type of necessity we demonstrate is a retrospective necessity

6. The transcendental perspective and ego that Husserl sought were, of course, never personal. Merleau-Ponty validates the program to discover the structures of intersubjectivity, but he also shows, through his frequent commentaries on Husserl, that the foundational logic that was pursued by Husserl bears a family resemblance to the *logos* of Being that was to become the main topic of existential phenomenology.

(not to be confused with Merleau-Ponty's "retrospective illusion"). Hegel's system is based on a similar type of necessity, for he attempts to prove that Being necessarily consists of certain "forms of consciousness" (i.e., transcendental structures that organize all aspects of existence) and that these have a necessary dialectical relationship one to the other (and that these conclusions can only be reached retrospectively given the present standpoint of the philosopher). The argument combines certain essential characteristics of Being and the ways in which it presently, or contingently, manifests itself, in order to disclose the structures and elements that must constitute Being. Thus the argument does not claim that given certain characteristics of Being it can be deduced that Being must consist of a plurality of clearings and have a categorically distinct social dimension; nor does it claim that one can predict Being's particular manifestations, for it establishes these structures of Being only "after the fact."

Further, this chapter will resemble a transcendental analysis and synthesis of Being, since its purpose is to reveal the "constitution of Being." That is to say, it will explicate and systematize the metaphysical grounds that Merleau-Ponty shows to be necessary if the subject and world as he describes them phenomenologically are to be possible. However, the spatio-temporal clearing and social dimension are not merely formal and transcendental structures of our understanding, but rather the material (flesh and stuff) and experienceable constituents of Being and the world.

Finally, it must be kept in mind that our overall argument is a construction which, although based on Merleau-Ponty's work, cannot be found there as such. Each stage and transition within the argument presents key positions of Merleau-Ponty's, and it is just these that it is our purpose to make comprehensible; but they occur in various contexts throughout his work. The systematization of his thoughts by means of a framework of core metaphysical issues should make their strength and coherence more obvious.

1. Being and Subjectivity

The term *clearing* will be central in this chapter, although it is one that Merleau-Ponty hardly uses. Though it is a Heideggerian term, its significance in Heidegger is not a major one, nor does it have the weight and precise sense we shall give it in Merleau-Ponty's name.[7] Ultimately we will justify its use by showing its effectiveness for clarifying and unifying Merleau-Ponty's metaphysics. However, we can begin by showing that it has a prima facie advantage over a group of closely related concepts on which Merleau-Ponty relies heavily.

I know of only one place where Merleau-Ponty makes direct use of the term *clearing* (more might be found). In an important statement on the *ekstase* of time or the dehiscence of subjectivity in the *Phenomenology of Perception*, he says: "Here a light [*lumière*] bursts forth, here we are no longer concerned with a being that reposes in itself, but with a being whose whole essence like that of light is to *make visible* . . . , to open itself to an Other and to go outside itself" (487). In a footnote he refers this use of *lumière* to Heidegger's *Gelichtetheit*.[8] The quotation includes many of the characteristics that define our use of *clearing*; that is, it is a dehiscence or an opening that splits off (*écart*) from itself (cf. *VI*123, *VI*146, and *VI*153) and a being-outside-itself or making-visible (cf. chapter 2.4). A second use, which comes close to being direct, occurs in *The Visible and the Invisible*: "My flesh and that of the world thus bring about clear areas, clearings [*comportent des*

---

7. Heidegger's usage is not precise (although it functions adequately in the different contexts in which he uses it). Not only does it change with Heidegger's "turn" (and Merleau-Ponty would favor to some extent the later use which makes the clearing more the action of Being than of *Dasein*), but its sense shifts in many works that lie within a single period. This has been shown adequately by a number of commentators, for example, A. De Waelhens (*Phénoménologie et vérité*, pp. 70 ff.) and Werner Marx (*Heidegger and the Tradition*, pp. 146 ff.). This equivocalness is advantageous for our purposes, for it allows us to develop the concept in a way that is distinctively appropriate to Merleau-Ponty, while still benefiting from the familiarity and intuitiveness that Heidegger has established for the term. Thus our use is in the tradition, but by no means, can it be taken to provide a Heideggerian interpretation of Merleau-Ponty.

8. This term is introduced in *Sein und Zeit* on p. 350, but it is used in the same way as *Lichtung*, which introduces the notion of clearing on p. 133 but which Heidegger then stops using in favor of the former term. Cognates of *éclaircir* better translate these terms than *lumière* (Boehm and De Waelhens use *lumière* as well in their translation of *Sein und Zeit*), for the light metaphor, which is better kept under control by *clearing*, too easily implies a dualism of light source and lit contents. *Lichtung* in *Ueber den Humanismus* is translated by Roger Munier as *éclaircie* (*Lettre sur l'humanisme*, p. 188) but by Frank A. Capuzzi and J. Glenn Gray as *lighting* (*Martin Heidegger: Basic Writings*, pp. 193 ff.).

zones claires, les jours], around which pivot their opaque areas" (*VI*195F).

The technical term of Merleau-Ponty's that comes closest to *clearing* is *field*. He says, for example, that "we are a field of Being" (*VI*240), "a field of experience" (*VI*110), and that "I am all that I see, . . . an intersubjective field" (452). In an important note he makes this programmatic statement: "There is no longer: —consciousness, —projections, —In itself or object. There are fields in intersection, in a field of fields wherein 'subjectivities' are integrated" (*VI*227). This states concisely the core of the argument of this chapter, which is to show that intersubjectivity is to be understood as the formal, natural, and social intertwining of clearings, and that Being by itself is just the field of all these fields (or the clearing of these clearings). He also says that his philosophy "leads to the rejecting of the notion of subject, or to the defining of the subject as a field, as a hierarchized system of structures opened by the inaugural *there is*" (*VI*239). It appears that, like Heidegger, Merleau-Ponty would like to stop using such terms as *subject, body, consciousness* and *cogito*, but he does not favor this kind of absolute linguistic legislation. Creative expression in philosophy and in ordinary language is achieved for him, rather, through the redefinition or rearrangement of the uses of sedimented terms. In spite of this overlap of sense, *field* is not the term we seek; it is too noematic and substantive, and thus it cannot sustain the crucial active, verbal, or process senses that *clearing* can.

Insofar as the cognates of the term *open* are closely connected to *clearing* (in ordinary language and in Heidegger) and are among the most frequently used terms in Merleau-Ponty's work, and because openness, or primordial contact, is a main theme of his philosophy (as we established in chapter 2.1), *clearing* is a natural and appropriate term for referring to the metaphysical status of the subject. *The open* will not do (although *opening* is a bit better), because it does not have the richness of *clearing* and clashes strongly with some dominant senses that *clearing* is able to capture. For example, an opening is something that is completely achievable and totally empty, something that has clear boundaries and is qualitatively homogeneous. It is also hard to conceive of how the open can progressively and shiftingly blend with the hidden, concealed, and closed.[9]

Our final justification for the use we shall make of the term *clearing* is that Merleau-Ponty uses often the phrase "natural light" in the same sense. Heidegger introduces the term by means of this phrase and Merleau-Ponty is well aware of the connection of the two.[10] Let us now begin to give a positive description of the subject as a clearing by stressing its global character.

A clearing is a spatio-temporal perspective on Being in its entirety. Thus when Merleau-Ponty states that Being "lets itself be captivated by one of its fragments" (*VI*141), he is telling us that Being as a whole reveals itself and has a hold on itself through one of its sectors (a subject). We discovered in our study of temporality that this figure through which Being clears itself is the present field. But we also learned, first, that this field holds all other fields simultaneously on its horizon and, secondly, that its entire past and indeterminate future are present within the field. Since these horizons cover Being, the clearing is "a unique structure that is *presence*" (430), but since they are organized differently through each present they are also essentially characterized as an "original perspective" (*VI*97). Yet we must be careful about some implications of the term *perspective* because "I am never fixed on any and am able to change points of

9. Heidegger believes just the opposite, for he favors making the open a whole whose parts are the clearing and the concealed (see, for example, "The Origin of the Work of Art" in *Poetry, Language and Thought*, p. 55).

Clearing, of course, has its own misleading connotations and some of the metaphors it carries may break down too easily. However, particularly in English, it is a term of such richness that it may be able to shape itself to the task we put to it. For example, consider only these three of its senses. First, a clearing as an opening in a forest is a useful metaphor as it is a place prepared within the wilds for human cultivation, and it shades off gradually into the darkness of the forest; yet, it does not organize the entire forest and only contains the beginnings of culture (it is not a settlement). Secondly, its sense of being at once a manifestation of the activity and a product of clarification, explication, and articulation, as well as being an openness, understanding, and reception of what is there, is a core sense; yet, this may suggest too easily the clarity, distinctness, and purity of cognition. Thirdly, the senses that it shares with its related term *cleaning* are fortuitous insofar as they imply making-ready and putting things in place, and, of course, brightening, unobscuring, defogging, unveiling, etc.; yet unhappy insofar as they may imply purity, translucence, emptiness, and finality.

10. Merleau-Ponty says, for example, that "even the light of consciousness is, as Heidegger says, *lumen naturale*, given to itself" (432) and that men "have in common a natural light or opening to being" (*Signs*, p. 239). Cf. *Being and Time*, p. 171 (*H*133). Some other uses of the phrase occur at *VI*xxxv, *VI*118, *VI*142, *VI*146, *VI*154, *Sense and Non-Sense*, p. 93, and *Primacy of Perception*, p. 10.

view" (*F*465–66). The sense in which he uses the term (e.g., 364, *F*406, 421, and *VI*98) is based on the fact that the "subject is in situation . . . is nothing other than a possibility of situations" (*F*467 and *F*465). Thus we should understand the way in which Being has a point of view on itself by means of the total "heirarchial system of structures" (*VI*239). These encompass all of otherness to some indeterminate and general degree; they are held and actualized by the present field, formally constitute our past, and protend our future. Therefore, our reliance on the concept of clearing does not run contrary to our initial assertion that the situation is the primary ontological unit. However, it is necessary to move to a more inclusive level of organization by taking the clearing as the main constituent or "building block" of Being. The clearing will remain a gestalt of structures, but of structures which, as we began to realize early, are centered and incarnated within the concreteness of a particular field.

Let us look more closely at the spatiality of the clearing. One can begin to see that the figure-ground relationship is basic in Merleau-Ponty's thought because it is the ultimate form through which Being can be given to itself as a whole. He tells us to understand that the "to be conscious = to have a figure on a ground—one cannot go back any further" (*VI*191); it is "the simplest '*Etwas*' " (*VI*192) because "it is *that separation* [*écart*] first of all that is perceptual *meaning*" (*VI*197). Whereas Hegel helped us to understand the Concept (Being) by showing us that the for-itself could be defined in "pure opposition" to the multiplicity of the world, Merleau-Ponty allows us to see how the for-itself is a "derived characteristic" (*VI*191): he shows us the continuity of the subject with Being, when it is taken as a point or instant of Being that splits off (*écart*) into this multiplicity. Being, taken either as a unified temporal thrust or as a global set of regions, splits off and diverges from itself by centering on a figure or field that makes it actual. Herein lies the usefulness of the metaphor used previously (chapter 1.4) that sees subjectivity as at the pinnacle of a figure which is fully continuous with the background to its farthest horizons.[11] Further-

---

11. Sartre uses to good effect a similar metaphor of the subject as the ideal limit of a contracting empirical center or vanishing point in order to understand the abstractness of the rationalist notion of the formal ego (*The Transcendence of the Ego*, pp. 41 and 54) and the givenness of the self of another (*Being and Nothingness*, pp. 255 and 295). It is important to note that Nietzsche too tries to envision the subject as merely a center or point of Power or Will (Being), in order to articulate the relationship of man and Being (*The Will to Power*, #'s 715, 488, 551n., 636, and 689).

more, we can form a concrete image of the world, space, and depth if we conceive of them as the scattering and divergence of this "point source" or as the figure spreading into its background. *Ecart* is, then, a putting in depth and the "inauguration" (*VI*140) of space, first, because this point encompasses otherness through its set of structures, and, secondly, because each of these structures has its own characteristic way of spatializing, while the present balance of all of these structures (the spatial level) constitutes the space of the present field.[12] A subject is possible because Being can only grasp itself by means of a particular focus which inherently opens on to an infinity of meanings. Thus *épaisseur* as the characteristic depth and denseness of Being, *écart* as its basic movement, and gestalt as its essential form are all intimately connected for Merleau-Ponty.

"The spectacle of the world that is my own . . . refers with evidence to typical dimensions of visibility, and finally to a virtual focus of vision, to a detector also typical" (*VI*146). The organization of my present field refers me to my own location in the field, but it does so as *any* perceiver who happens to be in that position. The "who" of prepersonal perception is the "perceiver in general" at this particular place or point. As we saw in chapter 1.4, our thrown regions of Existence are shared by and universal to all possible subjects. It is now clear that these regions can be manifest only if they are actualized at one point or are organized around one focus. ("Flesh is . . . adherent to *location* and to the *now*" [*VI*140]).[13]

When I see another within my field, I see him as a person like myself because he is another potential focus of these same dimensions; that is, I see another potential perspective of my own which is in fact actualized by another. As we shall note, this is only

12. Space should be understood as that which is "reckoned starting from me [*compté à partir de moi*] as point or degree zero of spatiality." Further, "depth and light . . . run through us and surround us" (*EM*59F).

13. "There is . . . no problem of the *alter ego* because it is not *I* who sees, not *he* who sees, because an anonymous visibility inhabits both of us, a vision in general, in virtue of that primordial property that belongs to flesh, of being here and now and of radiating everywhere and forever (*VI*187-88). *Flesh* becomes for Merleau-Ponty a name for Being, one, he says, that is primitive and that has not been spoken before. We can understand it by recalling that the senses and the body-subject (and Being) in the *Phenomenology* are the "milieu between the in-itself and the for-itself" (*F*246). Similarly, he states in *The Visible and the Invisible* that flesh which is "between the seer and thing is constitutive for the thing of its visibility as for the seer of his corporeity" (*VI*135).

possible because the natural world makes my body visible by referring back to it as the center of its levels and organization. The field, through its reversibility, locates its own focus and makes it visible as part of itself. As soon as the other acts within my present field (moves, manipulates, gestures, or suffers within it), he manifests a set of basic dimensions which locate him in the same space as myself (not, of course, a physical objective space, but one in which the subject moves and can exist). The other is experienced as a typical point of typical dimensions and space as an infinity of such perspectives. Since I know myself, at this level of the natural and prepersonal self, as a virtual focus, it is not difficult to see how I can recognize another as such. However, as Merleau-Ponty often insists, this only gives the other as a natural self, a manifestation of the *on*, or a mere "living other" (*F*406). He is not yet presented as an individual and distinctive personality or "human other" (*F*406).

We have thus far tended to understand the subject as a spatial field, but in order to understand the full subject we must also grasp it as the focus or present of a temporality. (We shall eventually see that the subject is still more than this, for it is also the focus of a social world and of history.) Merleau-Ponty states that what distinguishes the human subject from other organisms is its "historical inherence" (*F*69). It is because of this historicity of the subject that the other is given with a beyondness or "inexhaustible core [*fond*]" (*F*415). Let us examine the subject both as a spatial and a temporal clearing and attempt to discover how it is possible that such clearings can coexist and bear witness one to the other.

We have established that the subject is a figural present field which has the remainder of the simultaneous world generally on its horizon. This means that in every present the world as a whole is determined and cleared in a distinctive way. We can understand the subject as an historical field by recalling that this present field has a past horizon of other such fields. Each of these fields, in turn, presents a total and distinctive grasp of Being. Yet none of these present clearings of Being is separable; we have seen in detail how they are all modifications, outgrowths, and redeterminations of those that preceded them.

We can conceive of each present, then, as a highlighting and specification of the previously indeterminate and horizonal areas of Being and as a downgrading or disarticulation of the previously determinate features of the world. The clearing is a process which constantly changes its perspective or "relief" by altering the "determinate-indeterminate" system through which Being grasps itself. As a consequence, the world is radically dynamic and oscillates with these different systems. Furthermore, the objects within this world must have a similarly unstable being which includes and is defined by the entire range of their appearances within this determinate-indeterminate series (*VI*226). It is to the subject, then, that Merleau-Ponty would give the dubious metaphysical honor of being what has been called a "spatio-temporal worm." Unlike Strawson's "worm" (which is a basic particular that must always be at one of the coordinates of an objective space and time and which allows for the possibility of reidentification), the clearing does not require accepting a hypothesis about a link with its past (it is a continuous explication of this past); nor must it be precisely locatable in space in order to explain its coexistence with other such "worms" (it always spreads throughout Being). It is similar to Russell's "worm" in that it encompasses the whole world and changes its shape in every present, but dissimilar in not representing a private and monadic world.[14]

Given that the subject is a clearing and that a clearing encompasses Being, how can we understand that there can be many such all-encompassing clearings and that they can encounter one another? The others are possible because

the other is not enclosed in my perspective on the world, because this perspec-tive itself has no definite limits, because it slips spontaneously into that of others, and because they are together gathered into a single world in which we all participate as anonymous subjects of perception. (*F*406)

14. For Strawson's conception, see *Individuals*, e.g., pp. 206-08; for Russell's conception, see "The Relation of Sense-Data to Physics" (from *Mysticism and Logic*), in Arthur Danto and Sidney Morgenbesser, eds., *Philosophy of Science*, pp. 33-54, particularly p. 50.

The similarity of clearings to monads, and of Being as a system of clearings to a monadology is striking. Thus Merleau-Ponty observes in a working note that "Being . . . is to be sure not the god of Leibniz, the 'monadology' thus disclosed is not the system of monads—substances; but certain Leibnizian descriptions—that each of the views of the world is a world apart, that nonetheless 'what is particular to one would be public to all,' that the monads would be in a relation of expression between themselves and with the world, that they differ from one another and from it as perspectives—are to be maintained entirely" (*VI*222-23).

These different clearings can intertwine within one Being since each is an indeterminate and open-ended explication of Being. It is the "generality" of my horizons, of my present field, and even of myself as the focus of this field that allows others to be present to me.[15] The generality of my horizon does not come into conflict with another's figural determination of a part of it because my indeterminate claim can only be furthered by the other's specification of it. Even many subjects who share the same "landscape" (*VI*140) do not exclude one another, for this field is general enough to permit a multiplicity of perspectives, and these in fact support one another.

A field does not exclude another field . . . , it tends of itself even to multiply because it is the opening by which, as body, I am "exposed" to the world. . . . [Others] are able to slip into my field, multiply it from within, and appear to me to be prey to, and at grips with, the same world as I . . . because my relationship to myself is already generality . . . (and the other) is a generalized *I*.[16]

There is room for many clearings because Being is essentially finite: that is to say, Being can never exhaustively determine itself, not even in one detail or at one time; it can grasp itself as a whole only by means of the figure-ground structure; it is permeated by "emptiness," is "porous" (*VI*102), and "exists" only by degree. All clearings cover one and the same Being but set it in relief (*écart*) in ways which, though different, are essentially compatible and necessarily interrelated.

We have already noticed that the spatial positions of others are given to me as possible positions of my own. Conversely, my own past and future are given to me as other potential "selves" or the present fields of others. The others who are given to me as present fields are, therefore, in some sense actualizations of my own temporal horizons (and my present is a possible future or general past for them). "Two temporalities are not mutually exclusive" (433).[17] Of course, these presents will only merge in their general structures, but this is sufficient to give rise to a singular *on*, to an intersubjectivity that consists in the intertwining of all of these

15. *The Prose of the World*, pp. 136–38.

16. *La prose du monde*, pp. 191–92.

17. An alter ego is possible for man "because he is outside of himself in the world and because one ek-stase is compossible with others" (*Signes*, p. 215).

presents (we have learned that any present is alterity and flux and thus always leaves room for other determinations.) Therefore, when we share the same field, even though there will be a temporal shift or distance between our perspectives, these presents will be ecstatically bound to one another. Therefore, we can comprehend how temporality and spatiality are essentially inseparable. The spread between our positions is a temporal spread between presents.[18] Through my awareness of this spread I experience Being as a *lived* simultaneity of an infinity of presents or spatio-temporal clearings. Being, therefore, consists of, and is present to itself as, a multiplicity of clearings (it is flesh), not as a thing, or even as a universe of things.

What is given is not one fragment of time and then another, one individual flux, then another; it is the retaking [*reprise*] of each subjectivity by itself, and of subjectivities one by the other in the generality of a nature, the cohesion of an intersubjective life and of a world. (*F*515)

By examining visibility more closely and particularly the reversibility of the subject with his field, we shall see why it is *necessary* for Being to consist of a multiplicity of clearings.[19] By demonstrating, first, how the subject is made visible in the same action wherein the natural world is revealed, and, secondly, how his relationship with other subjects expands this natural visibility as well as giving rise to an historical-cultural world, we shall see what many subjects add to Being's comprehension and maximum articulation of itself, and hence why they are required. We have thus far shown that the clearing is the basic constituent of Being and that a multiplicity of such clearings is logically possible. We shall now establish that such a multiplicity accomplishes and satisfies the drive toward visibility which is the essential characteristic of Being that we discovered through our study of time. By means of this argument plus the phenomenological fact that there is an actual plurality of subjects in this world, which can be understood as a concrete

18. "Spatial profiles are also temporal: elsewhere is always something that one has seen or that one will be able to see; and even if I perceive it as simultaneous with the present, it is because it is part of the same wave of duration" (*F*329). "It is impossible to rigorously separate the present from what is only presented" (*F*382).

19. Let us recall that *visibility* is a very general term of Merleau-Ponty's that is used to refer at once to Being's drive to articulate itself and the corresponding inexhaustible structurability of otherness, to the logic of any of the four regions of Existence, and to the central fact that every structuring is a making visible both of itself and of its object.

manifestation of this multiplicity of clearings, we shall demonstrate that Being is necessarily constituted in this way.

Merleau-Ponty insists on the simultaneity of the visibility of the subject and the natural world because it makes the body-subject an intrinsic part of the field that it discloses. The important consequence of this fact is that it is the *field which clears itself*. The body must show itself when it makes the world visible; otherwise, we would have a case of a separable entity constituting Being rather than Being constituting itself. If the virtual focus of the clearing were not itself incarnate and as material as the rest of the field, then the subject would still be an external source of Being, at best as a pure transcendental ego and at worst as a distinct Cartesian substance. Similarly, we shall see that clearings clear one another, that is to say, that a subject makes other subjects visible while in the same action completing its own visibility. If it were not the case that each subject increased its own grasp of itself through making the others visible, then, again, we would not have a singular Being clearing itself. Instead, since the other would only make me visible *for* him (and him *for* me), Being would again be fragmented, but now into many private worlds or monads.

Merleau-Ponty has often demonstrated how the natural world reverses itself on the disclosing body and makes it appear as an "incarnate subject" (451). He says that the most "profound" sense of this "narcissism" of Being is "not to see the contour of a body that one inhabits in the outside as others see it, but especially to be seen by the outside, to exist within it" (*VI*183F). We can understand this reversibility by recalling some of the phenomenological studies through which Merleau-Ponty made it evident in his early work. In the previous chapters we learned that the field or "the common stuff of which all the structures are made is the *visible*" (*VI*200), that a particular field comes to light through its resistance to the subject's global set of structures, that the articulation of a present field is the expression of this set's maximum grasp of otherness, and that in general these structures are created and concretized through the contact of the subject and the world. We saw in great detail how by means of this same logic visual structures give rise to a prespatial field which makes space possible. The spatial levels which constitute space present the maximal and most balanced grasp of all the body's structures and anchor themselves within these prespatial givens.

Thus, for example, since the depth level of the field is determined by the degree of contact, grasp, or hold that the body has on the elements of the field, the "distances" with which its elements are given to the subject, being directly proportional to his phenomenological grasp of them, will necessarily place the body-subject at a particular point in the field. Furthermore, since this space is determined by the body's motor as well as by its perceptual capacities, the space between things and their extension will directly reflect (or make visible) the size, shape, position, and activity of the subject. "He who grasps them [any sensible entity] senses himself [*se sent*] emerge from them by a sort of coiling up or redoubling, fundamentally homogeneous with them; that he is the sensible coming to itself" (*VI*153F).

However, Merleau-Ponty notes that things only produce a "phantom of ourselves . . . by designating a place among themselves whence we see them" (*VI*143) and he characterizes the narrow reversibility of nature as "the plate glass of things with that feeble reflection" (*VI*143). Since the subject can only partially perceive himself and since the field's locating of his body can only be highly general and vague, the subject is not as visible to himself as are the other entities in the field. It is only when another occupies his field that he attains the same degree of existence and becomes completely ensconced in the field. In experiencing another, I perceive another structurer of my field, another perspective on it; thus I perceive myself from the other's point of view (and as the object-side of a structuring that is in fact visible to me). Furthermore, my present activity of structuring the world (see-ing, touch-ing, and spatializ-ing) becomes fully visible to me only insofar as the other's activity of making visible is visibly given to me.[20]

Merleau-Ponty's "ultimate" (*VI*140) descriptions of Being as a "circle," "wave," "coiling over," and "closing over upon itself" (*VI*140), as "pact," "fold," and "mirror arrangement" (*VI*146), gain their fullest expression through the relationship of two subjects. We shall see why it is through this relationship that Being makes itself maximally explicit. First, it is because the subject thus becomes fully

---

20. It should be noted that Merleau-Ponty maintains that there is no ontological distinction between the invisible and the visible, and that the most one can do to separate them is to characterize the invisible (structure) as the "obverse" of the visible (cf. *VI*149, *VI*151, and particularly *VI*152). To this extent, the title that was chosen for *The Visible and the Invisible* is somewhat misleading.

visible to itself; secondly, because its field gains added determinateness through the specifications which the other contributes;
thirdly, because its horizons are deepened and extended by being in
contact with the other's horizons; fourthly, because expression
becomes possible through this interchange, such that a socio-cultural
world can come into being, which in turn gives rise to an intersubjective world of ideas; and, finally, because Being can now begin
to explicate itself historically. It is for all of these reasons that it is
necessary for Being to split itself into a multiplicity of subjects or
clearings.

We should miss a great deal of Merleau-Ponty's metaphysics if we
failed to understand how it is possible to experience others to the
extent required above. Therefore we must digress in order to analyze
Merleau-Ponty's phenomenology of the perception of other persons.
We shall begin by establishing Merleau-Ponty's view that others are
given to us as a gestalt of conducts or gestures, and that these
gestures are intentions which can be visible to us. We shall then
discuss how it is possible to perceive gestures as such. This will be
followed by an explication of the metaphysical consequences of the
theory.

We do not perceive others as objective bodies nor their actions as
physical processes. On the contrary, others are available to us in the
same way as we are aware of ourselves, as body-subjects, and their
actions are given to us as structures, intentions, or manners of
being-in-the-world. Merleau-Ponty maintains that the smallest movement by the other (and we must recall that all concrete structures are
motor intentions) is given to us as a gesture, conduct, or
"comportment" (352, 369, and *CO*117). All of these terms indicate
that when we perceive the action of another, we perceive it on the
background of his present milieu. "A comportment outlines a certain
manner of treating the world" (*F*369). "The gesture . . . [brings]
certain perceptual bits of the world to my notice" (185). We perceive
the other as a source of situations and his individual gestures visibly
present us with "intentions" (352) and structures whose subject-side
and object-side are both necessarily given.[21] The other's action is

21. J. L. Austin's view is similar when he insists that actions and emotions are a "whole
pattern of events" which can only be abstractly distinguished into "occasion," "feeling" or
"impulse," and "manifestation." These three elements are clarified, when understood,
respectively as the object-side, subject-side, and actualization or incarnation of a situation.
Austin, "Other Minds," in *Philosophical Papers*, pp. 77-78.

given as animate and never simply as an objective physical movement because the perception of a body-subject immediately takes us into its field in such a way that we simultaneously perceive the objects at which it is directed and the way in which it structures them.[22]

> No sooner has my gaze fallen upon a living body in the process of acting than the objects surrounding it immediately take on a fresh significance . . . ; they are what this other behavior is about to make of them. Round about the perceived body a vortex forms. (353-54)

It is important to realize that this description applies not only to large-scale and overt gestures but to every movement of the body-subject. Thus even the other's perceptions are given to us as gestures which at least generally outline and organize a field, for as we have seen even perceptual activity is a form of motor intentionality. We have already discovered that the other is a possible present and position within our world, but we can now understand better that he presents us with a comprehensive modification of our field and that we perceive this partial duplication of our field in perceiving him. The field of which he is the virtual focus does not perfectly match mine, for it has different temporal and spatial horizons; in experiencing his variation on my present field, I am to some extent presented with these horizons, which in turn have a relevance to my own horizons (349). Therefore, the other is given to me as a clearing which permeates not only my present field but my entire world.

Given that "the other is open to me from the moment I define him and myself as 'conducts'" (CO117), it still remains to be understood how we can perceive others or their conduct "directly" (352). The theories of metastructures, incarnation, and innate existential regions allow us to comprehend how this type of perception is possible. We perceive, in the strict sense, the other as a body-subject because we use basically the same structures (those that constitute our own body-subject) which he is now using in order to perceive (in the strict sense) his actions. We share the same structures because the most basic structures of our regions are thrown and hence universal to all subjects. Furthermore, we also share a common

---

22. Since the body cannot be experienced in isolation from the field it structures, Merleau-Ponty cannot be accused of presenting a variant of behaviorism. Cf., for example, John W. Yolton, *Thinking and Perceiving*, pp. 36, 72, and 80.

history and culture which is for the most part responsible for the specification of these general regions and for the acquisition of our sedimented structures. Thus, when I perceive another, "the anonymous existence of which my body is the ever-renewed trace henceforth inhabits both bodies simultaneously" (354). We have seen that our metastructures consist of the concerns that are the articulation of our cognitive, motor-practical, or social-affective region. These structures give their significance to the natural world by modifying our lower-level and primary perceptual structures. They not only make it possible for us to be open to the features of the world which correlate with their particular interests (and to limit the openness of our perceptual region); but, as we saw at the end of our study of perception, they also guide and deepen our perceptual understanding of the natural world. Our senses will use whatever nonperceptual structures are available to them in order to grasp purely perceptual phenomena. For example, in perceiving the movements of any animate or inanimate entity, the motility of the eye or hand must anticipate the movements of its object and does so by relying on any of its own body's acquired capacities for movement. The transitional synthesis that is required to determinately perceive a moving entity is made possible by the senses integrating, or taking as their model, the motility of the body-subject. Our perceptual region uses any relevant structure which will aid it in grasping its object to the maximum degree.[23] In the case of perceiving others, we use metastructures that are identical to those that the other is now using merely in order to attain a maximum perceptual grasp of his actions. Secondly, since perceptual structures are a distinctive type of motor capacity, we use perceptual structures which correspond to those that the other is using in order to *see* his present perceptual activities. By calling on these capacities, perception immediately takes us to the intention that is occupying the other; his presence sets up an echo in our own body and the perception of the gesture is at one and the same time a being in sympathy with it.

To show the way in which the other's "gestures invade . . . [our]

23. "All that we are, all that happens to us can furnish us with explanatory tools for knowing the other . . . ; what happens to us does not happen only to us but to our entire vision of the world" (CO148).

world and guide . . . [our] look" (*F*464), Merleau-Ponty makes use of Husserl's phrase "intentional transgression" (*CO*24F),[24] describing the process as follows:

My body . . . discovers in that other body a miraculous prolongation of my own intentions, a familiar way of dealing with the world. (354)

This conduct, which I am only able to see, I live somehow at a distance. I make it mine; I retake it and comprehend it. (*CO*24F)

In his later works, he characterizes vision's distinctive mode of being-in-the-world as "having at a distance" (*EM*166). For example, he argues that I am in some sense kinesthetically present (to myself) in the distance at the place where I see the other acting, just as (but not to the same extreme degree to which) the child actually feels himself there where his visual image is within the mirror (*CO*134).

Therefore, not only do we use the same structures (from all regions) as the other is using in order to visually grasp his present actions, but these structures themselves have an essential visual side. We can grasp this visual character of any structure in the following ways. We have just seen in our discussion of natural reversibility that the field reflects the place and volume of the perceiver such that any movement he makes will have a spatial sense and be implicitly visible for him. Thus he will understand a conduct of his own simultaneously and inseparably as a patterning of the field and as a perceivable movement within the field. Merleau-Ponty's early studies of incarnation and his later ones on the phenomenon of "touching a touch" (perceiving a structuring) are meant to prove that any type of structuring has a perceptual significance. The incarnation of any structuring is given to me not as a physical sign of this conduct, but as the necessary visual manifestation of it. The actions of others will make this incarnation and perceptual sense determinate and actual for me.[25] It is in this sense that I *see* the other's intentions directly as intentions but within the distancing *logos* of vision; I do not "live" (356) them, as he does, but "re-enact" (351) them. It is because of this inherent visibility of our structures that there is no need to analogically infer the meaning of the other's gestures.[26]

24. See also, *Signs*, pp. 169 and 94.

25. "It is a question of becoming conscious of what might be called 'incarnation'" (*CO*120).

26. Another important consequence of this theory of gestures is that it demonstrates phenomenologically that one can reflect on a situation, take up a third-person perspective

Let us summarize what we have learned so far by making its metaphysical implications explicit. We have seen that it is not only possible for many clearings to coexist together, but that these clearings will necessarily blend with one another. Thus the mere presence of others deepens the determinations of my field (qualitatively specifying it and not merely quantitatively adding to it), expands its limits, and also further specifies my horizons. These expanded and deepened clearings belong equally to each and every subject, and this world of each must be the common and intersubjective world. Therefore, I am given to myself "as identical to my presence to the world and to others, such as I realize it now: I am all that I see, I am an intersubjective field" (452). As a result, by means of a multiplicity of clearings, Being greatly enlarges and develops its grasp on itself, both quantitatively and qualitatively, in terms of the natural world.

We have also learned that through the presence of others each subject is incarnated, becoming fully ensconced in the natural world, and also that his status as "structurer" or "revealer" of Being is made clear and visible to him. Since the clearing becomes aware of itself simultaneously as the source of the clearing and as that which is cleared, Being's consciousness of itself is not only expanded and deepened, but it becomes increasingly self-conscious of the manner in which it structures itself. It is only by means of a multiplicity of clearings that each clearing's visibility can be made explicit.

Another important consequence of this reversibility and inter-twining of clearings is that the natural world's permanence and stability are increased, or that its copresent determinations are somehow preserved. We have noticed that the natural world must be highly unstable if it is comprehended as a clearing. Similarly, if the clearing spreads over space and time and changes its grasp on itself in every present, then the being of natural entities within the world will be that of a constant flux, oscillation, or change (within the determinate-indeterminate system of each entity's structures). Although Merleau-Ponty stresses that the natural world is not phenomenologically given as a fully determinate and objective world, that no object "exists absolutely" but that "everything temporalizes

toward it, or view it from a distance. Therefore, contrary to what many of Merleau-Ponty's critics maintain, we can, without being fully involved in a situation, be aware of and describe both its subject-side and its object-side with the same degree of neutrality.

itself" (*F*383), he claims that the natural world presents itself in a much more highly determinate form than the world of a single clearing could make metaphysically conceivable. The interchange between a multiplicity of clearings makes possible the presence of a world with such a degree of determinateness and stability; that is to say, many clearings determine and expand one another's present spatial grasps and confirm and preserve one another's past determinations of the world.

Therefore, our lived natural world as it is phenomenologically given is essentially an intersubjective one, and it can only be founded on and manifest a Being that is constituted by a multiplicity of interrelated clearings. We have thus shown that Being must necessarily clear itself in more than one place, for such a multiplicity immensely expands Being's visibility, the drive toward which is its essential characteristic. Also, at one and the same time we have shown that Being must necessarily manifest itself by means of a natural world of the type Merleau-Ponty has described phenomenologically, and that our own world is thus metaphysically possible.[27]

It is necessary to add that the fully determinate world of objective thought and science is a limiting ideal which results from a cognitive sublimation of and abstraction from this intersubjective and semipermanent world. Once we see how intersubjectivity gives rise to a social world and cultural objects, we shall be able to understand better how the natural world can be further articulated and stabilized by means of the "facts" and "truths" that are constituted by the cognitive realm. The "prejudice of the objective world" arises because the ideal of a determinate world is taken to be actual, and this is done by understanding the world, strictly from a cognitive point of view, as implicitly containing a subject at every possible spatial and temporal point within the world. It is only in this way that the world could be cleared as exhaustively as this objectivist ideal requires (or equivalently, one omnipercipient subject would

27. It should be noted that, because of the unity among all the regions of Existence (cf. chapter 1.4), the phenomena we used to establish conclusions strictly relevant to the natural world often contained a social or practical significance as well. This did not damage our argument since all of these phenomena (e.g., gestures) contain, at a minimum, a natural or presentational nucleus, and it was the significance of this natural content that was pertinent to our main conclusions. Similarly, in the following analysis, we shall establish the necessity of sociality, or an interpersonal world, by using phenomena that also fall within the cognitive-linguistic and motor-practical regions.

have to be posited). However, the world can never attain this absolute degree of determination because such a plenitude directly contradicts the finitude, temporal spread, and clearing-character of Being. And it is precisely the clearing-characteristic of Being that founds this ideal and the *telos* of the world of objective thought.

This metaphysics of clearings is firmly within the existentialist tradition. Before ending this section we can make explicit the typical existentialist features of Merleau-Ponty's thought and thus see the common existentialist vision that lies at its source. It is obvious in such statements as:

This same ... nature that stuffs me [*me gorge*] with Being opens me to the world through a perspective, along with which I am given the feeling of my contingency, the anguish of being over-run [*dépassé*], such that although I do not encompass my death in thought, I live in an atmosphere of death in general. (*F*418)

We have discovered that subjectivity's individuality and the status it has within Being is that of a perspective or of one spatio-temporal clearing within a finite Being. Horror and despair result from such a recognition of ourselves because it implies that each of us is just one of an unbounded and dynamic multiplicity of similar perspectives that are all equally accidental, evanescent, and replaceable. In a Being that expresses itself in an oscillating and perpetually changing multiplicity and that is inexhaustible and incompletable, the greatest role that we can attribute to ourselves is that of a radically contingent and particular manifestation of Being.[28] My being is thus permeated by chance and contingency, and from the metaphysical point of view, I have as little intrinsic significance, purpose, and importance as objects within my field have for me.

"Each sensation ... is a birth and a death" (*F*250), for in the "blurring" (*F*329), or perspectival givenness, of every appearance I discover my own perspectival and given existence. This is like Heidegger's vision of death because I witness the nothingness of my projects and experience the indefinite but constant threat of

28. If these perspectives had even a minimal permanence and security, they would imply a system of monads which would constitute an infinite and fully determinate Being. Irrespective of how incomplete each perspective was by itself, as long as it represented an irreplaceable and atemporal fact about Being, it would imply that Being could be exhaustively expressed by a system of perspectives. (Merleau-Ponty has said occasionally that if one object were to exist in itself the whole of Being would be crystallized [e.g. 71].)

nonexistence. "Consciousness of life, taken radically, is consciousness of death."[29] We have already seen how Merleau-Ponty
distinctively develops this aspect of Heidegger's thought by
demonstrating how our contingency and thrownness are discoverable
by us in every phenomenon or situation, as all are specifications of
our primordial contact. Thus, for example, even the very ordinary
occurrence of being spatially disoriented can give rise to basic
existentialist experiences.

The instability of levels gives . . . the vital experience of vertigo and of nausea
which is the consciousness and horror of our contingency. The positing of a
level is the forgetting of this contingency and space is based on our facticity.
(F294)

A lack in the adjustment of our present global hold on the world
makes conspicuous the otherness of our field and gives us a glimpse
of our facticity. But because of the horror of this awareness, we
immediately articulate and organize the world in terms of secure
(sedimented) and approved (socio-cultural) structures. By making
ourselves "at home" in the world, putting it under our control and
making it non-other, we lose ourselves in the dependability of a
supposedly stable world which consists of a mere sum of
things-in-themselves. We thus flee and forget "the oneness of man
and the world which is, not indeed abolished, but repressed by
everyday perception and objective thought, and which philosophical
consciousness rediscovers" (291).

We have seen in this section that what "philosophical consciousness rediscovers" about subjectivity is that "my whole
essence . . . is *to make visible*" (F487); that "in the present, in
perception, my being, and my consciousness are at one . . . because
'to be consciousness' is here nothing but 'to belong to . . . ' " (F485);
that "the first truth is indeed 'I think', but only on the condition
that one understand by this 'I belong to myself' [a reference to
Heidegger] in belonging to the world [*je suis à moi en étant au
monde*]" (F466);[30] and that "true reflection gives me to myself . . .

---

29. *Sense and Non-Sense,* p. 66. Also, cf. pp. 67-70, where Merleau-Ponty clearly relates
his understanding of death to both Heidegger and Hegel. He makes a point of insisting that
our consciousness of death must give us "a sharper awareness of life" and must not become
the "empty and abstract universal" of all-encompassing nothingness. "Nothingness can exist
only in the hollow of being, and so consciousness of death carries with it the means for
going beyond it" (*Sense and Non-Sense*, pp. 69-70).

30. The meaning of this important statement is, equally, "I am in myself in being in the
world" and "I am at myself in being at the world."

as identical to my presence to the world and to others, such as I realize it now; I am all that I see" (*F*515). These most fundamental descriptions of our Existence are made possible, at least in part, by the kind of crises and limiting states of mind that Heidegger sees as necessary for an authentic encounter with Being. Merleau-Ponty affirms the place that existentialism has in his thought when he states: "The tacit *Cogito*, the presence of self to self, being existence itself, precedes any philosophy, but is known only in limit situations where it is threatened: for example, in the anguish of death or in the other's gaze on me" (*F*462).

These statements, which are central to Merleau-Ponty's metaphysics, must not be taken as mere metaphysical axioms or hypotheses, but as descriptions of our deepest experience. They thus have the intuitive and almost mystical sense characteristic of existentialist utterances, and these in particular convey the feeling of absurdity that some existentialists take to be intrinsic to their vision. Consciousness, as understood by Merleau-Ponty, is shown to be "absurd" because it is nothing more than a making visible or "general flight outside of self" (*F*479). It thus has no "ego," substantial identity, or selfhood in itself and lacks the purpose or intrinsic meaning that such natures would possess.[31] It is, instead, merely the drive to make everything conscious and "explicit" (407) and is an "insatiable being who appropriates everything that it meets" (*F*411). Its content can only come from a radically finite and contingent Being to which it must always be open and belong, and toward which it must transcend itself. Nor does its process of acquiring and giving meaning save it (or condemn it), for it is an infinite and inexhaustible specifying that can never complete itself nor make any final gains. Similarly, as we shall see in the following section, consciousness's ability to produce a socio-cultural world through its openness to others describes another kind of captivation and appropriation. "The whole of human history is, in a certain sense, stationary" (*EM*91-92*F*), and perhaps the most that sociality can achieve is the creation of new forms of inauthentic and herd-like existence which can help individuals better escape their otherness by more easily mistaking their sediments for absolute truths and eternal values. This vision of absurdity is multiplied immensely when the subject realizes

---

31. Camus demonstrates in *The Myth of Sisyphus* that it is in the disappointment of such crucial ideals and prejudices of Western thought that the experience of the absurdity of the universe arises.

that this life is the activity of Being itself, or, similarly, that there is nothing more to Being than the flux and the world that we find within ourselves. Because of his stress on our contact with Being in all its finitude, Merleau-Ponty can say that the truth of his phenomenology and metaphysics is that "man ... is the place of contingency."[32] He further describes the existentialist's vision when he asks rhetorically: "Is this the highest point of reason, to realize this slipperiness [cf. *F*398 and *F*462] of the soil under our feet, ... to call 'research' or 'quest' what is only trudging in a circle, to call 'Being' that which never fully is" (*EM92F*)?[33]

2. Being, Sociality, and History

We shall now turn to an examination of Merleau-Ponty's claim that sociality is a basic dimension of Being distinct from the natural dimension, because it is the capacity that clearings possess to interrelate in a way qualitatively different than the natural. This will take us to a consideration of the socio-cultural world and of history, which will be shown to be the forms in which this dimension necessarily manifests itself.

We have shown that Being must give rise to a subject and that it can, and in fact must, consist of a plurality of clearings that result in a highly articulated and stable natural world. But we have not yet been able to account for social transcendence and its correlative social world. Our discussion will show how sociality is *logically possible* given our present characterization of Being and given the way in which many clearings constitute it as nature. We shall see that there is still room for these clearings to relate as wholes (as unique and individual historicities) and to differentiate themselves ex-

32. *Signs*, p. 241.

33. It is interesting that Husserl asks the same questions in almost identical terms. "But can the world and human existence in it truthfully have a meaning ... if history has nothing more to teach us than that all shapes of the spiritual world ... form and dissolve themselves like fleeting waves, that it always was and ever will be so, that again and again reason must turn into nonsense, and well-being into misery [a reference to *Faust*]?" (*The Crisis of European Sciences and Transcendental Phenomenology*, pp. 6-7). Merleau-Ponty was probably aware of this statement. Yet, he affirms that such a state of affairs obtains for the most part, while Husserl denies it and lets the question lead him in the opposite direction, to the affirmation of a rationalist ideal.

tensively within the tension that thereby remains between them. Each will, thus, make itself visible as a total spatio-temporal clearing and become self-conscious of its own place or situation among a multiplicity of other such individuals. We shall establish the *necessity* (this is still the retrospective necessity we spoke of earlier) of Being having a distinctive social dimension and of manifesting itself as a social world which is ontologically distinct from the natural, by making three points: First, Being immensely develops its primordial drive to explicate itself, become self-conscious, and maximize its visibility by means of such a capacity. Secondly, sociality is a qualitatively new way for Being to make its clearings visible that is not reducible to their natural modes of interrelation, and thus is not a quantifiable expansion, or mere complication, of natural visibility. And, lastly, the uniquely interpersonal, which does exist and which Merleau-Ponty and others have phenomenologically described as such, is a contingent fact whose possibility can be demonstrated if there is such a dimension of Being.

The following will consist of an examination of Merleau-Ponty's claim that sociality is a "permanent field or dimension of existence" (362) and *"an actual structure in its own right"* (*CO45F*). Even outside the present context, this is one of Merleau-Ponty's most important claims, for he makes sociality a mode of thrownness and of being-in-the-world which is irreducible to natural situations and of equal importance. He can, therefore, argue that the social-historical world is as metaphysically significant as the natural world and that "naturalism" is fundamentally mistaken. Furthermore, through this analysis we shall come to understand what is perhaps the most important of Merleau-Ponty's metaphysical statements:

The absolute flux outlines itself [*se profile*] under its own look as "*a* conscious-ness" or as man or as incarnate subject because it is a field of presence—presence to itself, to others, and to the world—and because this presence throws it into the natural and cultural world from which it arrives at an understanding of itself. . . . We must grasp it . . . as a being which is in pursuit of itself outside. (*F515*)

We have thus far understood how Being, as a field of presence, comprehends itself as an "incarnate subject" (*F515*) through its reversibility with the natural world and other natural subjects. We have also begun to see how the clearing grasps itself as "*a* consciousness" (*F515*), for it experiences itself as *a* perspective or as just one more manifestation of the anonymous regions that it unifies. We shall now turn to the explanation of how its self-consciousness is further expanded through its reversibility with the cultural world.[34] As a result, it will understand itself as a man or a person who has a distinctive historicity or creativity (Existence) which, nonetheless, is also *a* manifestation of Being's own drive to transcend and articulate itself.

The difference between the "coexistence of psychophysical subjects in the natural world and of men in the cultural world" (*F*530 topic of *F*406-08) is that in the former we comprehend the other only in the way in which he expands my own field or adds determination to my own natural regions. We do reveal one another's particular gestures or structurings but only as duplicates or manifestations of our own capacities, and in a fragmented and atomistic way. Thus the other is not given as a unique individual or person, but as merely one gesture or a collection of gestures that allows me a better grasp of my own field. As another focus of my clearing, the other is at most "the very first of all cultural objects" (*F*401), for he acts as a *standard* extension of my body and gives me new directions and methods for dealing with the natural world (as, for example, a cane extends my own capacities). The other approaches the status of an objective symbol or, at best, an organic species; for he lacks the beyondness of a person and only serves to delineate certain predictable patterns within my field.

When the other is encountered as a person or man, he is comprehended as a distinctive expression of shared natural regions, that is, as a historicity which specifies and unifies these regions in a free and individual manner through its own temporality. He is treated as a creator of structures, as a unique system of sedimented structures which are not merely reproductions of my own. We deal with him as an original and active articulating of Being, not merely with his particular articulations of Being, and we thus perceive through his gestures a temporality and a freedom. A clearing that is recognized as a person is dealt with *as a whole*, for what is of

34. What Merleau-Ponty here and elsewhere calls the cultural world, he also refers to indifferently as the "social world" (e.g., *F*415 and *F*418). I prefer the latter as more precise, for it is social rather than cultural structures that are basic and these that are central to sociality.

importance here is the other's distinctive style, or accent, which shows through his particular actions.[35]

Therefore, it is not only through being parts of a common natural world and by means of this world that clearings are able to interrelate; they are also able to relate to one another directly as wholes. Sociality is this capacity of each clearing to interact and entwine with other unified spatio-temporal clearings. It is thus equivalently a dimension of Being which allows Being to reveal and articulate itself in a more profound way by relating, and thereby making visible, its perspectives as perspectives. Through the intertwining of these global manners of being in the natural world, Being clarifies and further determines the individuality of each. Thus it gives rise to a syntax and a development of the ways in which these clearings comprehend themselves and each other as individuals, and these are, respectively, society and history.

We can conclude that it is *possible*, given our conception of the clearing, that Being could articulate itself in a manner categorically different from the natural. This possibility can be confirmed and we can begin to make evident the *necessity* of sociality by examining the way in which Being "enlarges" (*VI*144) its visibility and comprehension of itself by means of this type of transcendence and reversibility.

Merleau-Ponty describes the new type of visibility that comes into being when one clearing recognizes another as such by stating that it goes "outside the [natural] world and its goals" and becomes "fascinated by the unique occupation of floating in Being with another life, of making itself the outside of its inside and the inside of its outside," thus giving rise to the "paradox of expression" (*VI*144). This floating is in a sense a playing with the individual's power of creating structures or is a making-visible for the pure purpose of making-visible (I make his making-visible visible and so on). It fascinates because it is another method of authentically and directly taking part in the essential flow and drive toward

35. Merleau-Ponty's study of Schneider's sexual incapacity gives us an example of the way in which one can conceive of being open to the natural but not the interpersonal. He shows that this accounts for Schneider's inability to relate to others emotionally, to desire human companionship and communication, to understand the other as a personality, and in general to take up any affective situation (156 ff.).

self-disclosure of Being. But, further, in treating the other as a unique spatio-temporal clearing, I become aware of a difference, "tension" (*F*412), or *écart* between our clearings. The attempt to articulate this tension and to make the other's beyondness explicit gives rise to a process of differentiation. Each begins to define himself as a person, or a historicity, through expressive exchanges and emotional relations with the other. Thus, like Hegel's account of the transition from "Consciousness" to "Self-Consciousness" in the *Phenomenology*, Merleau-Ponty's account sees this process as beginning with "desire" (*VI*144).[36] The articulation of this unique bond with others results in a whole new region of structures (e.g., emotions, passions, gestures, character traits, cultural and linguistic entities, classes, social roles, and ultimately historical epochs) which allows each person to achieve a degree of recognition and self-identity through a dialectical relationship with the other. "There is thus constitution and correlation of the other and myself as two human beings among all human beings" (*CO*25-26*F*).

Merleau-Ponty agrees with Hegel that Being gains its own self-consciousness by means of a creative intertwining of its subjects as "men" and in so doing builds a society whose constituent structures define the way in which this dimension of Being realizes and ontically manifests itself at a particular time. Since a clearing only becomes conscious of itself as a distinctive personality through its dialectical differentiation from other clearings, all clearings must develop this type of visibility reciprocally, and therefore Being reveals itself throughout its length in this way. Furthermore, since the structures that result from this differentiation are the articulations of a unique way in which clearings are open to one another, this capacity of Being to relate to itself perpetually determines itself and gives rise to a new type of multiplicity. Being thus follows its basic principle—to maximize its visibility and to articulate its otherness—in a categorically new way.

We are finally in a position to understand how sociality, like all thrown regions of Existence, is anonymous and gives rise to a social

---

36. "The social . . . envelops [*investit*] the individual, soliciting him and menacing him simultaneously, . . . each consciousness both finds and loses itself in its relationship with other consciousnesses . . . ; finally, the social is not a *collective consciousness* but intersubjectivity, a living relationship and tension among individuals" (*Sens et non-sens*, p. 157).

self which like the natural is a prepersonal *on*. We have seen that clearings not only reveal the natural world but that they are primordially open to other clearings as such. Thus every subject must have a "sympathy" (*CO*146) and "social sensibility" (*CO*141) which is a given and vastly general structure that unites him with others. Since "we are in contact [with others] by the sole fact of existing" (*F*415), as soon as we are in the presence of others we form a uniquely human relationship with them; and, as is the case with natural situations, the reality of each side is dependent on that of the other, with both being formed simultaneously.

The creative specification of this region gives rise at one and the same time to the personal self and to a social world. The logic of this specification is similar to that of the perceptual region's, except that its structures must be understood in terms of affective situations, emotional, cultural, and linguistic gestures, and character and personality traits. All of these situations are complementary and serve to differentiate the other from the subject. Many of these structures are also 'levels,' that is, similar to color levels. When the subject understands himself or another in terms of a trait, social role, or class (443-46), he dissects his social field into, and affirms within the social world, a coexistent series of such traits, roles, or classes. (Similarly, it is impossible for a single color to be either actualized or acquired without at least one other also being present.)

This does not make the individual a mere sum of such qualities but a complex gestalt of social differentiations. In embodying these structures through the constant process of understanding himself, he clears or manifests the entire social world. Furthermore, the particular structures which are "solicited" (*F*512) by those who are "close" to the subject, will determine the present social field and ultimately a "social space" (*F*508). The subject is therefore not only the focus of a natural world but equally the fulcrum of a social world. He is a distinctive perspective on his society for, although his society is defined by the common structures that all its members share, each subject organizes and manifests (and *can* authentically specify) these structures in a distinctive way. Conversely, his individuality is founded on, and can only be understood through the variation on, the structures that he shares with all the others. There is "a social coexistence," "One," or "functional and generalized existence" (*F*513), that is to say, a social self which is strictly parallel to the natural self of perception, "the *one* of corporeal life and the *one* of human life" (*VI*84). It is anonymous and universal to all subjects, a common stuff or flesh from which the individuality of the subject arises. Finally, we can now see how these social situations have the same reality, or ontological importance, as natural situations, for both are equally founded in thrown regions of Existence and necessary dimensions of Being. Sociality as a flesh becomes comprehensible as the society or social world in which every subject essentially inheres.

Sociality as a fundamental type of Being is not, of course, independent from Being's natural dimension but is closely related to it as a "metadimension," just as sociality, as an innate capacity of the subject, always metastructures his natural being-in-the-world. This *meta*-character is evident in a number of ways. First, we have seen that this type of structure links clearings to one another directly, instead of strictly by means of what is cleared. But, secondly, the clearings would not be able to communicate in this way if they did not already have a natural content, that is to say, if they did not already structure the natural world; for their differences as individual perspectives can only arise originally in terms of the manner in which each clears nature (*VI*83). Since it is the making explicit of each of these different manners that founds social interchange, all social structures (even the most "spiritual") must have a definite bearing on the way in which the natural world is cleared. Thirdly, since a society is constituted by its universal social and cultural structures and is thus a general social self, it can be defined by the types of concerns and preoccupations that determine the style and degree of its openness to nature. History, then, understood as the temporal development and differentiation of societies, will have this same *meta*-character. Therefore it must not be taken to include only the "spiritual" development of man, but also the way in which this development is integrated with the contingent demands of nature. Thus history is the historical development, or overall temporality, of Being as a whole.

We shall now turn to a brief examination of Merleau-Ponty's understanding of history and show that it is the culmination of his comprehension of Being as temporality and visibility. First, we shall show how Merleau-Ponty's concept of society implies the concept of history and then explain the individual's relationship to history and why history must have meaning.

That any society must be understood as an epoch, i.e., within the context of a history, can be shown in the following way. We have learned that every subject possesses a social general self which he shares with all others in his society and which in fact defines this society. Each society can be taken to have an individual character or style, at least to the extent that it is distinguishable from other societies—a style determined by the kinds and gestalt of the structures that constitute it. Since all of the subject's social structures (and ultimately his natural structures as well) are grounded in the anonymous structures of his society, he "lives" (F512) this style prereflectively in all situations, and he thus in fact unifies and balances these structures, making such a style possible. Since these social structures have the same logic as natural structures (being acquired through the specification of other structures and being themselves infinitely specifiable), each will have a temporal character; that is, each will be based on past structures that it has developed and will have protensions that indicate possible future modes of fulfillment. Society as the schema of all such structures must similarly carry a reference to the past structures and societies from which it has evolved and protend a future where the ambiguities of its present and past style will be further determined and re-organized. Any society can be considered as a historical epoch because there is a "concrete project of a future which elaborates itself in social coexistence and in the *on* before all personal decision" (F513), and, correlatively for the individual, "this functional and generalized existence makes of him a historical subject" (F513).

Hegel might well have written: "The subject of history is not the individual. There is an exchange between generalized existence and individual existence, each receiving and giving" (F513). Similarly, Hegel's final description of Being as Concept is in terms of the movement between a contingent or particular self and a general or rational self (society and history), where the role of the former self is only to account for the latter's actuality or appearance. However, Merleau-Ponty's essential departure from Hegel is made evident when he continues by asserting: "There is a moment where the sense that sketched itself out [*se dessinait*] in the *on*, and which was only an unstable [*inconsistent*] possibility menaced by the contingency of history, is retaken [*repris*] by the individual" (*F*513). We again see that, rather than making the general self absolute, Merleau-Ponty insists that it is radically contingent and has only "certain probable properties" (*F*512), its sense being equivocal, flabby, menaced, and only relatively stable.

Like natural space, social space is permeated by otherness and can never be exhaustively specified. Not only does this indeterminacy leave room for the individual's freedom to assume social space in his own particular way, but this otherness actually demands that the individual clarify and reorganize his present social situation. The individual's present historical self is constantly and directly challenged by the contingencies of nature (e.g., biological, ecological, and geographical changes and crises), of culture (e.g., obsolescence of tools, ambiguity of symbols, and conflicts within developing technologies), and of society (e.g., developing frictions between societies and subsocieties and the inconsistencies between the structures within any one society). Thus the individual must constantly retake and reassume this flux prereflectively; he either develops it to some extent, reaffirms it, or merely goes along with its present sense. Therefore, contrary to Hegel, some kind of preexistent society is not simply made actual through its embodiment by individuals, but these individuals perpetually reconstitute its sense, *"just because it is always lived history" (F*512).

Merely by prereflectively living his social situation, the individual is responsible for the movement of history in two ways. If his existence is predominantly authentic, his mode of life will to that extent take part in the creative organization and specification of his society. (Merleau-Ponty's analysis of the coming-to-be of class consciousness is an excellent instance of this [see, for example, 443-46].) On the other hand, if his existence is predominantly inauthentic, he will to that extent be imprisoned by his acquired social structures and thus only confirm, and be dominated by, the patterns that others are developing in his society.

Although personal authentic decisions or conscious historical choices can move history in a spectacular and obvious fashion, here too "there is an average and statistical significance of these projects" (*F*513). This follows because, if they are *historically relevant,* these free projects are motivated by the ambiguities within the general self, that is to say, by the present balance of social structures which points to privileged and probable modes of resolution. "We give history its sense, but not without it proposing it to us" (F513). World-historical individuals, for example, "artists and politicians," are thus the main movers of history, although they only realize a possible future that is already foreshadowed, rather than projecting or creating a totally new and free meaning.[37] However, to take one example, historians who reflectively thematize history can also have a profound effect on it, for they creatively specify its present ambiguous sense by making its previous and present stages explicit and by tracing their development. In a very strong argument for there being *"some* sense in history" (F531), Merleau-Ponty points out that free acts, if lacking a foundation in sedimented social structures, could have no historical value or relevance; thus they could only be understood as arbitrary, opportunistic, or anarchic (F512) and could not be assessed in terms of their historical responsibility or value. Because pure personal freedom—"the anonymity of consciousness" (F514)—is possible only on the ground of, or through the creative modulation of, one's thrown and acquired structures, the personal and the general selves are "two moments of a unique structure which is the concrete subject" (F514).[38]

Because subjectivity is necessarily grounded in the social, our prereflective grasp of society must reveal to some extent the direction of history. We can define this sense of history in terms of our own particular society, its origination in and differences from other present and past societies (which are all implicit in and loosely interwoven with our own), together with the protensions (the possibilities for clarification, confirmation, and development) that the whole implies. It is necessary that history anchor itself in and form about societies, because the subject can only grasp the world perspectively on the grounds of sets of given structures and, similarly, because Being grasps itself through clearings that

---

37. *Prose of the World*, p. 86, and *Signs*, p. 74.

38. It is worthwhile pointing this out, for contrary to many commentators we can see once again that it is not impossible for Merleau-Ponty to unite these two selves. In fact, such a unity follows from the main principles of his philosophy (for example, compare both the particularity of the natural object which can only be found in its general structures, and the open individuality of the world) and, of course, it is basic to temporality.

necessarily interrelate.[39] However, Merleau-Ponty does not run the risk of the infinite regress and extreme relativism of historicism, as his understanding of history might seem to imply. His positing of common thrown structures and the interweaving of all subjects in a present by way of their own sedimented structures allows for communication between epochs and the constant possibility of discovering a "historical truth" (F512). It is thus possible to understand epochs in their own terms better than those who lived in them and to find "patterns" that evolve through history. Furthermore, his insistence that the sense of history must be partial, ambiguous, and unfulfilled prevents him from being open to the similar refutation embodied in the questions: "How long is an epoch?" and "How extensive is a society?".[40]

Merleau-Ponty's concept of historical meaning (sens) necessarily implies a temporality that involves "progress," but one which is not very different from the value-free, purposeless, and nonteleological temporality which is found in the creative acquisition of any structure. Thus he states that authentic action is

in contact with Being, on behalf of which it opens a space of manifestation, but where all its own initiatives are inscribed, recorded, or sedimented, if only as errors surmounted, and take on the form of a history which has its sense, even if it turns in circles or marches in zigzags . . . [and is] capable of differentiating and of integrating double and even multiple meanings within a single universe. (VI125F)

Merleau-Ponty does not require a strong sense of progress, for he understands history as the concrete manifestation of Being's finite and never-ending drive to articulate itself. This process of visibility never conquers its otherness nor even completes itself in any one part; it always remains with "lacunae and fissures," losing almost as much as it gains.[41]

39. "History is not a power before which [one] must genuflect, it is the perpetual discussion that weaves itself between all speech, all valid [valables] works and valid actions; each from its own place and singular situation contesting and confirming the other, each recreating all the others. True history, thus, lives entirely from us, it is in our present that it takes the power to reconcile all the other presents to this one" (La prose du monde, pp. 121-22).

40. For example, R. Aron's modified historicism (perspectivism) is still open to these criticisms. Cf. "Relativism in History," in Hans Myerhoff, ed., The Philosophy of History in Our Time.

41. Primacy of Perception, p. 6.

In thought and in history as in life the only surpassings we know are concrete, partial, encumbered with survivals, saddled with deficits. . . . But, on a defined part of the route, there can be progresses; especially there are solutions excluded in the long run. (*VI*95)

We can only say that experience very probably ends by eliminating false solutions and by extricating itself from impasses. But at what price, and through how many detours?[42]

History has this drift and disjointedness, for although newly created structures are grounded on past structures, they cannot preserve or retain the whole of their ground's significance and thus will develop themselves in unrelated and disparate directions; furthermore, "no work is ever achieved absolutely" (*EM92F*). But there is some progress, for the new structures can cross out errors, negate alternatives, and complete particular processes, and they can always further specify the subject's general grasp of the world.[43] One can never describe a priori the exact course of history nor even specify a predetermined goal for its progress, but Merleau-Ponty does make it possible for the historian to disclose history's varying and contingent directions and for poets and politicians to create and exploit them—and the question of what precisely constitutes a progress in history is best left to them.

With this examination of history, we have achieved a concrete understanding of Being's own overall temporality and can finally comprehend the full implications of its being constituted by a multiplicity of clearings. Furthermore, it should now be obvious that Being's process of making visible and splitting into a multiplicity is not arbitrary or chaotic, for it is through the reversibility of this multiplicity that it maximizes its grasp on itself and ultimately yields a history. Although we discovered the temporality of Being through the subject's own temporality, this movement (*écart*) can be more completely understood at the level of history, where it appears as the thrust of an intersubjective Being or of "subjectivity in general."

42. *Signes*, p. 304.
43. "According to Hegel, as everyone repeats, all that is real is rational and thus justified. However, it is justified sometimes as a positive acquisition, sometimes as a pause, and sometimes as an ebbing withdrawal for a new surge. In short, all is justified relatively, as a *moment* of total history, on condition that this history make itself, and thus in the sense that our errors themselves are said to carry weight and that our progresses are our errors understood; which does not efface the difference between growth and decline, birth and death, regression and progress" (*La prose du monde*, p. 119).

What are "preontologically" understood as society and history thus give us essential phenomena for intuiting the way in which Being as a whole articulates itself over time. One must not, of course, take the individual's temporality to be separate from the temporality of history. Merleau-Ponty gives an excellent summary of the way in which we should understand this relationship when he states that I "am open to temporalities . . . and have a social horizon, with the result that my world is expanded to the extent of a collective history which my private existence retakes and assumes" (*F*495).

It should be noted that the previous arguments have established that particular histories and societies are the concrete manifestations of Being's distinctive social dimension, and Being must necessarily manifest itself; thus, they must be considered by any metaphysics and must have an ontological status not reducible to the natural world. As a corollary, as soon as one recognizes sociality as a thrown capacity for distinctive interpersonal relationships, one is committed to acknowledging that individuals must form societies which have a historical character and to seeing that their existence, as well as that of interpersonal phenomena such as sympathy, expression, emotional attachment, and moral involvement, cannot be reduced to natural phenomena, as, for example, the analytic social scientist wishes.

Let us be clear about the limits of Merleau-Ponty's claims concerning the metaphysical necessity of sociality. By making it an irremovable dimension of Being, he is not committed to holding that societies and histories as we experience them must exist. Rather, our social situations are contingent manifestations of sociality, which has to be concretized in some way or other, not necessarily in the ways with which we are familiar. Hence Merleau-Ponty does not have to claim, as, for example, Hegel and Marx do, that there is some form of ideal society and one direction in history. He is not even committed to seeing many specific types of movement in history. The actual organization and appearance of a society are not metaphysically necessary because, for one thing, societies and histories are metadimensions and thus extremely susceptible to the contingency, chance, and flux of nature and culture. Societies cannot be clear developments from and dialectical subsumptions of natural Being, as Hegel's are. Similarly, the cognitive-linguistic and the motor-practical regions cannot be considered as stages on the road to an absolute (as Hegel takes reason, practice, and science to be); for all of these regions are open to the contingencies of one another, and it is an essential part of Being's alterity that they can never be fully united, though they must always strive for such unity. Merleau-Ponty does hold that Being necessarily consists in these four dimensions (natural, social, cognitive-linguistic, and motor-practical) and that it is beyond comprehension how they could come into or go out of existence. Here metaphysics stops and Merleau-Ponty is satisfied to say that this "rationality" or *logos* of Being must simply be accepted (408-09).

If our proof that sociality is a necessary dimension of Being has been convincing, it may appear that we should supply similar arguments for the other regions of Existence. By briefly discussing each of these regions, we shall see that such a procedure would not be helpful. It is not applicable to the natural region, and for the cognitive-linguistic and motor regions it would be redundant and confusing.

Merleau-Ponty establishes the metaphysical foundations of the natural region (perceptual and motor-spatial) in other ways. We have argued at length that for Merleau-Ponty our natural capacities are thrown and in primordial contact with Being, and that these structures of the natural world are manifestations of a natural *on*, which is a dimension, or flesh, of Being. Similarly, through a phenomenological analysis of the body-subject, Merleau-Ponty establishes that subjectivity must be understood as the point or focus of such a natural field. Even if it were desirable, we could not reinforce our comprehension of the natural dimension by proving its necessity, as we have in the case of sociality. Such a procedure would be indefensibly circular, since we discovered the essential characteristics of Being that must be used in such a proof through the study of perceptual openness and the natural world. Similarly, we could not have arrived at this comprehension of Being by starting with one of the other regions and proving it to be a dimension of Being, for they are all metastructures and thus presuppose the description of the natural. We have learned that their *meta*-character is as important for understanding the way in which the dimensions of Being interrelate as was the theory of the primacy of perception for understanding the interrelation of the regional capacities of subjectivity.

Although this method of proof is available for the cognitive-linguistic and motor-practical regions, it would not be worthwhile to apply it. Our main task in this chapter was to become familiar with Merleau-Ponty's view of Being, and these further analyses would not significantly expand our present grasp of what is essential to Being. Also, by establishing the necessity of sociality as a dimension, we have already gone a long way towards demonstrating the metaphysical possibility and necessity of these other dimensions. They contribute to Being's visibility in the same way, for, as we have seen, society and interpersonal behavior are given to us in such a way that they are inconceivable without cultural objects and linguistic communication. Furthermore, the distinctiveness of the cognitive-linguistic and motor-practical regions, which prevents their reduction to sociality, satisfies, *mutatis mutandis,* the same kind of metaphysical requirements that we referred to in establishing sociality as a dimension. Besides being repetitious, such studies would be just an outline of Merleau-Ponty's phenomenology of these regions. Since the theory of the cognitive-linguistic region is so difficult and complex, it was best to leave its consideration to a chapter to its own. Similarly, we found that we could best deal with the most difficult aspect of motility, its intertwining with perception, by examining it along with perception. A complete description of motor-practical behavior would require another chapter, but since it is the best understood of the regions and has been given the clearest explication by Merleau-Ponty's commentators, this is not necessary.

One last question: Does this type of argument allow us to prove too much, that is to say, does it permit us to demonstrate that anything is a necessary dimension of Being? It does not. First, because in order to establish a region's possibility, the region must be shown to follow on Being's main characteristics and to qualitatively enrich them. Secondly, in order to establish a region's necessity, it must be shown phenomenologically that its structures are irreducible to those of the other regions. Merleau-Ponty's descriptions, which locate all phenomena in four categorically different regions of Existence, are quite convincing, and the claim for their distinctiveness is probably best settled phenomenologically rather than within the context of deep metaphysics.

Appendix

Translation of the Table of Contents of the *Phénoménologie de la perception* and Its Integration into the English Text

I have treated the list of topics that occurs in the table of contents of the French edition (*F*527-31) but appears nowhere in the English edition as subtitles and have located the places in the text where such subtitles would appear. It is useful to have these titles integrated into the text, for Merleau-Ponty indubitably had them in mind when he wrote and they usually state the conclusion or main point of their section unmistakably, succinctly, and in advance. They provide an important aid to comprehending the text, first because, as Merleau-Ponty often writes elliptically, his conclusions are not as plain as they should be, and second because, as the texts contain such a wealth of analyses, the overall organization which these titles disclose is sometimes lost to the reader.

The titles for the most part disclose the theme of Merleau-Ponty's paragraphs; thus the selection of locations for them was usually quite straightforward and can be taken as reliable. This fact makes their inclusion and distribution in the English edition particularly useful, as the original paragraph structure of the text (which helps disclose its organization) is broken up by the translator (often in an otherwise useful way). The location of the titles that break up individual paragraphs (indicated by a "line" index) is less certain. However, except for two or three, their location would not vary by more than ten lines.

277

The key is as follows: The first column of numbers gives the page and paragraph reference (counted from the first *full* paragraph) for the English edition, and the second column for the French edition (e.g., 3:1 *F*9:1 = page 3, paragraph 1, in the English, and page 9, paragraph 1, in the French). Occasionally, if the title occurs in mid-paragraph, the page number is followed by a line reference (e.g., 135: line 34).

Introduction: Classical Prejudices and the Return to Phenomena

Chapter 1. "Sensation"

Chapter 2. "Association" and "Projection of Memories"

Chapter 3. "Attention" and Judgment

Chapter 4. The Phenomenal Field

Part I: The Body

Introduction

Chapter 1. The Body as Object and Mechanistic Physiology

Chapter 2. The Experience of the Body and Classical Psychology

Chapter 3. The Spatiality of One's Own Body and Motility

Part II: The Perceived World

Introduction

Chapter 1. Sense Experience (le Sentir)

Chapter 2. Space

Chapter 3. The Thing and the Natural World

PART III: Being-for-Itself and Being-in-the-World

Chapter 1. The Cogito

Chapter 2. Temporality

Chapter 3. Freedom

Bibliography

1. Primary Sources

The following texts by Merleau-Ponty are listed in the chronological order of their original publication or, if they are lectures, of their delivery. The English editions precede the French whenever both have been used. For a fuller bibliography of Merleau-Ponty's books, articles, lectures, and essays in English, see R. L. Lanigan's bibliography in *Speaking and Semiology* (The Hague: Mouton, 1972); for works in French see bibliographies in T. F. Geraets, *Vers une nouvelle philosophie transcendantale*, and X. Tilliette, *Merleau-Ponty ou la mesure de l'homme.*

————. "La nature de la Perception." In T. F. Geraets, ed., *Vers une nouvelle philosophie transcendantale.* The Hague: Martinus Nijhoff, 1971, pp. 188-99 (written in 1934).

————. *The Structure of Behavior.* Translated by A. L. Fisher. Foreword by J. Wild. Foreword to the second French edition by A. De Waelhens. Boston: Beacon Press, 1963. (*La structure de comportement.* 2d ed. Foreword by A. De Waelhens. Paris: Presses Universitaires de France, 1967 [first edition 1942].)

————. *Phenomenology of Perception.* Translated by Colin Smith. London: Routledge and Kegan Paul, 1962. (*Phénoménologie de la perception.* Paris: Gallimard, 1945.)

————. *Humanism and Terror.* Translated by J. O'Neill. Boston: Beacon Press, 1969 (*Humanisme et terreur.* Paris: Gallimard, 1947.)

————. *L'union de l'âme et du corps chez Malebranche, Biran et Bergson: Notes prises au cours de Maurice Merleau-Ponty à l'École Normale Supérieure (1947-1948).* Collected and edited by Jean Deprun. Paris: Vrin, 1968.

————. *Sense and Non-Sense.* Translated, with an introduction, by H. L. Dreyfus and P. A. Dreyfus. Evanston, Ill.: Northwestern University Press, 1964. (*Sens et non-sens.* Paris: Nagel, 1966 [first edition 1948].)

————. *Maurice Merleau-Ponty à la Sorbonne: Résumé de ses cours établi par les étudiants et approuvé par lui-même. Bulletin de psychologie*, no. 236, vol. 18 3-6 (November 1964). (Contains student notes on courses delivered between 1949 and 1951.)

———.*Consciousness and the Acquisition of Language*. Translated by Hugh J. Silverman. Evanston, Ill.: Northwestern University Press, 1973 (translation of student notes from one of the above Sorbonne courses).

———."The Child's Relations with Others." Translated by W. Cobb. In *The Primacy of Perception*, edited, with an introduction, by J. M. Edie. Evanston, Ill.: Northwestern University Press, 1964. (*Les relations avec autrui chez l'enfant*. Les Cours de Sorbonne. Paris: Centre de Documentation Universitaire, 1967 [course delivered in 1950-51].)

———."Phenomenology and the Sciences of Man." Translated by J. Wild. In *The Primacy of Perception*, edited, with an introduction, by J. M. Edie. Evanston,Ill.: Northwestern University Press, 1964. (*Les sciences de l'homme et la phénoménologie*. Les Cours de Sorbonne. Paris: Centre de Documentation Universitaire, 1952 [course delivered in 1950-51].)

———.*In Praise of Philosophy*. Translated, with a preface, by J. Wild and J. M. Edie. Evanston, Ill.: Northwestern University Press, 1963. (In *Éloge de la philosophie et autres essais*. Collection Idées. Paris: Gallimard, 1960 [first edition 1953].)

———.*Adventures of the Dialectic*. Translated by Joseph Bien. Evanston, Ill.: Northwestern University Press, 1973. (*Les aventures de la dialectique*. Paris: Gallimard, 1955.)

———."Husserl et la notion de Nature: (Notes prises au cours de Maurice Merleau-Ponty)". Collected by Xavier Tilliette. *Revue de métaphysique et de morale*, no. 3 (1965): 257-69 (delivered in 1957).

———."La philosophie de l'existence." *Dialogue* 5 (December 1966): 307-22 (transcript of a lecture delivered in 1959).

———."Phenomenology and Psychoanalysis: Preface to Hesnard's *L'oeuvre de Freud*." In *The Essential Writings of Merleau-Ponty*, edited by A. L. Fisher. New York: Harcourt, Brace, 1969, pp. 81-87 (published in French in 1960 [Paris: Payot]).

———.*Signs*. Translated, with an introduction, by R. C. McCleary. Evanston, Ill.: Northwestern University Press, 1964. (*Signes*. Paris: Gallimard, 1960.)

———."Eye and Mind." Translated by C. Dallery. In *The Primacy of Perception*, edited, with an introduction, by J. M. Edie. Evanston, Ill.: Northwestern University Press, 1964. (*L'oeil et l'esprit*. Paris: Gallimard, 1964 [originally published as an article in 1961].)

———.*The Visible and the Invisible: Followed by Working Notes*. Edited, with a foreword and editorial note, by Claude Lefort. Translated by Alphonso Lingis. Evanston, Ill.: Northwestern University Press, 1968. (*Le visible et l'invisible: suivi de notes de travail*. Text established by Claude Lefort, with a foreword and afterword. Paris: Gallimard, 1964.)

———.*The Primacy of Perception*. Edited, with an introduction, by J. M. Edie. Evanston, Ill.: Northwestern University Press, 1964.

———.*Themes from the Lectures at the Collège de France 1952-1960*. Translated by J. O'Neill. Evanston, Ill.: Northwestern University Press, 1970. (*Résumés de cours: Collège de France 1952-1960*. Paris: Gallimard, 1968.)

_____.*The Prose of the World*. Edited by Claude Lefort. Translated by John O'Neill. Evanston, Ill.: Northwestern University Press, 1973. (*La prose du monde*. Text established and introduced by Claude Lefort. Paris: Gallimard, 1969.)

2. Secondary Sources Cited

Austin, J. L. *Philosophical Papers*. Oxford: Clarendon Press, 1961.

_____. *Sense and Sensibilia*. Reconstructed from the manuscript notes by G. J. Warnock. A Galaxy Book. New York: Oxford University Press, 1964.

Ayer, A. J. *The Problem of Knowledge*. Harmondsworth, Middlesex: Penguin, 1956.

Bannan, John F. *The Philosophy of Merleau-Ponty*. New York: Harcourt, Brace, 1967.

Barker, Stephen F. *Philosophy of Mathematics*. Englewood Cliffs, N.J.: Prentice-Hall, 1964.

Barnes, Hazel E. *An Existentialist Ethics*. New York: Knopf, 1968.

Barral, Mary Rose. *Merleau-Ponty: The Role of the Body-Subject in Interpersonal Relations*. Pittsburgh: Duquesne University Press, 1965.

Black, Max. *The Labyrinth of Language*. New York: Mentor, 1968.

Boudon, Raymond. *A quoi sert la notion de 'Structure'*. Paris: Gallimard, 1968.

Brandt, Richard B. *Ethical Theory: The Problems of Normative and Critical Ethics*. Englewood Cliffs, N.J.: Prentice-Hall, 1959.

Brentano, Franz. *The True and the Evident*. Edited by Oskar Kraus. Translated by Roderick M. Chisholm, Ilse Politzer, and Kurt R. Fischer. London: Routledge and Kegan Paul, 1966.

Carter, Walter B. "Review of F. Cowley's *A Critique of British Empiricism.*" *Dialogue* 7 (1968): 491-94.

Chisholm, Roderick. *Perceiving: A Philosophical Study*. Ithaca, N.Y.: Cornell University Press, 1957.

_____ .*Theory of Knowledge*. Englewood Cliffs, N.J.: Prentice-Hall, 1966.

Chomsky, Noam. *Language and Mind*. New York: Harcourt, Brace, 1968.

Cowley, Fraser. *A Critique of British Empiricism*. London: Macmillan, 1968.

Danto, Arthur, and Morgenbesser, Sidney, eds. *Philosophy of Science*. Cleveland: World Publishing, 1960.

De Waelhens, Alphonse. *Une Philosophie de l'ambiguité: L'existentialisme de Merleau-Ponty*. 2d ed. Louvain: Nauwelaerts, 1967 (first edition 1951).

_____ .*Phénoménologie et vérité*. Louvain: Nauwelaerts, 1965.

Edie, James M. "Can Grammar Be Thought?" In *Patterns of the Life World*. Edited by Edie et al. Evanston, Ill.: Northwestern University Press, 1971.

Fackenheim, Emil L. *Metaphysics and Historicity*. Aquinas Lecture, 1961. Milwaukee: Marquette University Press, 1961.

Fann, K. T., ed. *Symposium on J. L. Austin*. New York: Humanities Press, 1969.

Fodor, Jerry A., and Katz, Jerrold J., eds. *The Structure of Language: Readings in the Philosophy of Language.* Englewood Cliffs, N.J.: Prentice-Hall, 1964.

Geraets, Theodore F. *Vers une nouvelle philosophie transcendantale.* The Hague: Martinus Nijhoff, 1971.

Gerber, Rudolph J. "Merleau-Ponty: The Dialectic of Consciousness and World." *Man and World* 2 (February 1969): 83-107.

Gilchrist, Alan L. "The Perception of Surface Blacks and Whites." *Scientific American* 240 (March 1979): 112-24.

Gurwitsch, Aron. *The Field of Consciousness.* Pittsburgh: Duquesne University Press, 1964.

Hanly, C. M. T. "Phenomenology, Consciousness and Freedom." *Dialogue* 5 (Winter 1966): 323-45.

Hanson, Norwood Russell. *The Patterns of Discovery: An Inquiry into the Conceptual Foundations of Science.* Cambridge: Cambridge University Press, 1965.

Hare, R. M. *The Language of Morals.* A Galaxy Book. New York: Oxford University Press, 1964.

Hegel, G. F. W. *The Phenomenology of Mind.* Translated by J. B. Baillie. 2d ed. London: George Allen and Unwin, 1961.

Heidegger, Martin. *Being and Time.* Translated by John Macquarrie and Edward Robinson. New York: Harper and Row, 1962. (*Sein und Zeit.* Tübingen: Max Niemeyer, 1967. *L'être et le temps.* Translated by Rudolf Boehm and Alphonse De Waelhens. Paris: Gallimard, 1964.)

_____. *Lettre sur l'humanisme/Ueber den Humanismus.* Bilingual edition. Translated and edited by Roger Munier. Paris: Aubier Montaigne, 1964. ("Letter on Humanism." Translated by Frank A. Capuzzi and J. Glenn Gray, in *Martin Heidegger: Basic Writings.* Edited by David Farrell Krell. New York: Harper & Row, 1977.)

_____. *On the Way to Language.* Translated by Peter D. Hertz. New York: Harper & Row, 1971.

_____. *Poetry, Language and Thought.* Translated by Albert Hofstadter. New York: Harper & Row, 1971.

Heidsieck, François. *L'ontologie de Merleau-Ponty.* Paris: Presses Universitaires de France, 1971.

Henle, Paul, ed. *Language, Thought and Culture.* Ann Arbor: University of Michigan Press, 1966.

Husserl, Edmund. *Ideas: General Introduction to Pure Phenomenology.* Translated by W. R. Boyce Gibson. London: George Allen and Unwin, 1958.

_____. *The Phenomenology of Internal Time Consciousness.* Edited by Martin Heidegger. Translated by James S. Churchill. Bloomington: Indiana University Press, 1964.

_____. *Formal and Transcendental Logic.* Translated by Dorion Cairns. The Hague: Martinus Nijhoff, 1969.

_____. *Experience and Judgement.* Revised and edited by Ludwig Landgrebe. Translated by James S. Churchill and Karl Ameriks. Evanston, Ill.: Northwestern University Press, 1973.

_____. *The Crisis of European Sciences and Transcendental Phenomenology* Translated, with an introduction, by David Carr. Evanston, Ill.: Northwestern University Press, 1970. (*Die Krisis der europäischen Wissenschaften und die transzendentale Phänomenologie.* Edited by Walter Biemel. The Hague: Martinus Nijhoff, 1962.)

James, William. *The Principles of Psychology.* Authorized edition in two unabridged volumes. New York: Dover, 1950.

Jarvie, I. C. *The Revolution in Anthropology.* Foreword by Ernest Gellner. Chicago: Henry Regnery, 1969.

Kwant, Remi C. *The Phenomenological Philosophy of Merleau-Ponty.* Pittsburg: Duquesne University Press, 1963.

_____. *From Phenomenology to Metaphysics.* Pittsburgh: Duquesne University Press, 1966.

Langan, Thomas *Merleau-Ponty's Critique of Reason.* New Haven and London: Yale University Press, 1966.

Loux, Michael J., ed. *Universals and Particulars: Readings in Ontology.* Garden City, N.Y.: Anchor, 1970.

Marx, Werner. *Heidegger and the Tradition.* Translated by T. Kisiel and Murray Greene. Evanston, Ill.: Northwestern University Press, 1971.

Meyerhoff, Hans, ed. *The Philosophy of History in Our Time.* Garden City, N.Y.: Doubleday, 1959.

Moreau, Joseph. *L'horizon des esprits. Essai critique sur "La phénoménologie de la perception."* Paris: Presses Universitaires de France, 1960.

Nagel, Ernest, and Brandt, Richard B., eds. *Meaning and Knowledge: Systematic Readings in Epistemology.* New York: Harcourt, Brace, 1965.

Nietzsche, Friedrich. *The Will to Power.* Translated by Walter Kaufmann and R. J. Hollingdale. Edited with commentary by Walter Kaufmann. Vintage Books. New York: Random House, 1968.

Nowell-Smith, P. H. *Ethics.* Harmondsworth, Middlesex: Penguin, 1954.

Pitcher, George, ed. *Truth.* Englewood Cliffs, N.J.: Prentice-Hall, 1964.

Russell, Bertrand. *Logic and Knowledge: Essays 1901-1950.* Edited by Robert Charles Marsh. London: George Allen and Unwin, 1964.

Ryle, Gilbert. *The Concept of Mind.* Harmondsworth, Middlesex: Penguin, 1963.

Sartre, Jean-Paul. *The Transcendence of the Ego.* Translated by Forest Williams and Robert Kirkpatrick. Noonday Press. New York: Farrar, Straus and Giroux, 1957.

_____. *Being and Nothingness.* Translated by Hazel E. Barnes. New York: Philosophical Library, 1956.

Schutz, Alfred. *Collected Papers, Volume II: Studies in Social Theory.* Edited by A. Brodersen. The Hague: Martinus Nijhoff, 1964.

_____. *Collected Papers, Volume III: Studies in Phenomenological Philosophy.* Edited by I. Schutz. The Hague: Martinus Nijhoff, 1970.

Schutz, Alfred, and Luckmann, Thomas. *The Structures of the Life-World.* Translated by Richard M. Zaner and H. Tristram Engelhardt, Jr. London: Heinemann, 1974.

Skyrms, Brian. *Choice and Chance: An Introduction to Inductive Logic.* Belmont, Cal.: Dickenson, 1968.

Strawson, P. F. *Individuals: An Essay in Descriptive Metaphysics.* London: Methuen, 1964.

Swartz, Robert J., ed. *Perceiving, Sensing and Knowing.* Garden City, N. Y.: Anchor, 1965.

Tilliette, Xavier. *Merleau-Ponty ou la mesure de l'homme.* Paris: Seghers, 1970.

Toulmin, Stephen. *The Place of Reason in Ethics.* Cambridge: Cambridge University Press, 1968.

———. *The Philosophy of Science: An Introduction.* New York: Harper & Row, 1960.

Wisdom, J. O. "Observations as the Building Blocks of Science in 20th-Century Scientific Thought." In R. C. Buck and R. S. Cohen, eds., *Boston Studies in the Philosophy of Science.* Vol. 8. New York: Humanities Press, 1970.

Yolton, John W. *Thinking and Perceiving: A Study in the Philosophy of Mind.* LaSalle, Ill.: Open Court, 1962.

Zaner, Richard M. *The Problem of Embodiment.* The Hague: Martinus Nijhoff, 1964.

Index